T0299955

Labor, Industry, and Regulation during the Progressive Era

New Political Economy

RICHARD MCINTYRE, *General Editor*

Labor, Industry, and Regulation during the Progressive Era

Daniel E. Saros

Routledge
Taylor & Francis Group
New York   London

First published 2009
by Routledge
711 Third Avenue, New York, NY 10017

Simultaneously published in the UK
by Routledge
2 Park Square, Milton Park, Abingdon, Oxfordshire OX14 4RN

Routledge is an imprint of the Taylor & Francis Group, an informa business

First issued in paperback 2012

© 2009 Taylor & Francis

Typeset in Sabon by IBT Global.

Library of Congress Cataloging in Publication Data
Saros, Daniel Earl
    Labor, industry, and regulation during the progressive era / by Daniel E. Saros.
        p. cm. — (New political economy)
    Includes bibliographical references and index.
    1. Industrial policy—United States—History. 2. Steel industry and trade—United States—History. 3. Iron industry and trade—United States—History. I. Title.
    HD3616.U46S27 2009
    338.973009'034—dc22
                                                    2008033351

ISBN13: 978-0-415-99679-2 (hbk)
ISBN13: 978-0-415-54160-2 (pbk)

In loving memory of Earl C. Smith, who lost his life while working for General Tire and Rubber Company in Akron, Ohio on January 16, 1977

Contents

Figures

Tables

Acknowledgments

It is not possible for me to acknowledge every person who contributed to the successful completion of this project. The number is far too great and the contributions far too many to include a complete account here. Certain individuals cannot be omitted, however, and I will strive to recall the various influences that have sustained me throughout this project. I owe a special thank you to the economics faculty at the University of Notre Dame, which now resides in the Department of Economics and Policy Studies. Although I possessed a powerful drive to study heterodox economics as a first-year graduate student, it was the Notre Dame faculty that helped steer me in the direction that I expect will guide my scholarly path throughout the remainder of my life.

I am especially grateful to my dissertation director and friend, Professor Martin Wolfson, whose guidance ensured that I never lost perspective during my research. His assistance and encouragement were unceasing, and I will always be in debt to him for the role he has played in my intellectual and personal development. I would also like to thank the members of my dissertation committee for making the dissertation process so enjoyable and rewarding. Professors Charles Craypo, Kwan Kim, and William Leahy devoted considerable time to reading my dissertation and all made a number of valuable suggestions that have greatly improved the final product. Warm thanks also go to Professor Kali Rath for his official support that made possible the timely completion of the dissertation. I am indebted as well to Rita Donley for her assistance during the spring of 2003.

I also need to acknowledge Professor Virginia Shingleton who has supported me a great deal during my time at Valparaiso University in transforming this dissertation research into a book-length project. Without her encouragement during the summer of 2007, this book would not have been completed until somewhat further in the future. The helpful assistance of the staff at the Christopher Center for Library and Information Resources at Valparaiso University has also helped me obtain key sources needed for various chapters. Special thanks must be given to Professor Richard McIntyre of the University of Rhode Island for his very detailed comments and suggestions on an earlier draft. I am grateful as well to

Benjamin Holtzman at Routledge for his encouragement and assistance along the way. As usual, any and all errors are solely the responsibility of the author.

I must thank my parents, John and Linda Saros, for encouraging me to persevere throughout the most difficult period of this process. My grandmother, Virginia Smith, has also been a constant presence in my life for which I am most grateful. My brother Michael Saros and his wife Jennifer Saros have been important influences in my life as well. I would also like to thank my lifelong friends, Stephen Anway, Jared Cavileer, Nicholas Chordas, John Vogel, and Shawn Wilkoff for their support. I am grateful as well to the families of Carol and Doug Teter, Cheryl Bennett, Charlotte Armentrout, Beth Bonner, Janice Barnes; Jerry, Hanna, and Kayla Saros; Steve and Linda Saros, Derek Saros, Jason Saros, and my grandparents Angelo and Sophia Saros. Joe and Rita Hoult, Shelby Hoult, Keith Goudy, Walt and Jancy Hoult, Phyllis Yenawine, Aida Ramos, and Kimberly Burham were also very supportive and deserve my gratitude. Finally, I need to thank my lovely wife, Stacy Hoult-Saros, for always reminding me of the value of research that forces us to reconsider and rethink the social forces that have created our collective history as a nation.

Introduction

During the latter half of the nineteenth century, the American economy experienced a dramatic transformation in the social organization of capitalist production. As the harsh realities of capitalist society manifested themselves in the form of a global economic crisis, it became clear that the existing social structure was no longer capable of supporting stable economic growth. The dominance of the small business enterprise and its intensely competitive nature, the prevalence of highly skilled workmen and their considerable bargaining power, and a government that was unable or unwilling to effectively stabilize economic conditions all rendered continued economic expansion and capital accumulation increasingly difficult under the circumstances. The inability of businesses to earn consistent profits and accumulate capital rapidly led to numerous bankruptcies, falling commodity prices, poor working conditions, and the onset of a global economic crisis.

At the close of the nineteenth century, the U.S. economy embarked on its long-awaited recovery. Financial and industrial capitalists formed an alliance in an effort to create a new set of economic relationships through which stable profits would be ensured for the future. It was first necessary to eliminate the inherently destructive and inefficient competition that had contributed to the severe economic crisis of the past thirty years. This strategy required industrial capitalists to cooperate far beyond the gentlemen's agreements and pooling arrangements of the 1870s and 1880s. The inherent difficulties associated with the enforcement of such loose arrangements required a fundamental change in the pattern of property ownership itself. The solution required the combination of massive amounts of capital into the hands of a relatively small number of businessmen who strove to stabilize markets and encourage restricted competition rather than the fierce competition then prevalent. After the severe depression of 1893–1897, a wave of mergers led to the rise of large trusts and combines and marked a basic shift in the organization of capitalist production in the United States.

It is common for scholars and historians to identify early twentieth century America with the dominance of monopoly capital and restricted competition. This impression has often been misleading as in many cases competition became more intense as capital became increasingly concentrated. The tendency for competition to intensify was especially prevalent during the merger wave of the late 1890s when many businesses expanded operations to begin competing with former suppliers of raw materials or the former buyers of their semi-finished commodities. After the consolidation movement, the growth of the large corporation also failed to eliminate the competitive nature of the small and medium-sized rival. Smaller rivals continued to pursue higher profits and larger shares of the market than their larger competitor in many instances. New methods of restraining competition did become feasible, however, once a giant trust securely established itself as the leader of a particular industry. Disciplinary tactics and other means of persuasion were used to discourage smaller firms from returning to the intense price competition of the previous century. America's corporate leaders engineered a concerted effort to *control* the inherent instability of markets for raw materials, labor power, and finished commodities. The extent to which the leaders of industry were successful in their efforts to suppress the competitive spirit of the small and medium-sized rival carried important implications for the development of their industries.

While the leaders of the newly consolidated industries were struggling to directly modify the behavior of competitors, they were also engaged in a coordinated, national effort to influence governmental policy. Special organizations were formed during this period with the explicit goal of creating a national consensus on policy issues and drafting legislation for the further rationalization and stabilization of American industry. The National Civic Federation (NCF) founded in 1900 is the most notable example of an organization created by the leaders of big business with an explicit policy agenda in mind that ran counter to the ideological disposition of most business leaders in the late nineteenth century. Other organizations, such as the National Association of Manufacturers (NAM) and the American Anti-Trust League, continued to represent the traditional interests of small businesspeople during the early twentieth century. The conflict among large and small capitalists thus also manifested itself in the formation of such rival organizations. Each group sought to influence public policy with the ultimate goal of establishing greater control over business conditions in a manner that would best serve their economic interests.

As America's corporate leaders were attempting to modify the relationships among capitalists and influence the behavior of the state, the American workforce was in the midst of an enormous transformation. If the creation of a large class of wage laborers accurately describes changes in the American workforce during the mid-nineteenth century, then during the late nineteenth century America's wage labor force had its skills gradually eroded through the introduction of large-scale machinery and mechanized production processes. The creation of a large national labor market as immigrants from Eastern Europe entered the United States contributed further to the power of capital over labor in the sphere of exchange as well as production. The growth of labor organizations and the tense capital-labor relations led to numerous severe strikes during the late nineteenth century including the 1877 railroad strikes, the Haymarket Square riot in 1886, and a series of violent mine strikes in the western United States during the 1890s. The mechanization of production and the changing composition of the American workforce were significant factors leading to the intense conflicts of the period that continued throughout the progressive era.

The leaders of the consolidated industries at the beginning of the twentieth century were not blind to the role of labor conditions for their agenda of rationalization and stabilization for American industry. Corporate policies regarding wages, hours, and working conditions affected production costs and profits. Unlike the small business enterprises of the past, however, that always forced costs to the lowest level attainable in an effort to compete, the giant trusts and corporations were forced to proceed with much more subtlety. Constant pressure from the public, labor organizations, small business interests, and federal and state governments forced the corporate giants to engage in a balancing act. In many instances, the large combines refrained from exerting or displaying the full extent of their power over labor or their competitors.[1] Corporate welfare policies aimed at mollifying labor or industrial organizations that reassured competitors of the right to a peaceful coexistence with one another were frequent methods used to defuse hostile critics of the new social order.

In the context of this historical background, the precise nature of the alternative economic structure established at the beginning of the twentieth century becomes a question of considerable historical interest. How effectively this alternative structure managed to overcome the contradictions of its predecessor carries important implications for the ability of capitalism to survive its destructive tendencies. A sizable literature exists that has explored the historical development of this period in American history including Gabriel Kolko's *The Triumph of Conservatism* (1967) and James Weinstein's *The Corporate Ideal in the Liberal State: 1900–1918* (1968). This work has challenged traditional conceptions of the "progressive period" in American history by shifting its emphasis from middle-class and other social reformers to the manner in which business establishments used their power to shape social policy and protect existing property relations.

The work of historians has contributed greatly to our understanding of the development of American industry during this period. On the other hand, historians have not provided a systematic theoretical framework for understanding how the institutional structure of the period shaped the performance of the newly consolidated industries. Radical political economists have constructed a framework for the analysis of the economic history of capitalism known as *social structure of accumulation* (SSA) theory.

According to SSA theory, the history of capitalism may be comprehended as an alternating series of long periods of relative economic stability and growth (i.e., social structures of accumulation) on the one hand and economic crisis and decay on the other hand. A specific set of institutions forms the foundation of each SSA and defines its specific characteristics. For example, the relationships between capital and labor or between the state and capital help form the institutional environment of a particular SSA and thus help determine the conditions for economic growth and profitability. At the beginning of the twentieth century, the growth of monopoly power, the redefinition of capital/labor relations, the increased state regulation of the economy, and the development of a new economic ideology were all characteristic of a shift towards the creation of a new SSA in U.S. economic history.

Upon reflection, it is not at all clear why the hostile capital-labor relations of the late nineteenth century persisted throughout the progressive era when giant corporations were striving to eliminate the worst excesses of competition and free markets that had been associated with the late nineteenth century. The application of the tools of radical economic analysis to this period in American history has the potential to provide an explanation for this rather puzzling collection of historical facts.[2] SSA theorists have traditionally investigated the relationship between the institutional structure of capitalist economies and traditional measures of capitalist performance (e.g., output, profit rates). To comprehend the hostility of capital-labor relations in the United States during the early twentieth century, it is necessary to examine the relationship between their specific character and the level of economic performance they helped achieve. This necessity stems from the fact that periods of regulation, and the progressive period in particular, are often interpreted solely as reactions of the middle and lower classes against the worst excesses of free markets. Therefore, the reinterpretation of this period requires a reconsideration of basic business objectives and the extent to which hostile capital-labor relations contributed to enhanced profitability. Although it is not theoretically possible to isolate a single key institutional factor (e.g., capital-labor relations) when investigating the performance of a capitalist economy, it is theoretically necessary to include it in an overall explanation of that performance in a way that is coherent.

An analysis of the dialectical relationship between capital and labor during the progressive era, although interesting in its own right, may prove critical to an analysis of the present period in world history. The neo-liberal social structure was formed in the aftermath of the crisis conditions of the 1970s and early 1980s, complete with an unstable price level, high rates of unemployment, and social instability. The failure of neo-liberalism to revive global rates of capital accumulation and economic growth has led some contemporary theorists, such as David Harvey, to conclude that the creation of a new neo-liberal order had far more to do with the restoration of elite capitalist class power than with the stated goals of that ideological undertaking. In response to the contradictions inherent in neo-liberal thought and practice, new institutions and structures of elite class power may be forming under the ideological banner of neo-conservatism. To the extent that this process of social transition parallels the transformation of the U.S. economic structure at the end of the nineteenth century, our present scrutiny of the past may offer a dire warning of unintended and disastrous consequences in our future. These critical linkages and historical parallels are discussed at far greater length in the first chapter and in the conclusion.

The project of applying social structure of accumulation analysis to the progressive era is massive in scope. Like today, the U.S. economy during the early twentieth century was composed of many distinct industries each having its own specific institutional features. For example, while the steel and oil industries were highly consolidated by the early twentieth century, other industries retained a competitive structure such as the mining and apparel industries (Gordon et al., 1982: 158–159). Far-reaching historical statements should thus be made with considerable caution. It is for this reason that the present study concentrates on the institutional structure and performance of a single industry during the early twentieth century. The industry selected has been chosen because it has been, in many ways, the bedrock of American industry throughout much of the twentieth century. It also magnifies the puzzling historical facts alluded to above in that it was reorganized through consolidation at the beginning of the twentieth century in an industry-wide effort to control and stabilize markets and yet its treatment of labor culminated in one of the greatest strikes in American labor history. The American iron and steel industry is thus an appropriate choice for a detailed case study that aims to reconcile the seemingly contradictory coincidence of highly regulated markets and intense capital-labor conflict.

The application of what is essentially a macroeconomic theory of historical development (such as SSA theory) to the development of a particular industry (such as the iron and steel industry) is a relatively unusual approach. To the extent that they use industry histories, it is more common for SSA theorists to use them as a basis for theorizing about the exploration, consolidation, or decay of a particular SSA. The motivation for this research is the author's belief that the broad framework of SSA theory has the potential to help explain developments in the American iron and steel industry during a critical period in its history while concretizing our understanding of the institutional structure of early twentieth century America.

It should come as no surprise that the SSA literature and the literature pertaining to the history of the American iron and steel industry have not touched each other in any systematic or conscious way at the present time. One reason is that SSA theorists have traditionally neglected micro-oriented research, choosing instead to concentrate on macroeconomic issues. On the other hand, labor historians are more likely to let historical detail obscure the broader social forces that have helped determine labor conditions. Much can thus be learned about labor conditions in the iron and steel mills through the application of the SSA framework to the history of the iron and steel industry. If the dominant characterization of the SSA pertinent to this period in American history possesses general validity, then certainly it should be roughly consistent with developments in an industry as pivotal as the American iron and steel industry. The analysis may, in turn, encourage a more critical and concrete understanding of the claims of SSA theorists. Combining the insights of both literatures with the ultimate objective of understanding developments in the iron and steel industry is my main purpose.

The remainder of this work is organized in such a way that the theoretical framework of SSA theory and the general historical context of early twentieth century America are firmly established prior to the presentation and results of the case study. Chapter 1 thus provides an overview of social structure of accumulation theory beginning with its theoretical roots in the late 1970s. SSA theorists have traditionally emphasized particular aspects of American economic history to the neglect of others. The details of this scholarly history and reasons for the particular concerns of SSA theorists are examined. The more recent developments of David Kotz (2003) and Martin Wolfson (2003) are also discussed at length. The work of Kotz and Wolfson has created an opening for a generalization of SSA theory that has the potential to bring considerably more historical material within the scope of the SSA framework in a way that is consistent with the actual (often sluggish) growth of capitalist economies. Essential to this modified SSA framework is the notion that American capitalist development may be characterized as a history of alternating free market and regulated periods. A case study of the American iron and steel industry is proposed as a way of exploring the hostile capital-labor relations of the regulated progressive era. In addition, this chapter considers a number of alternatives to the direct application of the SSA framework. Ernest Mandel (1995) provides the definitive orthodox Marxist approach to long swings of capitalist activity whereas Michel Aglietta's (2000) pioneering work applies French regulation theory in a comprehensive way to American economic history. Although different, these alternatives to SSA theory share many of the same basic insights. A more subtle application of the notion of stages of capitalism is represented in the work of David Harvey (2005a), which is especially useful for illuminating the contemporary relevance of critical historical analyses of the progressive era.

Chapter 2 begins with a brief overview of the institutional structure characterizing the late nineteenth century American economy. This historical discussion is primarily included for the purposes of establishing a point of contrast for the very different institutional structure of the early twentieth century. In particular, the discussion establishes a connection between the set of institutions characteristic of the period and the world economic

crisis that led to its demise. The transition to the new institutional structure of the early twentieth century shifts the discussion to the work of
Terence McDonough who has attempted to provide an SSA account of the
period under investigation. Drawing upon the work of various historians,
McDonough's analysis is modified and extended to reveal an even greater
complexity of the institutional arrangement characterizing the early twentieth century U.S. economy. This part of the analysis concentrates on the
consolidation of American industry, the continued transformation of the
American workforce, the historical shift towards a more active economic
role for the federal government, and a basic shift in the dominant economic ideology. Finally, the extent to which this new institutional structure
overcame the poor performance of the late nineteenth century is explored
through an examination of traditional measures of capitalist performance.

Having described the theoretical framework that is used for the present study as well as the general historical context of the early twentieth
century, chapter 3 begins the case study analysis of the American iron and
steel industry. In the same fashion that chapter 2 explored the institutional
structure of the late nineteenth century, chapter 3 begins with an overview
of the competitive conditions prevalent in the iron and steel industry prior
to the consolidation movement. The shift from iron to steel production
and the consequences this change carried for the iron and steel companies
are explained within the context of a changing institutional environment.
By the time the Carnegie Steel Company was threatening to dominate the
markets for structural steel and finished steel commodities, the nature of
the industry was changing to one in which consolidation rather than competition served as the best means of economic survival. A wave of successful and unsuccessful mergers rushed through the iron and steel industry
during the late nineteenth century and culminated in the formation of the
world's first billion dollar business enterprise in 1901: the United States
Steel Corporation.

Having explored the events preceding the transition to the new institutional structure in the iron and steel industry, chapter 3 then explores key
institutional features of the new social structure. The changed character
of inter-capitalist relations in the industry during the early twentieth century involved a variety of efforts to mitigate the harmful effects of capitalist competition. The founding of an industrial organization known as the
American Iron and Steel Institute (AISI) in 1910 is a prime example of the
way in which U.S. Steel attempted to administer price and wage stabilization policies for the entire iron and steel industry. The slow purging of the
Carnegie steel men from the upper ranks of U.S. Steel to create room for
the new financial men is also explored as a sign of this institutional transition. The altered and often inconsistent behavior of the federal government during the anti-trust investigation of U.S. Steel, World War I, and
the steel strike of 1919 is recognized as a key factor in the development
of the industry. Throughout the analysis the role of economic ideology is

emphasized for the role it played in guiding the representatives of capital and the state. Finally, the consequences of the structure in general for the industry's performance are carefully linked to the institutional features summarized above.

Chapter 4 is devoted to the specific character of capital-labor relations in the American iron and steel industry during the early twentieth century. The reason for giving this institutional feature special treatment is that the treatment of labor in the steel industry appears to be entirely inconsistent with the industry's efforts to eliminate the harmful consequences associated with the unpredictability of markets. This chapter briefly traces the history of organized labor in the iron and steel industry prior to and during the transition to the new institutional structure. The decline of the Amalgamated Association of Iron and Steel Workers, especially after the establishment of U.S. Steel, is linked to a variety of harsh labor conditions including long hours, poor working conditions, irregular employment, an unequal distribution of the gains from productivity growth, and real wages that were stagnant for a growing class of semi-skilled steelworkers. This poor record for the industry with respect to its treatment of labor is even more confusing when one considers U.S. Steel's extensive welfare program, which included a stock subscription plan, a safety campaign, and a pension scheme to name only a few such programs. A resolution to this seeming inconsistency is developed in chapter 5 through an examination of the consequences of hostile capital-labor relations for the industry's performance and thus the basic objectives of the steel companies.

The book concludes with a general summary of major findings. One general conclusion is that capital-labor relations in the iron and steel industry during the early twentieth century have a puzzling dual character that is best comprehended within the context of the overall objectives of business. The progressive period has often been perceived exclusively as a regulated period in which reformers from below scored major victories in curbing the powers of big business. Capital-labor relations in the iron and steel industry, however, suggest that labor reforms originated largely from above and were consistent with the profit objectives of steel executives. It is thus concluded that the case study analysis of the iron and steel industry carries theoretical implications for our understanding of the regulationist institutional structure of the early twentieth century insofar as the industry was representative of American industry generally at that time. Armed with a new way of thinking about regulatory phases of American capitalism, it may be possible to then modestly rethink the post-World War II regulatory period as well as where the U.S. economy may be headed in future years. Two broad conclusions can then be drawn regarding the value of micro-oriented case studies to SSA theorists. Such studies can make possible valuable adjustments in macroeconomic theorizing within the SSA tradition at the same time that applications of SSA theory to specific industry histories have the potential to enlighten us about the development of various branches of social production.

1 A Theoretical Framework for the Historical Analysis of American Industry

To motivate the case study analysis of the American iron and steel industry during the progressive era, this chapter justifies the transition from the macroeconomic framework of SSA theory to the more micro-oriented character of an industrial case study. The chapter thus begins with a general overview of the basic concepts and terminology of SSA theory. The first section also provides a description of the social structures of accumulation that characterize American capitalist history according to most SSA theorists. The key institutions of each social structure of accumulation are briefly discussed to provide the historical background for the transition to a more concrete analysis in later chapters. The section also contains data on growth and investment rates for the long swings associated with each SSA because a primary strength of SSA analysis is its ability to relate the institutions comprising an SSA to traditional measures of macroeconomic performance.

The second section of the chapter then explores recent theoretical developments in SSA theory with special attention given to attempts to generalize the theory to account for long periods during which a stable set of institutions nevertheless gives rise to sluggish growth. It is argued that this attempt at generalization and greater abstraction actually creates an equal opportunity for its opposite: a more concrete, historical analysis. The second section also briefly explores the specific, contrasting capital-labor relations of the progressive and postwar periods to facilitate the analysis of capital-labor relations in the American iron and steel industry during the early twentieth century. The final section of the chapter concludes with a discussion of the methodological approach that is employed in the succeeding chapters and briefly considers alternatives to SSA theory.

1.1 SOCIAL STRUCTURE OF ACCUMULATION (SSA) THEORY

1.1.1 An Overview

Although first introduced decades ago, interest in social structure of accumulation (SSA) theory remains strong as evidenced by the First International

Conference on Social Structure of Accumulation Theory and Analysis held at the National University of Ireland in Galway in late 2006. When SSA theory was first conceived in 1978, David Gordon proposed the new framework as a way of comprehending the current economic crisis of the postwar U.S. economy. The inability of the U.S. economy to maintain rapid capital accumulation and economic growth had become apparent by the late 1960s and continued throughout the 1970s. According to radical political economists, the situation called for an explanation that attributed the current crisis to the growing inadequacy of the institutions that had made the postwar boom possible. As a result, much of the work of SSA theorists during the 1980s involved the detailed analysis of the postwar institutions and the manner in which their erosion brought on the prolonged economic crisis.

To better comprehend the value of the SSA framework as a tool for analyzing the development of American capitalism, it is first necessary to consider its basic structure. Simply defined, a social structure of accumulation is a set of institutions that promotes rapid capital accumulation (Kotz, 2003: 263). In their analysis of the postwar U.S. economy, Samuel Bowles, David Gordon, and Thomas Weisskopf argue that the institutions of an historically specific SSA provide capitalists with the stable and favorable external environment that is necessary to induce them to invest in production (1987: 47). The set of institutions may include virtually any historically specific institutional forms that condition the process of capital accumulation in a capitalist society. Among the relevant institutional forms, whose specific character will vary across time and place, are the relations between capitalists, between capital and labor, and between the state and capital. David Gordon, Richard Edwards, and Michael Reich have further classified the institutions of an SSA according to whether they fall in its inner boundary or outer boundary. Whereas the inner boundary separates the institutions most directly involved in the capital accumulation process (i.e., the "social structure") from the process of capital accumulation itself, the outer boundary separates this social structure from all other social structures in society (Gordon et al., 1982: 25). In any case, the examination of a particular SSA requires an analysis of the specific institutions comprising it and their implications for the rates of profit, capital accumulation, and economic growth.

In broader historical terms, SSA analysis provides a suitable framework for the inspection of "long waves" of capitalist economic activity. Such "long waves" or "long swings" have traditionally been of primary interest for SSA theorists. Each long wave consists of roughly 25 years of relatively stable capital accumulation and economic growth followed by roughly 25 years of economic crisis, stagnation, and decline. In their discussion of long swings, Gordon, Edwards, and Reich explain that the capitalist epoch may be characterized by a succession of social structures of accumulation (1994: 20). Each SSA then represents a historically specific stage of capitalism with its own institutions, its own dynamic, and its own sources of economic decline.

Because SSA theorists investigate the transitions from one SSA to the next, they are necessarily interested in the way they are constructed and tend to decay over time. Their traditional commitment to the multidimensional character of the capitalist accumulation process forces SSA theorists to reject single-factor theories of long swings (Gordon et al., 1982: 27). Hence, their analyses of economic crisis do not attribute reduced profitability and declining economic growth to the transformation of a single institutional form. For example, the oil price shocks of the 1970s are frequently cited as the exogenous factors responsible for the economic crisis of the postwar SSA. SSA theorists reject this perspective because they generally interpret the crisis as having its origin in the transformation of a variety of institutional factors whose harmful economic effects began to surface in the late 1960s.

With respect to the construction of new social structures of accumulation, SSA theorists generally do not rigidly establish boundaries between old and new SSAs. The stages of capitalism tend to overlap as old institutional forms are gradually transformed and new institutions are formed altogether. These institutional transformations are not automatic adjustments beyond all human control. According to Gordon, Edwards and Reich, the construction of an SSA requires "explicit and self-conscious actions by leading political actors" (1994: 25). One might also add that business leaders and labor leaders are also involved in the conscious transformation of the institutional forms that condition the process of capital accumulation. Brief mention has already been made of the way in which business leaders used the National Civic Federation (NCF) during the progressive era to influence public policy and combat the opponents of their economic agenda for industrial rationalization and stabilization. More recently, in the 1970s corporations mounted an aggressive antiunion drive through such organizations as the Business Roundtable (Bowles et al., 1990: 87). A number of corporate-backed think tanks were also formed including the Heritage Foundation, the Hoover Institute, the Center for the Study of American Business, and the American Enterprise Institute. This concerted effort to use the power of the business elite to defend the American free enterprise system was strongly recommended in a confidential memo that Lewis Powell sent to President Nixon in 1971, thus setting the stage for a significant advance in the ability of American capitalists to act as a class (Harvey, 2005a: 43–44). Representatives of business, government, and labor have repeatedly demonstrated that they are conscious of the political and class dimensions of their activities.

1.1.2 Social Structures of Accumulation in U.S. Economic History

The above description of SSA theory is only intended to introduce a broad outline of the basic concepts and terminology of that theoretical framework. Turning to the actual history of U.S. capitalism, it quickly becomes clear that the abstract institutional forms discussed above must be given a more concrete specification depending on the particular stage of capitalism being examined. This section provides a brief overview of the history of American capitalism that is consistent with the more popular applications of the SSA approach to U.S. economic history.

Radical political economists have traditionally argued that three social structures of accumulation have governed the pace of capital accumulation and economic growth during the last 150 years or so of American capitalist history. An early exception to this popular view among SSA theorists is found in *Segmented Work, Divided Workers* (1982), which is the first full-scale application of the SSA approach to U.S. history. Gordon, Edwards, and Reich identify four long swings in the world capitalist economy that are also relevant to the trajectory of the U.S. economy (1982: 9). The difficulty of obtaining reliable data for the late eighteenth and early nineteenth centuries, however, typically restricts the attention of SSA theorists to the three most recent SSAs in U.S. history to which we now turn.

SSA theorists have made a number of suggestions pertaining to the approximate timing of the various long swings in American capitalist history. Rather than become mired down in debates about the most appropriate dating scheme, an attempt by Gordon, Edwards, and Reich to approximate the timing of the long swings has been selected as a sample of the many possible approximations (1982: 43). The dating scheme presented in Table 1.1 has been selected because it offers a clear sense of the long-term trends in the rates of economic growth and investment.

The approximations in Table 1.1 only suggest an historical appearance that may or may not be best explained using the social structure of

Table 1.1   Boom and crisis in the U.S. economy: 1846–1988.

Long Swing	Phase	Output Growth Rate (%)*
I	Boom: 1846–1878	4.2
	Crisis: 1878–1894	3.7
II	Boom: 1894–1914	3.8
	Crisis: 1914–1938	2.1
III	Boom: 1938–1970	4.0
	Crisis: 1970–1988	3.12
Averages	Boom years	4.0
	Crisis years	2.97

SOURCE: *Adapted from Gordon et al., 1982: 43; the author has determined the boundaries of the crisis phase of the third long swing and computed its associated growth rate using data obtained from the U.S. Bureau of Economic Analysis (2003). Gordon et al. also regard these long swings as the second, third, and fourth long swings in U.S. history.*

* *The output growth rate is defined as the average annual growth rate of real gross domestic nonfarm product.*

accumulation approach. Detailed analyses of the institutional forms present in each period and their relationship to the rates of economic growth and capital accumulation are necessary to evaluate the usefulness of the framework for comprehending the historical evolution of American capitalism. For convenience, the terminology employed by Terence McDonough has been used throughout this study to identify the social structure of accumulation associated with each long swing. The successive social structures of accumulation characterizing U.S. capitalist history are, therefore, identified as the post-Civil War SSA, the monopoly capitalist (or monopoly) SSA, and the post-World War II (or postwar) SSA (McDonough, 1994: 103).

In the appendix to one of his articles, David Kotz provides a helpful summary of the key institutional forms associated with each of the three social structures of accumulation discussed above (1994a: 68). Although the dates Kotz uses to distinguish between the different SSAs are not exactly the same as those listed in Table 1.1, his list may serve as an appropriate guide to the institutional structure of each SSA. Rather than duplicating the entire list here, it may be helpful instead to refer to the highlights of each SSA to facilitate the transition to a more detailed historical analysis in the chapters that follow.

The post-Civil War SSA possesses an institutional structure that McDonough has associated with the primitive accumulation of capital (1994: 103). His reference to primitive accumulation is a reminder of the Marxist roots of SSA theory with its emphasis on class conflict and the economic transformation of society. According to McDonough, the pivotal years of the post-Civil War SSA marked the transition to the capitalist mode of production (1994: 126). It was during these years that capitalist relations of production were created where they were not already present. Kotz identifies a number of institutions that are associated with this social structure of accumulation. Among these institutions, he includes a competitive industrial structure, labor processes based on craft skills, one-person management of the labor process, and a philosophy of individualism (1994a: 68). During this period, price competition among capitalist firms was intense, workmen possessed considerably more bargaining power due to their skills than in later years, and the state adopted a relatively laissez-faire approach to the economy. This social structure of accumulation began to collapse towards the end of the nineteenth century.

The monopoly capitalist SSA was created in the aftermath of the crisis of the post-Civil War SSA. Its key institutional features were formed in an effort to overcome the inability of the earlier institutions to create an environment suitable for profitable investment. After the widespread bankruptcies and falling prices of the 1890s, businesspeople were eager to end the competition they now perceived as highly destructive. Close links between industrial and finance capital were thus established and a highly concentrated industrial structure resulted from an alliance between the two forms of capital. According to McDonough, the monopoly market structure that resulted can be regarded as the "lynchpin" of the monopoly capitalist SSA (1994: 104). The concentrated nature of American industry is also the first on Kotz's list of key institutions for the early twentieth century (1994a: 68). In their analyses of the early twentieth century social structure of accumulation, SSA theorists have assigned great importance to the consolidation of industry.

Major changes in the organization of the labor process and labor markets occurred as well during this time. A large, homogenous labor force consisting of a new class of semi-skilled workmen developed as the production process became increasingly mechanized and a large number of Southeast European immigrants entered the U.S. in search of work. At the same time, the new corporations were devising welfare programs for employees while joining the state in the repression of trade unions. The new corporate liberal philosophy served as a rationalization for the paternalistic behavior of big business and its claim to social responsibility. The U.S. government was also becoming increasingly interested in the regulation of business and in the imperialist expansion of the United States. These tendencies manifested themselves in the creation of governmental regulatory agencies, federal antitrust suits, and America's entry into the Spanish-American War in 1898. According to David Harvey, the late nineteenth and early twentieth centuries are marked by the rise of bourgeois imperialisms, which required the partial incorporation of the bourgeoisie within the state apparatus in order to cope with capitalist crises of over-accumulation (2005b: 42). The need to find profitable outlets for surplus capital created tensions within the international sphere that eventually exploded in inter-imperialist rivalry and world war.

America's entry into World War I led to severe labor shortages due to the discontinued inflow of foreign labor and the conscription of workmen for military service. Once these conditions combined with increases in the cost of living to breathe new life into the labor movement, the end of the war brought on a series of industrial strikes that included the great steel strike of 1919. The widespread failure of these strikes undermined the labor movement and led to a renewal of laissez-faire government despite the continued dominance of large consolidations throughout the 1920s. Unfortunately, most SSA theorists have not emphasized the distinctive character of the 1920s in their analyses of the early twentieth century. The conditions persisted during the 1920s until the crash of 1929 brought on an important period of institutional restructuring that was not firmly established until America emerged victorious at the end of World War II.

Radical political economists have devoted a disproportionate amount of their analytical efforts to the investigation of the post-World War II SSA and the institutional failures that led to its demise. This tendency has been acknowledged by a number of SSA theorists. Terence McDonough, for example, admits "much of the historical work done within the SSA framework examines recent history, seeking to explain the demise of the postwar

SSA in the 1970s and after" (1994: 101). It may seem strange that a theoretical framework constructed for the purpose of examining the development of capitalist society over very long periods of time would be used in this relatively narrow fashion. The reason becomes clear, however, as soon as it is remembered that radical political economists have an explicit political and economic agenda that involves the introduction of greater democratic control over the social processes of production and distribution. This reform agenda necessitates a theoretical and practical preoccupation with the most recent developments of capitalist society. As Bowles, Gordon, and Weisskopf claim, "[l]iving in the United States draws our gaze to the future, not the past" (1990: 16). It should come as no surprise then that the postwar SSA is the most explored SSA in the literature. The reader is thus asked to excuse the brevity of the summary of the postwar SSA's key institutions provided below.

Although SSA theorists generally reject single-factor theories of long swings, Terence McDonough argues that the construction of a new SSA involves a central organizing principle. According to McDonough, these unifying principles are "historically contingent and unique to each SSA" (1994: 103). For example, the oligopolistic market structure of the monopoly capitalist SSA served as the organizing principle around which that SSA was constructed. As McDonough explains, a specific institution during the postwar period cannot be identified as the organizing principle of the postwar social structure of accumulation. Instead, the "social influence of the war itself" constituted the organizing factor of the postwar SSA (1994: 115). Therefore, the war itself created the social and economic conditions necessary for the development of a new set of institutions that would foster rapid capital accumulation and economic growth during the early postwar period.

In their classic analysis of the postwar social structure of accumulation, Bowles, Gordon, and Weisskopf identify four key institutional sets as having provided the basis for capital accumulation in the postwar era. They refer to these sets of institutions as: the Capital-Labor Accord, Pax Americana, the Capital-Citizen Accord, and the Containment of Inter-Capitalist Rivalry (1990: 9). The Capital-Labor Accord served as an unwritten contract between capital and labor that guaranteed the right of workers to share in the productivity gains of the postwar boom in exchange for management's control of the production process. The cooperative relations lasted for a time until the groups that were excluded from the Capital-Labor Accord and denied a share in the postwar gains (e.g., women, minorities) challenged the existing relations. Such working class resistance ultimately led to the collapse of the accord after the mid-1960s (Bowles et al., 1987: 48–49). Similarly, Harvey concludes that the spreading of the benefits of consumerism to the lower classes followed from the increasing power of labor within the capital-labor pact but that the urban unrest of the 1960s proved that minorities were not included sufficiently to maintain stability (2005b: 58). Ernest Mandel (1995) offers a distinctively Marxist explanation for the restructuring of postwar capital-labor relations, whose approach to long waves is reviewed at greater length later in this chapter. In Mandel's view, a continuous rise in the organic composition of capital occurred at the same time that the rise in the rate of surplus value began to slow thus making a fall in the rate of profit unavoidable from the standpoint of capitalist relations of production (1995: 64, 73). Aglietta's analysis is largely consistent with Mandel's view in that he pinpoints barriers to the extension of surplus labor within the framework of current labor processes as a key factor responsible for the crisis that began in the mid-1960s (2000:87). In any case, reduced corporate profitability and worker resistance to the bureaucratic control and strict supervision of the production process made the Capital-Labor Accord unsustainable from the perspective of management.

Pax Americana includes all of the economic and political institutions that assured United States' capitalist power in the postwar world economy. The Bretton Woods-GATT system established near the end of the war created an international capitalist economy with the United States as the acknowledged leader in the spheres of global trade and investment. Throughout this period, the United States sought to encourage propertied classes and dominant elites wherever they existed (Harvey, 2005b: 55). Chomsky (2003) and others have carefully documented many of these instances. Nevertheless, Bowles, Gordon, and Weisskopf argue that United States' hegemony faced serious challenges from developing countries both militarily (e.g., the Vietnam War) and economically (e.g., OPEC) beginning in the mid-1960s (1987: 49). Hence, this institutional adjustment also contributed to the crisis of the postwar SSA.

The Capital-Citizen Accord involved increased state regulation of the conflict between capitalists' profit-seeking activities and the public's demand for the social responsibility of large corporations. Harvey refers to the entire postwar era as one of embedded liberalism to distinguish it from the neo-liberal era that followed, defining embedded liberalism as a form of political-economic organization in which market processes and corporate activities are surrounded by a web of social and political constraints (2005a: 11). By the mid-1960s, the balance was threatened, however, as the citizenry began to push for government regulation that would ensure occupational health and safety, environmental protection, and consumer product safety (Bowles et al., 1987: 50).

The Moderation of Inter-Capitalist Rivalry also helped create a favorable environment for the investment of American capital after World War II. The devastated European and Japanese economies allowed U.S. capitalists to reign supreme until their recovery was well underway after the mid-1960s (Bowles et al., 1987: 50). Increased domestic competition, however, eventually undermined the ability of American capitalists to maintain the high profits of the early postwar era. The Bush administration's imposition of tariffs on imported steel in 2002 made it all too clear how the U.S. position of strength in manufacturing has been shattered in industries it once dominated.

The collapse of the institutions of the postwar SSA led to economic crisis, institutional restructuring, and conservative economic policy that aimed to restore the power of American capital. This brief review of the three most recent social structures of accumulation in U.S. history thus ends with the current neo-liberal era that remains a subject of considerable debate amongst radical political economists.[1] In Harvey's view, a major characteristic of the neo-liberal regime is the way in which the U.S. shifted the balance of power within the bourgeoisie from production activities to institutions of finance capital (2005b: 58). With the collapse of the international gold standard regime, New York was able to maintain its status as a power center of global finance by means of petrodollar recycling and the establishment of the U.S. dollar as the world's oil reserve currency. This transition was necessary in Harvey's view because it allowed the U.S. to continue in its quest for "spatio-temporal fixes" for its over-accumulation problem. That is, the need to find profitable outlets for surplus capital cannot be satisfied within the fixed geographical boundaries of the nation-state. As a result, either a temporal solution may be found through the investment of surplus capitals in long-term capital projects (as China is rapidly pursuing) or a spatial solution may be found through the investment of surplus capitals in the territories of other states, particularly developing nations that lack their own surplus capitals (2005b: 109). The neo-liberal insistence on the removal of all barriers to the free flow of goods and capital coupled with U.S. dollar hegemony thus supports western capital's pursuit of profitable employment on the world stage even when its rapid withdrawal may lead to financial crises in the host countries. The alternative to such "fixes" would be the devaluation of capital in the U.S., which would force American capitalists to bear the costs of over-accumulation crises and cause economic dislocation at home.

Another critical feature of the neo-liberal era is what Harvey refers to as accumulation by dispossession. This concept is closely linked to Marx's notion of the primitive or original accumulation of capital. Harvey is careful to point out, however, that an ongoing process of forceful separation of the mass of the population from land and the means of production should not be associated strictly with an earlier stage of capitalist development (2005b: 144). The privatization of the ejido lands in Mexico in the 1990s, of water resources in post-apartheid South Africa, and of most major industries in Iraq (except for oil) since the 2003 U.S. invasion are part of this process of drawing new resources and labor-power into the realm of capitalist exploitation. According to Dumenil and Levy, U.S. corporations have been efficient at pumping excess profits from the rest of the world back into the U.S. economy (Harvey, 2005b: 223). Accumulation by dispossession has thus helped to redistribute income towards the upper classes even if it has a dismal record of restoring rapid economic growth.

Drawing developing countries into the neo-liberal regime has required a combination of financial coercion as well as covert and overt military force. The Mexican debt crisis of 1982 resulted from a combination of high interest rates in the United States and massive lending of recycled petrodollars to the developing world. The IMF thus offered debt rescheduling in return for structural adjustment (e.g., social spending cuts, relaxed labor laws, privatization) (Harvey, 2006: 23). Incidentally, 1984 was the first time in the World Bank's history that it granted a loan to a country in return for neo-liberal reforms (Harvey, 2005a: 100). Developing countries were also pressured to adopt neo-liberal reforms insofar as they were offered preferential access to the huge U.S. consumer market (2006: 32). These far-reaching changes in the structure of global economic relations were all the while defended with an ideology of free market fundamentalism that had completely driven Keynesian theory from the IMF and World Bank by the early 1980s.

Despite the introduction of restrictive monetary policy and the anti-union campaign launched by U.S. corporations in the 1970s, conservative efforts to end the economic crisis and revive the rapid capital accumulation of the postwar SSA have largely failed. According to Bowles, Gordon, and Weisskopf, the uninterrupted U.S. expansion from 1983 to 1990 does not provide sufficient evidence for the claim that the conservative economic policies of the 1970s and 1980s succeeded in restoring a favorable environment for profitability and capital accumulation (1990: 4–5). The authors explain that the growth rates of GNP and productivity were not restored to their pre-crisis levels, nor did the United States keep pace with the other advanced industrialized economies during the 1980s in terms of productivity growth or investment share (1990: 6). These claims, however, are not without their critics. According to Harvey, the high rates of return on foreign investments resulting from neo-liberalization helped fuel much of the growth in the 1990s (Harvey, 2006: 33). Robert Brenner further argues that the U.S. established the conditions for the revival of profitability in the 1980s, primarily by means of the striking turnaround of its manufacturing sector within the global economy (2002: 50–93). Given these disputes, the analysis of this latest phase of American capitalist development has thus become a major concern for all theorists interested in the historical analysis of the various stages of capitalism.

In more recent years, a new stage of capitalist development has begun to emerge from the troubled conditions that the widespread adoption of neo-liberal policies has created. The end of the 1990s economic boom and the election of George W. Bush in the United States have paved the way for a new neo-conservative doctrine to serve as the ideological rationale for a new kind of imperialism. Neo-conservatism is like neo-liberalism in that it also maintains that freedom and human welfare are best enhanced by the proliferation of free markets in commodities and capital (Harvey, 2005b: 201). Unlike neo-liberalism, however, the primary objective of neo-conservatism is the establishment of and respect for order, both internally and upon the world stage (190). Whether this objective is entirely consistent with the advocacy of unrestricted markets is something that remains to be seen. This shift appears especially important when one considers that the regulated structure of the progressive era arose in reaction to the free market environment of the late nineteenth century, which advocated unrestricted individualism in the realms of consumer choice and capitalist competition. The implications of this parallel are explored at greater length in the conclusion.

1.2 RECENT DEVELOPMENTS IN SOCIAL STRUCTURE OF ACCUMULATION THEORY

To grasp the relevance of the postwar crisis and the subsequent period of institutional restructuring to the analysis that follows in later chapters, it may be instructive to briefly explore a number of theoretical developments within the SSA tradition during the last decade. David Kotz, Terence McDonough, and Michael Reich have compiled a collection of articles that surveys the expansion of SSA theory to a variety of topics of concern to radical economists in a book titled simply *Social Structures of Accumulation* (1994). This *expansion* of SSA theory includes more detailed expositions of the institutional features of the postwar social structure of accumulation as well as the greater recent attention paid to earlier social structures of accumulation. For example, Randy Albelda and Chris Tilly argue that race and gender need to be incorporated into SSA analysis in a more fundamental way (1994: 213). They further contend that "proletarianization" and "integration" are more appropriate terms to describe the experiences of women and men of color during the postwar era than "segmentation" (218). Martin Wolfson has also contributed to the expansion of SSA analysis with his analysis of the way that the financial system contributed to the rapid growth of the postwar SSA by promoting stability, enhancing profitability, and managing class conflicts (1994: 134). Terence McDonough's analysis of the monopoly capitalist SSA (1994) has already been discussed above and provides yet another example of the broad scope of the current research in this area.

Although the expansion of social structure of accumulation analysis has encouraged radical political economists to investigate the characteristics of earlier SSAs in American history, more recent theoretical developments are necessary to demonstrate the relevance of the postwar SSA for these earlier periods. Martin Wolfson (2003) and David Kotz (2003) have recently advocated the *generalization* of SSA analysis in an effort to account for the fact that the U.S. economy has been unable to restore rapid capital accumulation and economic growth in the neo-liberal era. Bowles, Gordon, and Weisskopf recognized this puzzling fact as early as 1987 when they noted that conservative economic policy in the 1980s failed to restore the rate of profit even though it succeeded to some extent in reforming the key institutions of the postwar SSA (1987: 52). Although Bowles, Gordon, and Weisskopf attribute the economy's sluggish growth to "the inherent contradictions of conservative macroeconomic policy" (52), Wolfson and Kotz advocate a much more general solution to this theoretical problem.

Expressed in the simplest terms, the generalization of social structure of accumulation analysis requires the abandonment of the notion that a set of institutions must give rise to rapid capital accumulation and economic growth. Wolfson and Kotz thus advocate a modified SSA framework through which the history of capitalist development is understood in terms of a series of successive "institutional structures" (Kotz, 2003: 264; Wolfson, 2003: 258) that do not necessarily promote rapid capital accumulation. Kotz defines an institutional structure as "a coherent set of economic, political, and cultural/ideological institutions that provides a structure for capitalist economic activity" (264). Therefore, SSA analysis no longer requires an exclusive emphasis on social structures of accumulation. This broader framework is thus capable of classifying the neo-liberal period as a stable institutional structure that nevertheless fails to promote rapid capital accumulation and economic growth.[2] It may be objected, however, that this new terminological distinction possesses the unwelcome characteristic of suggesting that an institutional structure that is characterized by sluggish growth and capital accumulation is not at the same time "socially" structured. For this reason, we might identify such a period as a *social structure of stagnation*. Granted, such an institutional structure is not created for the purpose of undermining rapid capital accumulation but that is nevertheless the consequence of institutional reform in particular historical periods. It is the fact that a particular balance of class forces leads to the social construction of a stagnating capitalist economy that justifies this particular label.

The puzzling character of the neo-liberal institutional structure as relatively stable and yet plagued with sluggish growth by historical standards has led to a welcome generalization of SSA theory that extends over the entire history of capitalist development. The modifications to SSA theory, however, extend beyond a simple allowance for weaker aggregate economic performance. Specifically, the institutional structures appear to alternate according to whether the principle of the free market or the principle of regulation dominates (Wolfson, 2003: 259). Kotz classifies a given institutional structure as either a "liberal institutional structure" (LIS) or a "regulationist institutional structure" (RIS) depending on the tendency that dominates during that particular period (2003: 264). According to Kotz, regulationist institutional structures appear to be better for capital accumulation than liberal institutional structures (265). Wolfson also recognizes this tendency, arguing that a regulated structure is a social structure of accumulation because it experiences economic growth (261).[3] In contrast, liberal institutional structures tend to be social structures of stagnation. It is essential to remember that it is fundamentally an empirical question whether regulationist institutional structures are social structures of accumulation while liberal institutional structures are social structures of stagnation. Whether they are consistently linked is a question that only historical investigation can answer. In addition, the distinction between liberal and regulationist institutional structures is purely structural whereas the distinction between social structures of accumulation and stagnation is performance-based. Hence, the generalization of social structure of accumulation analysis involves a modification of the theory at both the level of structure and the level of performance.

The inspiration for this modified social structure of accumulation framework is found in Karl Polanyi's *The Great Transformation* (2001). Originally published in 1944, Polanyi's book examines the historical transformation of human society from one in which the economy was subordinate to society to one in which the new industrial interests continually sought to subordinate society to the logic of the free market. The newly emerging class of industrial capitalists used the free market ideology, championed by classical political economists, to rationalize the commodification of land, labor, and money. Among Polanyi's central theses, however, is the claim that self-regulating markets never work (Stiglitz, 2001: vii) and will destroy human society and the natural environment if they are allowed to expand unchecked (Block, 2001: xxv). Fortunately, the movement towards laissez-faire is offset by a protective counter-movement as all groups in society (at one time or another) participate in resisting the transition to a self-regulating market economy (Block, 2001: xxviii). Recently, John Micklethwait and Adrian Wooldridge have explained that "[l]ooking back through history, most periods of gaudy capitalism have been followed by a reaction" (2003: 155). Both Wolfson and Kotz also acknowledge the relevance of this "double movement" in their analyses of alternating institutional structures (Wolfson, 2003: 258; Kotz, 2003: 268). The liberal institutional structure may be interpreted as the free market phase and the regulationist institutional structure as the protective counter-movement through which society restrains the excesses of the free market.

The relationship between recent attempts to generalize SSA analysis and Polanyi's analysis from over a half century ago is deeper yet. Polanyi's arguments were developed in direct response to Austrian economists such as Ludwig von Mises and F.A. Hayek, who continued to defend market liberalism even as the stability of the world capitalist economy began to crumble. Polanyi's challenge to Mises extends back to the 1920s (Block, 2003: xx). Similar to the social structure of accumulation theorists who seek to untangle the complexities of economic crisis, Polanyi sought to explain how the prolonged peace in Europe from 1815 to 1914 suddenly ended in world war and economic collapse (Block, 2003: xxii). This "Hundred Years' Peace," as Polanyi aptly phrases it, represented the dominance of free market institutions, and its end marked the inevitable response of class forces seeking to restrain the self-regulating market economy. Extending the analogy between SSA analysis and Polanyi's work, it is worth noting that Polanyi identifies four institutions whose demise led to the collapse of nineteenth century civilization. The institutions include the balance-of-power within the international system, the international gold standard, the self-regulating market, and the liberal state (Polanyi, 2003: 3). It is through a similar theoretical lens that the notion of alternating institutional structures should be interpreted.

The classification of institutional structures as either regulationist or liberal necessarily introduces a more concrete description of institutions at the relatively abstract level of basic terminology. It is no longer sufficient to refer only to social structures of accumulation as a set of institutions capable of promoting rapid capital accumulation and economic growth. The alternation between free market periods and regulated periods involves the greater specification of the institutions underlying an institutional structure. Therefore, the surprising implication of the generalization of SSA analysis is its further *concretion*. This book advances the concretion of SSA analysis to the realm of historical application. The specific method employed to accomplish this task in the case of the American iron and steel industry during the early twentieth century is elaborated later in this chapter.

The specification of alternating institutional structures has led David Kotz to identify their differences along four dimensions that he labels as "state-economy relations, capital-labor relations, capital-capital relations, and the character of the dominant ideology" (2003: 264). Kotz explains that in a liberal institutional structure, the state adopts a laissez-faire approach to economic activity, capital is on the offensive with respect to labor, cut-throat inter-capitalist competition dominates, and the glorification of the free market is expressed in the dominant ideology. On the other hand, in a regulationist institutional structure, the state actively regulates business, capital-labor relations involve an element of cooperation and compromise, inter-capitalist rivalry is muted, and the dominant ideology reflects suspicion of the free market and support for an active government (264). Hence, this new conceptualization of social structure of accumulation analysis necessitates a more specific initial description of the institutions governing capital accumulation.

Martin Wolfson's contribution to the generalization of social structure of accumulation analysis also involves a certain degree of institutional specification in the construction of the theory's basic framework. Wolfson argues that "all the stable institutional structures of a capitalist society . . . represent the (temporary) stabilization of the central contradictions of capitalism" (2003: 258). These contradictions include the contradiction between capital and labor as well as those between capital and the state and between competing capitalists (258). During free market periods, capital dominates labor whereas during regulated periods, labor is strong enough to prevent capital from completely dominating economic relations. Among the contradictions in Wolfson's framework are several not listed among Kotz's four institutions, namely the struggles for unity within the working class and the contradictions between financial and non-financial capital (258). This theoretical shift of emphasis away from institutions and towards contradictions also serves as a reminder of the way in which social relations constantly threaten to usher in the forces of social change. These social processes periodically explode in economic crises and create the series of alternating institutional structures that is the subject matter of this discussion.

It is now possible to consider the consequences that the concretion of social structure of accumulation analysis carries for the historical breakdown of U.S. economic history. Earlier in this chapter, U.S. economic history was discussed in terms of a series of three overlapping social structures of accumulation as the economic crisis of one set of institutions occurred simultaneously with an institutional restructuring that gave rise to a new set of growth-promoting institutions. The modified SSA framework advocated by Wolfson and Kotz suggests the need for a new historical arrangement that organizes the history of American capitalism in terms of alternating regulationist and liberal institutional structures. This task involves reference to both the changing institutional forms in U.S. history as well as the changing aggregate performance of the economy through time.

Table 1.2   Alternating institutional structures in U.S. economic history: 1900–2001.

Institutional Structure	Period	Output Growth Rate (%)	Investment Rate (%)*
Progressive Era Regulated Institutional Structure	1900–1916	3.70	.23
Post World War I Liberal Institutional Structure	1920–1932	.31	-12.50
Post World War II Regulated Institutional Structure	1947–1973	3.98	5.55
Contemporary Liberal Institutional Structure	1980–2001	3.05	1.71

David M. Kotz, *Review of Radical Political Economics*, Vol. 35, No. 3. pp. 263–270, copyright © 2003 by Union for Radical Political Economics. Reprinted by Permission of SAGE Publications, Inc.

SOURCE: *The entire table is excerpted from (Kotz, 2003: 267) with the exception of the investment rate, which the author has computed using data from the U.S. Bureau of the Census (1960), the U.S. Bureau of Economic Analysis (2003), and the U.S. Bureau of Labor Statistics (2003).*

NOTE: *All figures have been adjusted for inflation.*

* *The investment rate is defined for the first two periods as the estimated average annual growth rate of real gross private capital formation. For the two most recent periods, the investment rate is defined as the annual average growth rate of real gross domestic private investment.*

Kotz concludes his article with one particular dating scheme that interprets U.S. capitalist history in terms of a series of alternating institutional structures (2003: 267). A portion of this scheme, along with the annual growth and investment rates for each institutional structure, has been provided in Table 1.2. Rather than two social structures of accumulation characterizing American capitalist history since 1900, Table 1.2 indicates that this history is better captured with a series of four alternating institutional structures. A number of years have not been assigned to any particular period because, during these years, the gradual erosion and replacement of earlier institutions meant that no identifiable institutional structure was firmly in place. The rates of output growth and investment suggest that regulationist institutional structures provide a more favorable environment for economic growth and capital accumulation than liberal institutional structures. This expectation is consistent with the expectations of both Wolfson and Kotz (Wolfson, 2003: 261; Kotz, 2003: 265). The progressive era and post-WWII regulationist institutional structures may, therefore, be correctly labeled social structures of accumulation whereas the post-WWI and contemporary liberal institutional structures may be identified as social structures of stagnation.

McDonough (2008: 168) is somewhat critical of this particular dating scheme on the grounds that Kotz characterizes the post-WWI LIS as a period of slow growth which nevertheless includes the Roaring Twenties. Only by extending the period into the Great Depression, McDonough argues, is Kotz able to characterize the institutional structure as one exhibiting slow growth. It is an objection worth considering. At the same time, it should be remembered that business cycle fluctuations are to be expected within the period during which an institutional structure is in place. The rapid accumulation that occurs on the basis of a changed set of institutions may be undermined rather quickly by those same institutional characteristics. To the extent that a distinct set of institutional features were in place from 1920 to 1932, the period as a whole may be considered one of sluggish growth. This question requires a more detailed treatment than is possible here.

1.3   CAPITAL-LABOR RELATIONS IN TWO REGULATIONIST INSTITUTIONAL STRUCTURES

As explained above, the generalization of social structure of accumulation analysis leads to certain expectations about the nature of the institutions that govern capital accumulation and economic growth. Hence, the institutional characteristics of each institutional structure listed in Table 1.2 should conform to our expectations. Unfortunately, the dangers of making broad assertions in the field of macroeconomic history quickly rise to the surface upon closer inspection.

Regulationist institutional structures consist of stable institutions that evolve in direct response to the excesses of free markets that threaten to destroy society if they are permitted to grow unchecked. As a result, the institutional features of the Progressive Era and Post-World War II Regulated Institutional Structures should be similar to a certain extent. Social structure of accumulation theorists have acknowledged, however, that the institutional characteristics of the two periods diverge considerably. David Kotz, for example, contrasts the core institutions of the progressive era with the core institutions of the post-World War II expansion (1994a: 65). In particular, Kotz identifies the dominance of monopoly/finance capital, the repression of trade unions, and an aggressively imperialist foreign policy with the early twentieth century U.S. economy. In contrast, he associates militarization of the economy, peaceful collective bargaining, and the U.S. ascent to a dominant global position with the postwar era. Kotz is not alone in recognizing the difference between the two periods. Bowles, Gordon, and Weisskopf (1990), for example, also contrast the restructuring in 1900 with the restructuring after World War II. In the first period, the large corporations:

> . . . so successfully restored their economic and political power . . . that they reigned virtually unchecked during the 1920s. After the second period of restructuring, in contrast, the new SSA involved a much more complex balance of forces—with significant concessions to organized labor and substantial improvements in income security. Popular forces thus had a much greater effect on the second institutional transformation than they had on the first. (1990: 26)

Radical historians, such as Garbriel Kolko and James Weinstein, base their critiques of traditional accounts of the progressive era on the common assertion that the reforms of the period originated largely with middle class and agrarian social movements. In the above quotation, Bowles, Gordon, and Weisskopf also seem skeptical of this popular interpretation of the progressive era reforms. If the leading corporations of the newly consolidated industries had a significant role in the reforms of the progressive era, then the source of reform may be helpful in distinguishing between regulationist institutional structures.

The stark contrast between capital's treatment of labor during the progressive era with its treatment of labor during the postwar era is especially puzzling given that regulationist institutional structures are created to restrain the destructive character of free markets. Labor unions would be expected to participate in the construction of a RIS given that workers have much to gain from regulating the conditions of labor that have most likely deteriorated during the previous free market period. For example, when defining the limited capital-labor accord of the postwar SSA, Bowles, Gordon and Weisskopf explain that corporations retained control over "the essential decisions governing enterprise operations" (e.g., decisions pertaining to production, technology, plant location, investment, and marketing) (1990: 56). At the same time, unions were acknowledged as the legitimate representatives of workers' interests. They would pursue labor's economic goals (e.g., a greater share in productivity gains, greater job security, and improved working conditions). Specifically, the postwar practice of "productivity bargaining" linked wage gains to productivity growth (1990: 83). Wolfson also supports the view that during the postwar period, capital traded union recognition for union acceptance of management control of decision-making (2003: 260). In Harvey's view, the coupling of wages with productivity gains resulted from the pushing and cajoling of labor into a general compact with capital (2005b: 51). In any case, the capital-labor accord finally began to break down when workers, such as women and minorities who were excluded from the productivity gains of the postwar era, began protesting (1990: 57). While noting the objections of Lichtenstein (2002) and others, it may be argued that capital accepted the existence of organized labor to a certain extent and tolerated the influence that labor unions possessed over the distribution of economic gains in the early postwar period more than in earlier periods.

During the progressive era, on the other hand, capital assumed an aggressive stance towards organized labor despite the characterization of it as a regulationist institutional structure. Rather than the limited cooperation between capital and labor one might expect, the progressive era is marked by the refusal of corporations to recognize the legitimacy of unions. An open-shop drive initiated by capitalist corporations eliminated unions in all the trustified industries with the exception of the railroads and established a new balance of power between capital and labor by 1904 (McDonough, 1994: 110). The reorganization of the labor process through the introduction of mechanized production further eroded the bargaining power of trade unions, which depended primarily on the skill base of their membership.[4] Although corporations developed a series of welfare policies to share their gains with employees, the extent of this sharing rested largely with the corporations due to the general exclusion of unions from the process.[5]

This chapter has briefly surveyed the development of social structure of accumulation analysis from its inception through its more recent generalization. The concept of an institutional structure has led to the formation of specific expectations about their characteristics. Drawing attention to the contrasting capital-labor relations of two regulationist institutional structures is of great significance given the status of that relation as one of the central contradictions of capitalist society. Kotz's assertion that more cooperative capital-labor relations should characterize regulated periods (2003: 264) does not account for the differences in the capital-labor relations of the Progressive Era RIS and the Post-World War II RIS. Ironically, part of the solution may also be found in one of Kotz's earlier suggestions. In a manner consistent with Wolfson's assertion that institutional structures involve a temporary stabilization of capitalist contradictions, Kotz has argued that capital-labor conflict can be stabilized either through capital's commitment to bargain with labor or through its determination to outright oppose labor as in the neo-liberal period (1994a: 55). In other words, relatively cooperative labor-management relations are not, after all, a necessary feature of regulationist institutional structures. The only requirement is that some sort of controls be imposed on the labor market and labor conditions so as to consciously shape the outcomes and thus prevent those that would occur if the market were left largely unregulated. The motivation for this study of early capital-labor relations in the American iron and steel industry is the curious fact that capital elected to dominate labor within an institutional structure that constitutes a reaction against the free market.

An issue to be explored in greater detail then is that the systematic suppression of labor may characterize a RIS. This approach gives rise to the possibility of two distinct forms of regulationist institutional structure. On the one hand, the restraints in the marketplace may be the result of a protracted struggle that gives rise to a highly complex balance of class forces thus creating the conditions for the realization of modest working class objectives within a capitalist society. This form of regulationist institutional structure is consistent with the post-WWII SSA that is frequently alluded to in the literature pertaining to the subject. On the other hand, capitalists may be in a position to impose direct market controls and regulations without regard to the aims and needs of the working class as a result of the weakened position of organized labor and the inability or unwillingness of government officials or the public to intervene on the behalf of workers. It is this sort of institutional structure that best explains how capitalists severely suppressed workers within the context of the progressive era regulationist structure.

This entire discussion, of course, appears to smack of a contradiction when recalling Polanyi's notion of the double movement. No such contradiction exists, however, because reactions against the free market are not the reactions of the working class and the poorer classes alone. Capital also participates in this reaction against the free market, the unrestricted spread of which would undermine the entire social fabric. The nature of the regulationist institutional structure that forms in response to the dangerous tendencies of the unrestricted market depends completely on the class struggle and whether capital or organized labor emerges as having the upper hand in negotiations pertaining to the conditions and terms of exploitation. Similarly, the state in a regulationist institutional structure should not necessarily be expected to be either interventionist or laissez-faire. In a later chapter, it is shown that in the case of the steel industry during the progressive era, a relatively laissez-faire stance on the part of the federal government provided capitalists with the freedom to impose their own particular regulatory apparatus on the industry. Paradoxically, a laissez-faire stance may actually contribute to the regulated structure of social relations.

This clarification of the notion of regulated periods raises a number of significant issues. In particular, if a specific RIS involves capital's harsh suppression of labor, then the interpretation of its oppressive character when indications of capital-labor cooperation appear to exist is an additional challenge that necessarily follows. Furthermore, the possibility that capital may elect to *consciously* dominate labor within the context of a regulated institutional structure in which market forces are restrained renders the exploitation of labor by capital even more apparent and thus even more subject to the legitimate attacks of critics of the capitalist mode of production.

1.4 METHODOLOGY

Although this modified SSA framework is well suited to the exploration of the subject matter at hand, it should be noted that SSA theory is not without its critics. Ernest Mandel argues that even though the theory of long waves is of Marxist origin, Marxists eventually "turned their backs" on it after it was further developed by Kondratieff, Schumpeter, and others (1995: 1). Mandel has attempted to revive a distinctly Marxist theory of long waves by arguing that Marxists must consider three separate time frames in their discussion of fluctuations in the average rate of profit. In addition to the industrial cycle, the traditional emphasis of orthodox business cycle theory, and the entire life span of the capitalist system, which brings attention to the long-term tendency of the rate of profit to fall, he advocates a renewed emphasis on the long waves of 20–25 years (9). Mandel's theory differs from SSA theory in that it is an asymmetric theory of long waves in which depressive long waves have their origin in the internal logic of capitalist development, arising from the falling tendency of the rate of profit. At the same time, expansionist long waves can be explained only in terms of extra-economic factors (e.g., the class struggle, state intervention, military confrontation) that raise the rate of surplus value and so serve to counter the tendency towards a falling rate of profit. It is thus an eclectic combination of determinism and non-determinism that maintains an emphasis on the internal laws of capitalist development within Mandel's theory while creating a space for revolutionary social transformation. By his own admission, Mandel's criticism of Gordon's theory of stages of capitalism may have been exaggerated (116). In any case, it offers an alternative to SSA theory that is more firmly grounded in orthodox Marxist theory.

One of the greatest and most direct challenges to SSA analysis is the one that historian Nelson Lichtenstein (2002) has put forward. Lichtenstein's attack concentrates primarily on the claim that a labor-management accord was struck in the decades following World War II. To strengthen his critique, Lichtenstein cites the fact that strike levels were historically high during the 1940s and 1950s and that even if industrial relations stability existed in some core industries (e.g., automobiles, steel), such stability did not exist in sectors where wages were low, output labor intensive and management decisively anti-union (Lichtenstein, 2002: 99). Perhaps the greater point is that insofar as any sort of accord did exist, it must be remembered that it was in the context of a capitalist system that is defined, in part, by a contradictory relationship between wage labor and capital in which labor is always subordinate to capital. Lichtenstein clarifies by saying that "[a]t best it was a limited and unstable truce, largely confined to a well-defined set of regions and industries. It was a product of defeat, not victory" (99). This unstable truce was certainly a failure in that labor had not achieved the elimination of the contradictory dynamic between itself and capital in the aftermath of the Great Depression and its replacement with a more just set of social relations. From the standpoint of American capitalist social relations, with its long history of repressing organized labor, however, the decades following World War II were a victory for the labor movement, but it is critical to keep in mind that within a capitalist economy, no capital-labor cooperation, in the strong sense, is even conceivable because it is inherently illogical. Capital-labor "cooperation" should always be understood in the weaker sense to mean that labor, possibly with state backing, is able to achieve modest gains and that capital is somewhat resigned to the fact that some gains need to be shared to maintain stable industrial relations.

During the 1970s, another general research program, known as regulation theory, developed within the field of radical political economy. Michel Aglietta's (2000) groundbreaking application of this approach to American capitalist development is also more firmly rooted in orthodox Marxian theory than the SSA approach. Aglietta posits a theory of social regulation as a complete alternative to general equilibrium theory in that regulation theory seeks to formulate in general laws the way in which the determinant structure of society is reproduced (2000: 13–14). Capitalist crises may then be interpreted as "ruptures" in the continuous reproduction of social relations (19). The Marxist roots of Aglietta's regulation theory are present in how he defines the notion of a regime of accumulation, which he regards as an intermediate concept that is less broad than the more general principle of capital accumulation. Simply defined, it is a form of social transformation that increases relative surplus value under stable conditions (68). Aglietta also distinguishes between two distinct forms of accumulation regime (71). The predominantly extensive regime of accumulation is one in which relative surplus value is obtained by transforming the organization of the labor process. In contrast, the predominantly intensive regime of accumulation appropriates relative surplus value by creating a new mode of life for the wage-earning class by greatly expanding the sphere of commodity production, for example. Within this theoretical framework, the progressive era occurred within the context of an extensive regime of accumulation whereas the post-WWII era occurred within the context of an intensive regime of accumulation.

The social structure of accumulation school in the United States shares many of the concerns of the Parisian school that spearheaded the development of regulation theory. In particular, regulation theorists favor the dynamic notion of the regulation of capitalism as opposed to the static notion of reproduction that many orthodox Marxists and neoclassical economists tend to favor (Jessop, 1994: 329). Like social structure of accumulation analysis, regulation theory is also a theory of long waves (1994: 330). David Kotz has also investigated the similarities and differences between the two schools of thought. Among other points, Kotz emphasizes that both theories explain the long run process of capital accumulation in terms of the set of institutions that affect it (1994b: 86). Both theories also explain capitalism's development in terms of a series of stages, consider economic crises to be transitional between stages, and use an intermediate level of analysis that is neither highly abstract nor very narrow (1994b: 86–87). The intermediate nature of both regulation and SSA analysis is especially relevant to the methodological approach adopted for this research.

The intermediate nature of theoretical analysis does not prohibit abstract thought or concrete research. On the contrary, regulation theory involves three levels of analysis that may be classified according to decreasing degrees of abstraction. According to Boyer and Saillard, the three levels include the analysis of modes of production and their connections, the description of the social and economic patterns that allow long-term accumulation to occur between structural crises, and the analysis of the specific configurations of social relations for any given era or geographical location (2002: 38). Regulation theorists seek to describe institutional forms as well as analyze their permanent transformations. Institutional forms serve as the basis of observed social and economic patterns and thus permit "a passage from micro to macroeconomics" (38–39). The intermediate nature of theoretical analysis thus does not forbid, but rather inspires, concrete analyses of the historical development of capitalism.

Social structure of accumulation theorists are also careful not to let the intermediate character of SSA analysis interfere with their concrete investigations of capitalist history. Gordon, Edwards, and Reich have clearly stated their commitment to specific analyses of economic history:

> [A] final specification of the character of production at any point and time cannot depend solely on analysis at an abstract level but must also focus on more concrete determinations. (1994: 12)

They further explain that many historians have followed the example of E.P. Thompson in Britain and Herbert Gutman in the U.S. in placing nearly exclusive emphasis on concrete and specific analyses of the daily lives of workers and employers in particular periods and locations. The authors admit to the extreme value of these studies yet also claim that "their broader meaning remains ambiguous" (Gordon et al., 1982: 22). The intermediate level of analysis found in social structure of accumulation theory implies that the broad historical context and social meaning of capitalist economic activity must never be forgotten.

This investigation of the specific character of capital-labor relations in the American iron and steel industry during the progressive era takes seriously the general methodological approach discussed above. The combination of the case study approach and social structure of accumulation theory requires the prior elaboration of the historical and theoretical background to facilitate a more detailed analysis of the industry. This unique approach to radical political economy is necessary to reveal the social significance of the industry's development without losing sight of it beneath a thick layer of historical minutiae. Furthermore, insofar as case study work should internalize theorizing practices (Harvey, 2006: 115), every effort has been made to rely on SSA theory as a guide for the investigative reconstruction of the development of the steel industry during the late nineteenth and early twentieth centuries. Whenever this process has led to modifications in the theoretical perspective being used, they have been foreshadowed in this chapter and expanded further in the conclusion.

This chapter has provided the theoretical categories and overview of American capitalist history necessary to place the Progressive Era Regulated Institutional Structure among the other institutional structures in U.S. economic history. Chapter 2 continues the transition to a more micro-economic analysis of the iron and steel industry by examining the structure and performance of the Progressive Era RIS in greater detail. The nature of capital-labor relations, inter-capitalist relations, state-capital relations, and the dominant ideology are explored at length. Certain expectations regarding the performance of the institutional structure are also tested against the available evidence. For example, Kotz explains that "[w]hen a social structure of accumulation is established, and class conflict and competition become more stable, profit rates should rise as well as becoming more predictable" (1994a: 56–57). Rapid economic growth should also characterize the period given its status as a social structure of accumulation. In terms of distribution, a RIS is expected to diverge from a LIS, which tends to benefit the capitalist class by driving wages down and increasing income/wealth inequality (Kotz, 2003: 266). The period as a whole must be explored carefully to provide an accurate historical backdrop to a more concrete analysis of labor and industrial history.

With the theoretical framework and historical context firmly in place, Chapters 3 and 4 are devoted to a detailed analysis of industrial and labor conditions in the iron and steel industry during the early twentieth century. Chapter 3 explores the way in which the steel companies, the imperialist state, and the dominant ideology functioned to create and reinforce a stable environment for capital accumulation and economic growth in the iron and steel industry. The consequences of the industry's institutional structure for its rate of profit, growth rate of output, and pricing policies are explored in detail. The manner in which the regulatory program of the steel industry eventually led to a harsh reaction by the forces of organized labor, which had been stifled by the industry during the progressive era, is developed at length in chapter 4. The history of capital-labor relations in the iron and steel industry reveals that its regulated features during the progressive era created a volatile situation in which labor conditions did not improve sufficiently (and, by some measures, worsened) and thus led to the industrial strike of 1919. Rather than lose sight of the historical context of this key American industry, it is essential to turn now to an investigation of the main features of the Progressive Era Regulationist Institutional Structure.

2 The Structure and Performance of the Progressive Era Regulationist Institutional Structure (RIS)

Whenever the history of human civilization is written, one is inevitably drawn to processes of social change and the human conflicts that are, almost invariably, responsible for their development. Historical analysis, therefore, tends to be political and is frequently colored with a particular ideology. Radical political economists take advantage of this characteristic of historical analysis by rewriting conventional histories to create an alternative social vision to the one currently dominant in capitalist society. This chapter draws together the attempts of radical historians and economists to provide an alternative vision of American capitalism during the progressive era (i.e., 1900–1916) and offers criticisms of more standard interpretations of the period. More importantly, the chapter highlights the role that regulation played during this period and demonstrates how hostile capital-labor relations reveal the contradictory nature of regulation within a RIS.

The first section of the chapter provides a brief overview of the liberal institutional structure of the late nineteenth century. Sections two through six correspond to the historical description of five general institutional categories as they developed during the progressive era. These institutional categories include inter-capitalist relations, state-capital relations, the dominant ideology, the financial system, and capital-labor relations. Section seven then pays special attention to the relationship between the institutions of the period and the aggregate economic performance to which they contributed. The theoretical framework developed in chapter 1 provides the lens through which the historical developments in this chapter are examined.

2.1 THE LATE NINETEENTH CENTURY LIBERAL INSTITUTIONAL STRUCTURE (LIS)

The late nineteenth century U.S. economy is best described as a liberal institutional structure. In an effort to define the boundaries of the period, this institutional structure may be said to have lasted from the first year after the post-Civil War Reconstruction ended in 1878 to the year of the panic of 1893, which began the transition to the progressive era regulationist institutional structure. The main structural features that characterize American capitalism today were being formed during this critical period in U.S. history.

Capitalist competition was of the cutthroat sort in many industries and a prolonged period of deflation caused many businesses to fail. In the railroad industry, for example, freight wars and bankruptcies were common. As Peter Gourevitch (1986) has explained, the hard times that began in 1873 derived directly from the preceding good times. According to the logic of investment cycles, the push to earn profits through new investment squeezes profit margins to the point where investment halts, causing demand to drop and leaving factories with a large production capacity but without buyers for their products (Gourevitch, 1986: 72). Thomas McCraw argues further that scholars typically underestimate the problem of industrial overcapacity during the period, which was relevant to the trust movement, the protective tariff movement, the railroad rate problem, and the imperial quest for foreign markets to absorb surplus production (1984: 67–68). Hence, just as the hard times of the late nineteenth century followed naturally from the earlier good times, the same hard times would create conditions for a renewed period of growth and profitability in the twentieth century.

Capital-labor relations often erupted in violent confrontations as well. Examples of such confrontations were numerous and included the 1877 strike on the Baltimore and Ohio Railroad, the 1886 Haymarket Square Riot, and the 1892 Homestead steel strike. Furthermore, the American labor movement was growing rapidly in response to the homogenizing transformation of the American workforce. Workers no longer controlled the nature of the labor process but were required to adjust to the demands of mechanized production and skill reduction. Labor organizations, such as the Knights of Labor founded in 1869 and the American Federation of Labor founded in 1886, sprang up to represent the interests of workers in this rapidly changing industrial climate.

The relationship between capitalists and the American government was laissez-faire in many respects during the period. The federal government was certainly supportive of western settlement and the development of the railroad industry, but it was miniscule by today's standards. Militarily, it was slow to recover from the Civil War, and most government revenue was derived from tariffs and excise taxes on liquor and whiskey. Government regulation of business was in its infancy, and any variation in the legal environment across state lines could send capital rushing from one state to another. Such migrations of capital were already occurring in the middle of the century, for example, when George Smith moved his Wisconsin Fire and Marine Insurance Company to Wisconsin after the Illinois state legislature outlawed the issuance of circulating notes of small denominations

(Tuttle and Perry, 1970: 166). A more notable example was the relocation of the Standard Oil Trust to New Jersey after the Ohio Supreme Court ruled that it was behaving as a monopoly in violation of state antitrust laws in 1892.

The dominant ideology used to rationalize the prevailing social structure in the late nineteenth century praised the individual as the most basic unit of society and as having a potential that could only be fully realized within the American social structure. It was a philosophy that offered a rationale for poverty and hope for the working class. Furthermore, the ideology of individualism extended into the realm of capitalist competition where individual firms competing with one another would generate the greatest possible benefits for society. The dominant ideology of the late nineteenth century LIS thus supported the doctrine of laissez-faire and a minimal economic role for government. Even though each of these institutional characteristics persisted to some degree well into the progressive era, each was dethroned as a dominant feature and replaced with a new structural characteristic that was better able to foster rapid capital accumulation and economic growth in the early twentieth century.

2.2 THE CENTRALIZATION OF CAPITAL: INTER-CAPITALIST RELATIONS

The economic crisis of the late nineteenth century initiated a massive transformation of American society. In response to the instability and stagnation of the 1870s and 1880s, firms sought to insulate themselves against competition and the threat of bankruptcy by forming combinations, syndicates, and trusts (Gordon et al., 1982: 106). An early sign of this centralization of capital occurred when John D. Rockefeller formed Standard Oil through the takeover of rival firms in 1870. The trend continued when James Duke's cigarette business in Durham, North Carolina merged with four competitors to form the American Tobacco Company in 1890 (Micklethwait et al., 2003: 66). The growth of large firms continued throughout the late nineteenth century in other industries, including the meat packing industry, the telephone industry, and the iron and steel industry.

By the end of the nineteenth century, the transformation of American society developed rapidly along these lines. The merger era included U.S. Steel, American Cotton, National Biscuit, American Tobacco, General Electric, International Harvester, AT&T, and United Fruit (Micklethwait et al., 2003: 66). During the period of greatest consolidation between 1898 and 1902, 3,653 mergers were recorded and between a quarter and a third of the entire U.S. manufacturing capital stock was consolidated (Gordon et al., 1982: 107). As Figure 2.1 indicates, the number of recorded mergers in the manufacturing and mining sectors achieved its highest levels with 1,208 mergers in 1899 and 423 mergers in 1901.

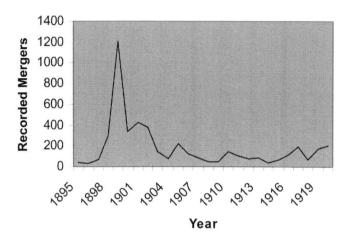

Figure 2.1   Number of mergers in manufacturing and mining in the U.S.: 1895–1920.
SOURCE: U.S. Bureau of the Census, 1960: 572.

The gross assets involved in mergers in the same sectors also soared as shown in Figure 2.2, reaching nearly $2.3 billion in 1899 and more than $2 billion in 1901.

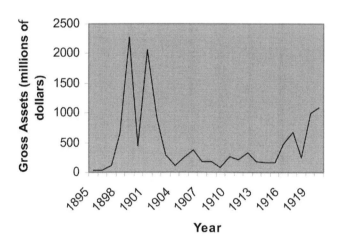

Figure 2.2   Gross assets involved in mergers in manufacturing and mining in the U.S.: 1895–1920.
SOURCE: U.S. Bureau of the Census, 1960: 572.

As the next chapter explains, the formation of the United States Steel Corporation in 1901, the world's first billion dollar business enterprise, is largely responsible for the high levels in that year. After 1902, both measures of industrial consolidation remain at relatively low levels until the 1920s, which was also a decade of expansion and consolidation. The most mergers since the 1880s and 1890s occurred during the 1920s (Henretta et al., 2000: 741). Merger waves thus appear to occur prior to the formation of new regulationist institutional structures: a possible indication of the inadequacy of liberal institutional structures in creating the conditions for economic growth and stability.

The merger movement of the late 1890s was not confined to industries in the eastern United States. Although hydraulic mining damaged the environment, it also helped transform western mining into big business. "[A]s elsewhere in corporate America, the western metal industries went through a process of consolidation" (Henretta et al., 2000: 526). The western mining industry joined the rush to combination during the merger wave at the turn of the century. The Amalgamated Copper Company took control of the Anaconda Copper Mining Company and other Montana mining firms in 1899. The same year, the American Smelting and Refining Company consolidated most of America's lead-mining and copper-refining properties, and San Francisco became the capital of the western mining empire (Henretta et al., 2000: 526).

This brief overview of the pattern of business concentration in the late nineteenth century indicates that a major transformation of U.S. business enterprises began late in that century and culminated in a wave of mergers from 1898 to 1902. It is difficult to overstate the magnitude of these changes. Prior to the 1880–1920 period, no manufacturing industry, let alone a single manufacturing enterprise, had reached sufficient size to affect masses of people and major factories usually employed no more than a few hundred workers with the largest manufacturing enterprises usually capitalized at less than one million dollars (McCraw, 1984: 64). The causes of this transformation are complex, but it is possible to identify several key factors. Among the main causes of the merger movement according to Gordon, Edwards, and Reich (1982: 106–107) was the completion of the national rail network in the 1880s, which created a national market for goods that justified massive concentrations of capital. They also include the growth of an industrial stock market in the 1880s and the 1889 New Jersey holding company legislation that provided the legal model facilitating corporate consolidation.

Another key reason for the merger movement is one that Gabriel Kolko identifies and may be added to Gordon et al.'s list of causes of the merger movement. Kolko refers to this factor as "an impetus to eliminate competition" (1967: 24). This factor explains most clearly how the economic crisis of the late nineteenth century culminated in the merger wave of the late 1890s. The cutthroat price competition of the previous liberal institutional structure destroyed business confidence and led to a transformation of the prevailing institutional structure. A key reason for the intense competition for buyers may be the problem of overcapacity characteristic of the period. The tendency for production technology to far outrun similar developments in distribution, marketing, and consumer purchasing power led to serious periodic imbalances between the nation's production capacity and its ability to consume, leading businesses to combine to limit output and raise prices (McCraw, 1984: 65–66). This conscientious withdrawal of efficiency to maintain profits even when working people are in need of the additional production is a technique the great social theorist Thorstein Veblen would eventually call the "sabotage of industry by business" (Hunt, 2002: 330). Consolidation was thus a means of confronting the excess capacity problem and stabilizing markets.

A final cause of the merger movement that should not be overlooked involves the search for a special kind of profit that arose with the development of an industrial stock market. According to Micklethwait et al., the merger wave "was, if anything, the work of 'stock promoters'" (2003: 69). Kolko also identifies the drive for promoter's profits[1] as a key influence in the merger wave (1967: 24). The growth of the stock market was very rapid as the nineteenth century came to an end. "The total amount of capital in publicly traded manufacturing companies increased from $33 million in 1890 to more than $7 billion in 1903" (Micklethwait et al., 2003: 69–70). The power of investment bankers, like J.P. Morgan, was considerable and enduring. They charged huge fees for the underwriting services they provided and frequently maintained control of the combines by serving as directors after the mergers were completed (Henretta et al., 2000: 659). Historian Howard Zinn cites an early twentieth century U.S. Senate report, which explains that Morgan and Rockefeller sat on the boards of 48 and 37 corporations, respectively (Zinn, 2003: 258). Based on the *expected* profits of the new consolidations, the profits of stock promoters frequently exceeded the amount that their return justified.

At the beginning of this section, the suggestion was made that the economic crisis of the late nineteenth century was the key factor responsible for the merger movement. Gordon et al.'s short list of causes, therefore, does not clarify *specifically* how the economic crisis of the late nineteenth century contributed to the merger movement. The railroad industry, for example, contributed to the merger wave in other ways aside from the fact that it created a national market for goods. The transcontinental railroad was completed in 1869, and yet the great postwar railroad boom did not begin until 1878 when the economy began to recover from a recession that began in 1873. Forty thousand miles of track were laid west of the Mississippi River during the 1880s (Henretta et al., 2000: 511). The federal government made railroad construction the work of private enterprises, and the state and federal governments actively assisted them. State governments bought railroad bonds and the federal government provided land grants and the corporate form of business organization necessary for the firms to raise large amounts of capital (2000: 545). The importance of the railroads for national economic success thus led to government support for the large scale of railroad enterprises.

The railroads' huge requirement for capital was a major factor in the development of the New York Stock Exchange. Between the end of the American Civil War and the 1890s, Wall Street existed to finance the railroads. The railroads primarily issued bonds to raise capital (Henretta et al., 2000: 546). Because they were funded largely by debt, the narrow equity base of the railroad companies encouraged bankruptcy (Micklethwait et al., 2003: 62). During the last quarter of the nineteenth century, over 700 railroads went bankrupt (2003: 61). As a result of the many railroad bankruptcies of the 1890s, Wall Street investment bankers, such as J.P. Morgan, reorganized the industry through mergers (2000: 547). Hence, the development of the railroad industry demonstrates how the spike in bankruptcies during the late nineteenth century economic crisis contributed to the reorganization of industry and the large-scale concentration of capital.

Figure 2.3 reveals that a significant relative increase in the number of bankruptcies occurred generally throughout the economy in the 1890s. In 1896, the failure rate for U.S. business enterprises reached its highest level in nearly twenty years at 133 per 10,000 concerns. The average liability per failure for U.S. business enterprises also rose to nearly $23,000 in 1893— its highest level since 1875. This volatile and uncertain business environment thus strongly encouraged business owners to seek greater stability

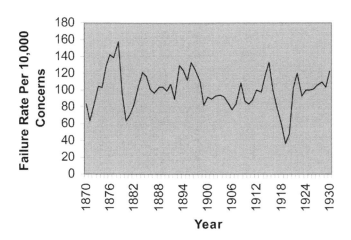

Figure 2.3   Failure rate for U.S. business enterprises: 1870–1930.
SOURCE: U.S. Bureau of the Census, 1960: 570.

and certainty because the existing social structure was no longer deemed suitable for profitable growth.

Much like the causes of the merger movement, the consequences that flowed from industrial consolidation were varied and complex. One immediate consequence of the merger movement was the overwhelming share of the market won by the newly consolidated corporations. According to Gordon, et al. (1982: 108), International Harvester controlled 85% of the agricultural machinery market in 1904. Similarly, the United States Steel Corporation controlled about 60% of the steel market in 1902. The power of large corporations continued well into the progressive era. By 1910, 1% of U.S. manufacturers produced 44% of U.S. industrial output (Henretta et al., 2000: 659). Even though the newly consolidated corporations never achieved a *total* monopoly in their industries (see Kolko, 1967: 8), the final section of this chapter demonstrates empirically that they managed to create a more certain and stable environment for corporate profitability.

Other significant consequences of the merger movement for the progressive era are more closely linked to the remaining institutional characteristics discussed in this chapter. For example, corporate consolidation permitted the large-scale concentration of capital necessary for business enterprises to mechanize their production processes and homogenize their workforces. Their dominating presence in national markets and the harsh working conditions they created threatened small businesspeople and individual farmers as well as more socially conscious Americans. The result was the formation of a multi-class alliance that sought to oppose the large corporations and included small businesses, middle class reformers, and socialists (Gordon et al., 1982: 109–110). These consequences of the merger movement are discussed in greater detail below.

Another consequence of the merger movement was the harsh reaction of the general public to the giant corporations and the federal government's response to their growing power in American life. The Muckrakers were practitioners of a new style of reform journalism that exposed corruption in American life (Henretta et al., 2000: 642). In 1902, the muckraking journalist, Ida Tarbell, exposed Standard Oil and its many abuses of corporate power (Micklethwait et al., 2003: 73). According to Henretta et al., The Pure Food and Drug Act of 1906 was also a victory for muckraking journalists (2000: 639). The pressure created by such reform-minded journalists pressured the federal government to investigate corporate abuses of power. In 1906, Roosevelt initiated an antitrust suit against Standard Oil, which the U.S. Supreme Court ordered dissolved in 1911. In 1911, American Tobacco was also divided up into several separate companies. This standard interpretation of the role of the state in the progressive era contains an element of truth, but it also requires substantial modification as explained in the next section.

A final consequence of the merger movement that should not be overlooked involves the internal reorganization of the business enterprise that was required. In his 1937 article, "The Nature of the Firm," Ronald Coase argued that firms exist to minimize the transaction costs associated with the coordination of particular economic activities (Micklethwait et al., 2003: xxii). Furthermore, the internalization of many independent business units within one enlarged enterprise during the managerial revolution allowed for the administrative coordination of flows of goods between units. According to Alfred Chandler, "[t]he savings resulting from such coordination were much greater than those resulting from lower information and transactions costs" (1977: 7). Chandler's emphasis on the savings that resulted from the administrative coordination of managerial enterprises is insightful. Henretta et al., for example, trace the beginning of the managerial revolution to the 1850s when Daniel McCallum recognized the need for a formal administrative structure in the railroad industry to operate large-scale complex enterprises successfully (2000: 550).

Another important result that Chandler obtains strengthens the argument that technological advantage may have had something to do with the consolidation movement. Specifically, he finds that horizontal integration succeeded in *center industries* (e.g., steel, oil), which are capital-intensive, technologically advanced, and characterized by scale economies (McCraw, 1984: 73). In contrast, labor-intensive industries were rarely dominated by a small number of firms, and mergers in such industries were much less successful (Chandler, 1990: 140). In such *peripheral industries* as textiles, apparel, lumber, furniture, leather, and publishing and printing, firms remained relatively small and owners often continued to participate in their management (1990: 141). In terms of the American structure of industry, this basic pattern remained relatively stable throughout the twentieth century.

At the same time, the internal reorganization of firms should not be viewed entirely in terms of cost reduction and increased efficiency. In Chandler's view, the visible hand of management was more efficient than the invisible hand of the market (Micklethwait et al., 2003: 60). This statement assumes that an efficiency improvement is the best explanation for the rise of the managerial enterprise. The alternative view presented here is that the stable profits and predictable business environment that were the primary goals of corporations in the progressive era are equally necessary to explain how the managerial enterprise became the dominant form of business organization. It is also far from clear whether the managerial enterprise achieved business efficiency. Historical and statistical evidence suggest a poor record for corporations, especially with respect to technical progress (Blair, 1972: 228). Even Chandler was forced to concede "that merger itself was not enough to assure business success" (1977: 338).

For McCraw, contemporary critics of big business lacked the experience and the vocabulary of modern mainstream economics that could clarify the efficiency gains of large enterprises and were thus forced to rely only on their personal sensibilities and traditional political ideologies to guide them (1984: 78). Nevertheless, by his own admission, the majority of prosecutions were aimed at loose cartels of small companies during the first twenty years of the Sherman Act (1984: 79). Additional political factors may have thus played a role in the stifling of centralization in the so-called peripheral industries. It is certainly true that many trusts were unsuccessful in peripheral industries and failed. McCraw thus accuses the muckraking lawyer, Louis Brandeis, of confusing cause with effect when he argued that some trusts failed because they did not gain control of their markets (1984: 100). The technological disadvantage (i.e., diseconomies of scale), however, may not be the only causal explanation for their failures although it was certainly a contributing factor in many cases. Other possible explanations may include the inability or unwillingness to successfully participate in predatory pricing, illegal railroad rebating, etc. In any case, the 1920s marked the completion of the management revolution. By that time, large-scale corporate enterprises with bureaucratic structures had mostly replaced the family-operated businesses of the nineteenth century (Henretta et al., 2000: 741), particularly in center industries.

The consequences that flowed from the centralization of capital all carry important implications for the claim that an evolving regulatory framework served as the basis of the early twentieth century U.S. economy. The new consolidations regulated themselves to an extent by creating a professional class of managers to bring greater certainty to their markets and by using their market power to maintain stable prices. Large corporations also sought to establish greater control over their workforces through the mechanization of production. When business failed to regulate itself to the satisfaction of the public and radical movements began to prosper, the federal government often intervened, armed with antitrust law. As capital sought to overcome the failings of the late nineteenth century LIS, many other segments of society reacted negatively to capital's new vision for the U.S. economy.

2.3   THE REGULATORY STATE: STATE-CAPITAL RELATIONS

The economic role of the state and the legislative efforts of American business enterprise were so closely intertwined during the progressive era that no attempt is made in this section to disentangle them entirely. The federal government also possessed many regulatory characteristics during the late nineteenth century. In fact, "[t]he Civil War . . . brought into being an activist state" that included a national banking system, massive subsidies for interregional railroads, free homesteads for settlers, an expanded postal system, and improvements in rivers and harbors (Henretta et al., 2000: 495). A key difference between the post-Civil War institutional structure and the progressive era institutional structure, however, was the degree to which the capitalist class learned to exploit the cooperative tools of the federal government for its own advantage during the progressive era.

Part of the reason for the increasingly expansive role of the federal government in the late nineteenth century was variation among U.S. states in the laws affecting business. In 1889, for example, New Jersey created the most liberal incorporation law in the United States. When the Ohio Supreme Court ruled that Standard Oil was a monopoly in 1892, the Standard Oil Trust relocated, becoming Standard Oil of New Jersey in 1899. Two-thirds of all U.S. firms with at least $10 million worth of capital were incorporated in New Jersey by 1901 (Micklethwait et al., 2003: 68). Other states, such as Delaware, began to retaliate in a general "race to the bottom" as their legislatures sought to attract capital (2003: 69). By the early twentieth century, business leaders were eager to assist legislators in the drafting of a federal incorporation or licensing law that would eliminate the uncertainty created by inconsistent state incorporation laws.

The movement towards a more expansive government was relatively slow, however, during the final decades of the nineteenth century. No small part of this slow development can be attributed to the prolonged recovery of national politics in the postwar era. The Democratic Party was in shambles after the American Civil War (Henretta et al., 2000: 479). The slow recovery of the Democratic Party began with the presidential pardoning of many ex-Confederates by President Johnson, a Jacksonian Democrat. In the 1874 congressional elections, the Democrats finally regained control of the U.S. House of Representatives for the first time since the South seceded from the Union and took control of seven normally Republican northern states (2000: 499). Because the old Whigs in the South could not join their Northern Allies in the Republican Party due to that party's hostility towards them, they joined with the Democrats and helped sustain the Gold Democrats in a battle with the populists for control of the Democratic organization in the south (Gourevitch, 1986: 110). The Civil War played a crucial part in putting the industrialists in control of both major political parties by the end of the nineteenth century in that it accelerated the pace of industrialization and so tipped the internal balance of power in the Republican Party towards the industrialists (1986: 110). The political shifts during the late nineteenth century thus also helped establish the political conditions necessary for big business to play a leading role in the structural reforms of the progressive era regardless of the party in power.

In the mid-nineteenth century, Democrats favored states' rights and limited government whereas Republicans typically favored federal assistance for economic development. After Reconstruction, however, party differences became unclear and neither party clearly dominated politics from 1876 to 1892 (Henretta et al., 2000: 577). The Republican Party in 1894 was trying to break the multi-class alliance of farmers, workers, and middle class reformers by offering tariffs as a safeguard against domestic unemployment (Bowles et al., 1990: 21). According to historian Samuel

Hays, the 1894 and 1896 elections signaled "one of the greatest blood-less political realignments that this country has ever experienced" (1990: 22). The wealthy Cleveland iron maker and Republican Party leader, Mark Hanna, raised a great deal of money for the 1896 campaign and helped ensure McKinley's victory over William Jennings Bryan (2000: 592). With the exception of President Wilson's two terms in office, this electoral shift marked the dominance of the Republican Party in national politics for the next thirty-five years.

After President McKinley was assassinated in 1901 and the final round in the great wave of consolidations was coming to an end, Theodore Roosevelt became President of the United States. Roosevelt considered America's great corporations to be natural and inevitable developments. His assault on forty-five giant U.S. firms during his presidency earned him the title, "trust-buster," and yet he was not anti-business (Henretta et al., 2000: 661). Actually, in the Northern Securities case, Roosevelt asked neither for the dissolution of the company nor for the restoration of competition (Kolko, 1967: 67). As Roosevelt's Commissioner of Corporations, James R. Garfield directed the Bureau of Corporations much to the satisfaction of big business (1967: 77). In Roosevelt's view, the federal government should regulate big business, not try to break it up (2000: 662–663). He sought to control the excesses and benefits of the new system rather than destroy it outright (Weinstein, 1968: 156). In this respect, he was a key player in the formation of the progressive era RIS. During his presidency, he managed to temporarily stabilize the contradictory state-capital dynamic.

In general, Roosevelt distinguished between "good" trusts, such as U.S. Steel and International Harvester, and "evil" trusts such as Standard Oil and American Tobacco (Kolko, 1967: 113, 122). The key difference was whether a corporation would cooperate with the federal government in ful-filling its greater, social responsibilities.[2] To assist business in doing so, the Roosevelt Administration formed the Bureau of Corporations in 1903 to perform the same type of sunshine-commission role pioneered by Charles Francis Adams in Massachusetts during the nineteenth century (McCraw, 1984: 80). This new government bureau seemed aggressive only because prior to its establishment during the early years of the Roosevelt adminis-tration, scarcely anything had been done to enforce the provisions of the Sherman Act (Tuttle and Perry, 1970: 438). Soon the Morgan-controlled companies began to establish informal agreements with the Bureau of Cor-porations (1967: 119). To avoid prosecution, they would provide the Bureau with confidential business information and correct any abuses discovered by the government. According to Kolko, "Roosevelt was consciously using government regulation to save the capitalist system, perhaps even from itself" (1967: 130). Hence, the abstract character of Polanyi's "double movement" had real consequences during the progressive era.

Although Taft was indebted to Roosevelt for his political success and the House of Morgan for sizable campaign donations during his 1908 campaign, he destroyed what Kolko has called the détente system that governed state-capital relations during Roosevelt's Presidency (1967: 164–165). Taft turned out to be a greater trustbuster than Roosevelt, with whom the title is most often associated. A total of sixty-five anti-trust cases were initiated under the Sherman Act during Taft's adminis-tration versus only forty-four cases under Roosevelt (1967: 167). By 1911, Taft had initiated an anti-trust suit against U.S. Steel and was commit-ted to similar action against International Harvester (Weinstein, 1968: 148). From 1908 to 1912, Taft thus disrupted the state-capital balance Roosevelt had struggled to maintain.

Despite Taft's more aggressive treatment of trusts, the antitrust suits filed during Taft's presidency did not entirely undermine the power of the large corporations they targeted. According to Kolko, the Standard Oil dissolu-tion plan was "designed to fail" as the Standard empire was largely rein-tegrated over the next fifteen years (1967: 167). Similarly, when American Tobacco was dissolved in 1911, "the three giants created by the dissolution increased their share of the cigarette market from 80 per cent as one firm in 1909 to 91 per cent in 1913" (1967: 169–170). Taft's actions, neverthe-less, posed a threat to the new institutional structure, and it needed to be protected. As Kolko explains:

> Under Roosevelt it had been possible to attain a significant measure of stability, at least for the Morgan interests, without legislation. Taft, however, vividly illustrated the need for a more formal, predictable, and permanent basis for the relationship of the large corporation to the national government. (1967: 172)

The politics of the presidential election of 1912 were the direct consequence of Taft's failure "to establish the political conditions necessary for eco-nomic stability" (1967: 190). Hence, the Republican Party split in 1912 over the disagreements between Taft and Roosevelt and paved the way for the conservative reformer, Woodrow Wilson, to restore a measure of order and stability to the American social structure.[3]

During Taft's administration, the Democratic Party began to make a strong comeback. The Democrats became the majority party in the U.S. House in 1910 for the first time since 1892 and possessed firm control of both houses of Congress in 1912 (Henretta et al., 2000: 665–666). Although Wilson won the Democratic nomination as a reformer, he accepted the exis-tence of large corporations much like Roosevelt (2000: 665). According to Weinstein, their differences during the 1912 campaign were largely rhetori-cal (1968: 162). Wilson's New Freedom was about government regulation and in his eight years as a trustbuster, he initiated substantially fewer cases than Harding and Coolidge during their two terms (Kolko, 1967: 257).

Wilson's Presidency also followed Roosevelt's lead insofar as he tried to stabilize the worst excesses of progressive era capitalism. Unlike the progressive Republican Robert M. La Follette who yearned for America's return to a highly competitive economy, Wilson considered the era of free competition to be over and viewed large-scale business organizations as "normal and inevitable" to a certain extent (Weinstein, 1968: 163). He also understood that the intense social conflicts of the progressive era required a strong capitalist state to stabilize the contradictory relations of capitalism. Wilson thus "looked to the federal government to act as regulator and social mediator of the existing system" (1968: 157). During World War I, Wilson pushed this principle to its limits as capitalist social relations threatened to undermine America's war effort.

Underlying the above discussion of presidential politics was an inconsistent treatment of trusts by the judicial and executive branches of the federal government throughout the progressive era. To understand the evolution of antitrust law and its consequences for the institutional structure of the progressive era, it may be helpful to begin with the Interstate Commerce Act of 1887 that established the Interstate Commerce Commission (ICC) to oversee and regulate the railroads. The ICC established the precedent within government that trusts should be regulated, not busted. Although the ICC made railroad regulation a permanent part of national policy, as the nation's first regulatory agency it also had little effect on the industry during its first twenty years (Henretta et al., 2000: 537). With 22,000 railroad workers killed or injured in 1889 according to the ICC's own records, the industry remained extremely dangerous (Zinn, 2003: 256). The greatest significance of the 1887 legislation that created the ICC was the formation of the prototypical federal regulatory agency after which most of the federal regulatory commissions were patterned (McCraw, 1984: 61–62). The Sherman Anti-trust Act of 1890 appeared to challenge this treatment of trusts insofar as it seemed to outlaw any attempt to monopolize trade (McDonough, 1994: 108). This perception is misleading, however, since the Sherman Act of 1890 was a common law doctrine that was not strictly enforced during the 1890s. Its application in the courts was limited to "unreasonable restraints of trade," thus greatly restricting its application.

The strict interpretation of the Sherman Anti-trust Act began with the Trans-Missouri Freight Association case of 1897. Justice Peckham, who wrote the majority opinion in the case, argued that the Sherman Act "could not be interpreted to legitimate a category of 'reasonable' restraints since it explicitly outlawed every restraint of trade" (Bork, 1978: 22). During this period of the Sherman Act's strict interpretation (i.e., 1897–1911), Roosevelt needed to be very selective in his choice of targets for antitrust prosecution (Henretta et al., 2000: 661). This narrow application of the Act persisted until Justice White established the "rule of reason" in the Standard Oil case of 1911, and "reasonable" restraints of trade were again permitted (Weinstein, 1968: 63).

It is no coincidence that this critical shift in the judicial treatment of corporate consolidations occurred during Taft's presidency. During the progressive era, it appears as though one branch of the federal government always intervened to ensure the survival of monopoly capital. When Roosevelt left the presidency and the détente system left with him, the U.S. Supreme Court modified its stance on the trust question. Hence, the antitrust suit initiated against U.S. Steel during the Taft administration ended in the Steel Corporation's acquittal in 1920. The separation-of-powers principle is most often interpreted as a fundamental safeguard for American democracy. In the context of the changing antitrust policies of the progressive era, however, that principle of American government served to prevent the free market excesses that were revealed during the economic crisis of the late nineteenth century.

In the discussion of national politics and antitrust policy above, one may be left with the impression that the federal government acted independently during the progressive era. By contrast, historians have typically emphasized the role of middle-class reformers as the primary source of state regulatory action during the progressive era. Another possibility is that business leaders became very much interested in federal regulation during the progressive era. According to Gabriel Kolko, "business action in the federal political sphere was motivated by . . . the structural condition within the economy, . . . which imposed the need for rationalization on many American industries" (1967: 59). Early in the progressive era, reformers began pushing for regulation of utilities and large corporations began to favor state and federal government regulation to stabilize their industries (Weinstein, 1968: 23–24). Specifically, between 1905 and 1908, the National Civic Federation (NCF) completed substantial work and obtained considerable agreement on trust regulation, workmen's compensation, and the ownership and operation of public utilities (1968: 24). Business also favored federal regulation in the insurance industry where insurance companies opposed costly state regulation (1967: 89–90) and in the meatpacking industry where the big meat packers favored meat inspection laws to gain access to export markets (1967: 98).

Generally speaking, all social classes within a RIS favor some form of regulation to save capitalist society from its destructive tendencies. Certainly, progressive reformers "from below" contributed to the increased federal regulation of the progressive era. Despite these victories, large corporations cooperated with conservative unionists and representatives of the public through the NCF to draft legislation in many of the key areas mentioned above. Although many of these attempts failed to change existing law, their contributions were often embodied in later legislation.

Examples of the legislative efforts of big business abound during the progressive era. The Hepburn Bill of 1908, for example, was the organization's attempt to amend the Sherman Act, which had become increasingly burdensome to large corporations. The bill was intended to reduce the level of uncertainty large corporations felt with respect to the legality of their agreements. It would grant the Bureau of Corporations the power to sanction business transactions that were not ruled unreasonable under the Sherman Act (Weinstein, 1968: 79). The bill was essentially the creation of the House of Morgan (Kolko, 1967: 134). Surprisingly, the bill contained a provision that excluded labor from coverage under the Sherman Act, and it was ultimately this provision that led to Roosevelt's opposition to the bill and its eventual failure (1967: 135, 137).[4] This effort on the part of the business community to reduce uncertainty was part of its larger plan of creating an institutional structure capable of supporting rapid capital accumulation and economic growth. The Keynesian roots of social structure of accumulation analysis are thus relevant to our understanding of the progressive era RIS.[5]

Business leaders also favored a federal incorporation or federal licensing law as well as the establishment of an interstate trade commission as embodied in the Newlands bill (Kolko, 1967: 173, 175). Although the Newlands bill was not politically viable, it demonstrates again that business favored regulatory legislation and gave their early support to the formation of an agency like the Federal Trade Commission (FTC) in 1914. The claim that business interests heavily influenced progressive era reforms may appear controversial. Nevertheless, even in his general history of American enterprise, John Dobson admits that business support was certainly essential for much of the success of progressive era reformers (1988: 207). Identifying the source of these reforms is the key to understanding the role of business in the shaping of the regulatory environment of the progressive era.

In 1914, legislation was finally passed that provided a more secure environment for capital accumulation than had previously existed. Two laws captured the essence of the Hepburn and Newlands bills that had previously failed. The Clayton Anti-trust Act, an amendment to the Sherman Act, specified discriminatory pricing and exclusive contracts as illegal. The Clayton Act also outlawed interlocking directorships when they restrained trade (Micklethwait et al., 2003: 73–74). At the same time, the Democrats were sure to exempt labor unions from antitrust litigation (Dobson, 1988:210). Like the earlier Hepburn bill, however, historians generally agree that the Clayton bill did not free unions from prosecution under the antitrust laws (Kolko, 1967: 263). At the same time, the Clayton Act did allow trade associations to stabilize prices within their industries (1967: 268). It thus possessed benefits for business that led to its relatively favorable reception in the business community.

The Federal Trade Commission Act of 1914 was also passed to enforce the Sherman and Clayton Acts (Henretta et al., 2000: 667). The law stated that the FTC would determine which methods of competition were unfair and therefore unlawful and could then order offenders to "cease and desist" from using such unfair methods (McCraw, 1984: 214). At the same time, it was a vague and unclear law and failed to exclude businessmen from membership on the five-member commission (Kolko, 1967: 267).

When the commission was formed in 1915, it consisted of individuals with business backgrounds or long pro-business records and thus served as a buffer against public criticism of business (1967: 271). The agency would "prevent the evils of socialism" and "eliminate uncertainty," according to businessmen (1967: 176). It also conducted "conference rulings" that served as a guide for businesses with respect to the legality of their actions (1967: 272). Businessmen favored the new commission because they antici-pated receiving so-called "advance advice," which would help them avoid tedious and self-defeating legal proceedings (1984: 129–130). Firms were especially attracted to the FTC's position on trade associations and export trade associations, in particular, because the commission permitted them to be used to stabilize prices and eliminate competition (1967: 275). Both laws were anticipated by business leaders in the NCF and had their wide-spread support because they would create a more certain and favorable business environment.

In addition to regulating the giant trusts, another major area of progres-sive era reform involved regulation of the railroad industry. According to Dobson, this form of regulation turned out to be the most effective reform of the period (1988: 207). A series of legislative actions were taken to pro-hibit a variety of unfair competitive railroad practices and to authorize the ICC to investigate complaints of unfair practices. This legislation included the 1903 Elkins Act, the 1906 Hepburn Act, and the 1910 Mann-Elkins Act. Surprisingly, much of this legislation was viewed favorably by the railroads much as the newly consolidated corporations looked upon much of the new trust legislation with favor. In fact, these laws were met with little opposition from the industry because they offered railroad companies protection from unfair competition and helped insulate them from many customer complaints (1988: 209). Again, capitalist enterprises are not nec-essarily opposed to government regulation when it can be molded to serve their interests—both their immediate interests and their long-term interests in safeguarding their positions of power in society.

Around the same time business leaders were using their influence to sup-port federal regulation of business, government agencies were establishing cooperative relations with business and labor in an effort to reduce class tensions. For example, the U.S. Commission on Industrial Relations, an organization sponsored by Taft and continued by Wilson, attempted to conciliate workers and radicals between 1913 and 1915 (Weinstein, 1968: 172–173). Wilson chose labor lawyer, Frank Walsh, to serve as chairman of the Commission on Industrial Relations. Although Walsh was evidently more concerned with social justice than the stabilization or rationalization of industry, he sought justice within the existing social structure and never supported the transformation of basic social relations (186–187). Walsh actually shared with business leaders in the NCF "a vision of a socially responsible society in which cooperation and genuine accommodation between social classes would be possible" (189). The Commission created the impression that "unions and radical intellectuals possessed real power over social policy" (213). It thus served as another organization committed to stabilizing the central contradictions of U.S. capitalism during the progressive era.

During World War I, a number of boards and agencies, directed by the nation's business leaders who were recruited for their economic expertise, tried to rationalize and coordinate the economy (Henretta et al., 2000: 719). The Fuel Administration, the Food Administration, the War Industries Board, the War Labor Policies Board, the National War Labor Board, and the Committee on Public Information were a few of the wartime boards established for this purpose. One governmental organization aimed specifically at stabilizing contradictory class forces during the war was the American Alliance for Labor and Democracy (AALD) established on April 4, 1917 and directed by the chairman of the Committee for Public Information (CPI), George Creel. The organization was the federal government's primary attempt to win labor support for the war effort (Weinstein, 1968: 240). The war thus gave a major boost to the state's economic activities that had been gradually expanding during the progressive era.

When the United States entered World War I, the regulated character of the progressive era became even more pronounced. The Webb-Pomerene Act of 1918 permitted manufacturers to form export trade associations while enjoying an exemption from the Sherman Anti-trust Act (Weinstein, 1968: 218–219). With government support for cooperative business arrangements, agencies like the Price Fixing Committee of the War Industries Board (WIB) were free to pursue the dual goal of stable prices and suitable profit margins (223–224). According to Weinstein (251), "the idea of government-business partnership had . . . gained considerable ground" by the end of the war.

Once the war ended, however, state-capital relations were modified yet again to provide support for the liberal institutional structure of the 1920s. The extensive cooperative business-government structure established during the war was rapidly dismantled in its aftermath, reflecting "the unease that Americans felt about a strong bureaucratic state" (Henretta et al., 2000: 717). Nevertheless, "during the 1920s the Harding and Coolidge administrations embraced a philosophy of business-government partnership, believing that unrestricted corporate capitalism would provide for the welfare of the American people" (2000: 703). Kolko agrees with this characterization noting that "the unity of business and the federal government continued throughout the 1920's and thereafter, using the foundations laid in the Progressive Era to stabilize and consolidate conditions within various industries" (1967: 287). During that time, the Republican agenda included federal assistance for corporations but not state support for progressive reforms, and the FTC mostly ignored the nation's antitrust laws (2000: 739). Hence, the LIS of the 1920s differed considerably from the LIS that gave rise to the progressive era RIS in that business and government in the 1920s related to one another as partners in the new institutional structure.

2.4 THE PHILOSOPHY OF SOCIAL RESPONSIBILITY: THE DOMINANT IDEOLOGY

During the late nineteenth century, the philosophy of individualism was pervasive both in popular writings and in academic circles. The rags-to-riches tales of Horatio Alger and Andrew Carnegie's book *Triumphant Democracy* (1886) praised the potential and determination of the American individual (Henretta et al., 2000: 578). During the same period, the British philosopher, Herbert Spencer, adapted Charles Darwin's theory of natural selection to human society. The American sociologist, William Graham Sumner, was the main proponent of Spencer's social Darwinism in the United States (2000: 579). The philosophy provided a rationale for the poor state of the common laborer relative to the wealthy robber baron and for the relative hardships of the struggling business compared to the enormous success of the rising monopolies.

To fully grasp the role of the philosophy of individualism in American history and the subsequent ideological transformation that took place, it is necessary to review the development in the United States of the classical liberal political ideology of which individualism is an integral component. As Louis Hartz explains (1986), the classical liberal ideology is so deeply embedded in American society that there has never even been a liberal movement or a real "liberal party" in America. Instead, the "American way of life" has served as a nationalist articulation of Locke (Hartz, 1986: 19). Few Americans in the nineteenth century, therefore, had experience with opposing ideologies or the Lockean roots of the prevailing American ideals. It is precisely in John Locke's *Second Treatise on Civil Government*, however, that the central elements of liberalism were molded into a coherent intellectual tradition for the first time (Gray, 1995: 13). According to Locke, the natural laws that God has granted to us guarantee us a natural right to liberty and the acquisition of property. Locke thus associates the right to personal property with the right to individual liberty in a way that differs from both Spinoza and Hobbes (1995: 14). Such ideas were to have a profound effect on the framers of the U.S. Constitution and the structure of the American polity.

One natural consequence of this alleged relationship between private property rights and individual liberty was that economic interests would play a role in the drafting of the American Constitution. Charles Beard's (1986) controversial interpretation of the U.S. Constitution as an economic document provides support for the thesis that the Lockean link between property rights and liberty is enshrined in the Constitution itself. The prime example of this concern is reflected in the fact that the framers contemplated placing virtually the entire national tax burden on consumers via the imposition of indirect taxes (e.g., tariffs on foreign trade, excise taxes). The apportionment of direct taxes on the basis of population would serve as a last resort when indirect taxes failed to raise the required revenue. Personal property would thus be assured a generous immunity from such burdens as Congress had attempted to impose under the Articles of Confederation (Beard, 1986: 58–59). While protecting the economic interests of the framers of the Constitution, Beard's analysis suggests how the document also served to protect all holders of property and wealth throughout the early life of the nation.

The classical liberal basis of the American Constitution extends far beyond the collection of taxes, sometimes straining that ideology to its limits. The *Federalist* authors deemed armies and navies to have vital economic functions insofar as trade and commerce are the fundamental causes of war between nations. That is, the army and the navy are to serve as instruments of defense in protecting America against the commercial and territorial ambitions of other countries as well as in the forceful opening of foreign markets (Beard, 1986: 59). The Constitution thus granted the Congress the power to raise and support military and naval forces. It further granted Congress control of foreign and interstate commerce, thus laying the groundwork for a "wide sweep" for free trade throughout the entire American empire (60). In the *Federalist*, Hamilton specifically argued for the reciprocal advantage that would accrue from free trade over a wide geographical area (60–61). In terms of state rights, Madison argued that the federal judicial control of state legislatures was essential for the protection of property rights. States were thus forbidden to impair contractual obligations (61). As a result, states could not interfere with labor contracts, in particular, thus providing a safeguard against states that might meddle with fundamental social relations in the new republic.

The extreme depth with which the philosophy of individualism was embedded during the first century of the new American nation has much to do with the absence of a feudal past. For Hartz, its lack of a feudal past explains the absence of a genuine revolutionary tradition in America and thus the absence of a tradition of reaction (1986: 16). As a result, American liberalism never acquired a concept of class in its bourgeois form (1986: 18). The absence of a class struggle within the context of a well-defined precapitalist mode of production strengthened the trend towards individualism and stifled opposing ideologies. According to Alexis de Tocqueville, who visited the country in the mid-nineteenth century, individualism is stronger at the close of a democratic revolution than at other periods because it is at that time that men are most disposed to live apart, as those who had been higher on the social scale view their equals as oppressors and those who had been lower on the social scale are uneasy about their newly acquired independence (1986: 7–8). For de Tocqueville, Americans were at a great advantage because they arrived at a state of democracy without having to endure a democratic revolution and were thus born equal instead of becoming so (1986: 8). De Tocqueville's observation suggests that individualism and egotism should have been weaker in the new republic. The persistent strength of individualism in nineteenth century America, rather than stemming from the onset of greater political equality due to democratic revolution, may have had more to do with the trend towards greater labor market equality due to industrial revolution as skill differentials narrowed and worker control of the production process faded with the emergence of a more homogeneous national workforce.[6]

The decline of classical liberalism as a reputable political and economic doctrine paralleled its relative decline in the United States as the liberal institutionalist structure of the late nineteenth century came to an end. As John Gray explains, this intellectual shift took place gradually over the course of many decades. According to Gray, the first rupture in the development of classical liberalism may be attributed to Jeremy Bentham, who founded the Utilitarian tradition that ultimately led him to condone illiberal government intervention (1995: 28). After John Stuart Mill had completed this rupture by creating a system of thought to legitimate such interventionist tendencies, L.T. Hobhouse attempted a synthesis of the philosophies of Mill and T.H. Green in his *Liberalism* in 1911 (30–32). The new revisionist liberalism, as it has been called, emphasized social harmony and distributive justice in contrast with the classical liberal ideal of free and unfettered markets. If any fault can be found in Gray's account of the historical development of liberalism, it is his claim that the century preceding World War I was an era of almost uninterrupted liberal progress and yet the illiberal tendencies at work in liberal societies were made dominant nearly overnight with the outbreak of the war. Although Gray expresses fresh doubts about his commitment to liberalism in the second edition of his book (vii-x), he does not seem to seriously consider the possibility that warfare was the inevitable consequence of a classical liberal global order rather than a result of its failed realization.

As a political philosophy with European roots, a comparative analysis of the paths of development of American and European liberalism seems in order. To appreciate the uniqueness of an American society without feudalism, it must be studied in conjunction with a European society where the feudal structure did survive (Hartz, 1986: 15). Terry Eagleton's (2005) analysis of the development of criticism in England since the seventeenth century provides a helpful point of comparison for such a study. Eagleton borrows the notion of "the public sphere" from Jurgen Habermas to argue that modern European criticism was born of a struggle against the absolutist state in the seventeenth and eighteenth centuries (2005: 8–9). In such an historical setting in which literacy is still restricted and commodity production has not made available cheap periodicals and pamphlets to the mass of the population, the bourgeois public sphere may flourish. Circulation may thus proceed without a breath of exploitation in the public sphere where no social classes exist at all (Eagleton, 1976: 17). In the American case, of course, the object of criticism was a colonial power abroad rather than an absolutist state at home. Nevertheless, the creation of a public sphere allows for a bourgeois equality to exist in the sphere of political discourse. All may participate but only because the class-determined criteria defining significant participation are always in place (1976: 26). These ideal American and British public spaces were historically specific and were rapidly undermined in their infancy.

Eagleton attributes the decline of the bourgeois public sphere in England to an inevitable conflict between the forces of literary production and the social relations of literary production. The veritable explosion of literary periodicals in mid-eighteenth century England and their greater availability with the expansion of market forces caused the ideal equality of the public sphere to rapidly disintegrate (Eagleton, 2005: 30–35). Furthermore, as social and political interests that were in direct conflict with the rational norms of the bourgeois public sphere began to make their way into that discursive space, its further disintegration became inevitable. Such interests cannot be acknowledged as legitimate because they fall outside the realm of the sphere's accepted discourse, and yet they cannot be dismissed because they pose a material threat to the sphere's continuing existence. The nature of the class struggle thus threatens to strip the bourgeois public sphere of all ideological credibility (35–37). It was the intense labor struggles of the late nineteenth century that signaled the death knell of the pure individualist philosophy in America and the sphere in which it was expressed.

Within this context, the rags-to-riches tails of nineteenth century America may be interpreted as attempts to maintain the individualist slant of the American public sphere. Such tails were concurrent with the rise of the "man of letters" in nineteenth century England who sought to explain and regulate economic, social, and religious change as much as to reflect it, thus rendering it less ideologically fearful. According to Walter Bagehot, the readership of the man of letters must have its opinions molded by intellectual simplification (Eagleton, 2005: 48–50). As Howard Zinn explains, the Horatio Alger stories of "rags to riches" were mostly a myth and a useful myth for control (2003: 254). Aside from the intensely libertarian efforts of writers like Thoreau (1970), for example, in "Civil Disobedience," the individualism of nineteenth century America would come to an end along with the public sphere that supported it as muckraking journalism and social criticism followed from the intense class struggles of the late nineteenth century.

The class-based ideology of the bourgeois public sphere thus came under fierce attack as a result of the work of Henry Demarest Lloyd, Louis Brandeis, the contributors to *Collier's Weekly*, and many others. In popular magazines such as *Cosmopolitan, American, McClure's*, and *The Saturday Evening Post*, the worst excesses of capitalism were revealed by Ida Tarbell, Lincoln Steffens, Burton Hendrick, Ray Stannard Baker, and others (Tuttle and Perry, 1970: 439). Despite attempts to control education and the political quality of teachers by means of loyalty oaths, teacher certification, and citizenship requirements, a literature of dissent and protest arose (Zinn, 2003: 263–264). In the 1890s, over a thousand Populist journals were in print, one of which had a circulation of 100,000 readers (2003: 292). For Eagleton, any attempt to recreate the bourgeois public sphere in the midst of class conflict, the dominance of the commodity, and an economy, which passed from liberal capitalism to its statist and monopolistic state, was doomed from the outset (2005: 76). The sphere was only possible in the phase of liberal capitalism. From that point forward, criticism would retreat to the universities and lose political and social significance.

The decline of American liberalism as a political and economic ideology in its original formulation can be interpreted in terms of the distinction between the economic base, consisting of the forces and relations of production, and the superstructure, which consists of the legal, ideological, religious, aesthetic, and cultural dimensions that help reproduce the dominant mode of production in a given society. Elsewhere, Eagleton has explained in Marxist fashion that the function of ideology is to legitimate the power of the ruling class in society and that the dominant ideas in any society are the ideas of its ruling class (1976: 5). Furthermore, ideology is not a set of doctrines but rather the values, ideas, and images, which tie humans to their social functions and so prevent them from obtaining a true knowledge of society as a whole (16–17). In this sense, the ideology of individualism was becoming less convincing and thus less effective as a means of legitimating and rationalizing the power of the American capitalist class.

Art then is part of the superstructure of society insofar as it embodies dominant modes of thinking in a multitude of forms. It is thus ideological in nature although it is never a mere reflection of the ruling ideas (Eagleton, 1976: 5–7). Literature, for example, challenges the very ideology it confronts (17). It is through this lens that we might better understand the work of an Upton Sinclair as both historically captive to the dominant ideology and yet creating distance between itself and the same ideology. Art then helps us to gain experience of the historical situation thus allowing us to 'see' the nature of ideology and allowing us to move towards a complete understanding of it (18). In the first half of the twentieth century, therefore, American literature both reflected and contradicted the ruling ideology helping to undermine the ruling ideas of the past and solidifying a fresh set of ruling ideas for the future.

The classical liberalism of the late nineteenth century was a suitable ideology for an institutional structure based on free competition, a vastly unequal distribution of income, and a minimal economic role for the federal government. The progressive era regulationist institutional structure, however, required an ideology with a drastically different character. It needed to rationalize the very existence of the huge consolidations created during the merger wave of the late 1890s. In addition, the new ideology needed to defend the growth of a federal government aimed at rationalizing and stabilizing the markets in which the large trusts participated as well as the subordinate position of workers within the trust-dominated economic system.

The architects of this new ideology were, by necessity, those actors in the economy who would benefit the most from it during the progressive era. According to James Weinstein, liberalism in the progressive era was the consciously created product of the leaders of giant corporations and financial institutions (1968: xv). By 1918, the large corporations and giant banks emerged as the victors in the progressive era struggle among various social classes for political power. "Corporate liberalism" is the name Weinstein gives to the political ideology U.S. corporations used to rationalize their dominant position in the new economic structure (1968: 3). The new corporate ideology emphasized the obligation of the large corporation to behave in a socially responsible manner towards all classes of society in an effort to maximize social welfare.

Writing in modern times, Micklethwait et al. claim that "companies have become more ethical: more honest, more humane, more socially responsible" (2003: xx). The authors do not emphasize the ideological origin of this changed character of companies in the progressive era. The notion that corporations possess social obligations was not entirely new in the early twentieth century either. "Throughout the nineteenth century, legislatures revoked charters when the corporation wasn't deemed to be fulfilling its responsibilities" (46). The key difference, however, between the nineteenth and twentieth centuries in this respect is that the notion of corporate social responsibility during the progressive era was developed and trumpeted by corporations themselves. The state, however, continued to pressure corporations to act in a socially responsible manner. Philadelphia, for example, informally required corporations to fulfill their social obligations in exchange for entry into society (76). At the same time, the regulatory arm of the federal government became a means for corporations to implement their ideological agenda in practice.

As the previous section discussed, it was through the National Civic Federation that business leaders influenced public policy during the progressive era. It was also within this organization that large corporations devised the new philosophy of social responsibility that would inspire much of its proposed legislation. The National Civic Federation (NCF) was an organization created by large corporations in 1900 to build a national consensus among business, labor, and the public. Although the organization established the principle of tripartite representation in public affairs (i.e., representatives of business, labor, and the public) (Weinstein, 1968: xv), big businessmen dominated the NCF from the very beginning (8). For example, Andrew Carnegie and George Perkins, partner to J.P. Morgan, were directly involved in the organization's leadership from the outset. As

Weinstein explains, the NCF raised the class-consciousness of business leaders (10). In 1910, George Perkins argued that corporate officials were becoming more like statesmen (10). Unfortunately, the paternalistic business leaders in the NCF refused to acknowledge the obvious contradiction between their new role as quasi-public officials (i.e., not elected) and the most basic principles of representative democracy.

Strength for the claim that U.S. corporations dominated the NCF during the progressive era may be found in the NCF investigation of "government by injunction." An injunction is essentially a court order to require persons to refrain from committing a particular act. Many judges were willing to grant employers labor injunctions that would prohibit unions from conducting strikes or boycotts (Henretta et al., 2000: 653–654). As Weinstein explains, the injunction was one of the few issues almost entirely motivated by labor's concerns. Labor feared that employers were using the courts to stop strikes and wanted legislation that limited the injunction, but because business leaders refused to compromise on the issue, no action was ever taken (Weinstein, 1968: 28). When the AFL turned to politics in 1906 with the drafting of its "Bill of Grievances," it demanded from Congress immunity from court attack for unions and then became allies with the Democratic Party (2000: 654). Hence, the cooperative public face of the NCF was often inconsistent with its deeper, paternalistic nature implicit in the rhetoric of social responsibility.

It is also important to understand that the new corporate ideology did not primarily originate among leaders in government. The corporations were specifically ahead of the courts in developing a new ideology. For example, a court ruling in 1911 declared New York's conservative compensation law unconstitutional much to the displeasure of America's corporate leaders (Weinstein, 1968: 55–57). Theodore Roosevelt was angry about the decision on the grounds that such decisions added "immensely to the strength of the Socialist Party" (Zinn, 2003: 353). Nevertheless, the determination of the NCF resulted in all but six U.S. states having effective compensation laws by 1920 (1968: 11). Business, rather than government, was mainly responsible for the ideology of social responsibility and the wave of regulatory legislation to which it gave rise in the progressive era.

Business leaders were drawn to the NCF's ideology of social responsibility and recognized the importance of the new organization as a means of achieving their economic goals. Membership rose from 1,500 in 1907 to more than 5,000 in 1912 (Weinstein, 1968: 35). One reason is that trust regulation was a primary concern of NCF business leaders during the progressive era. This preoccupation was perfectly appropriate for the founders of a new corporate ideology. As Robert Bork claims, "[a]ntitrust is a subcategory of ideology" (1978: 3). Specifically, the NCF was eager to reestablish the common law interpretation of the Sherman Act as is clear from its 1907 conference on trusts in Chicago (1968: 74). Its role in generating support for antitrust reform was reviewed in the previous section and is equally relevant to its ideological position. By supporting conservative anti-trust legislation, the business community could demonstrate that it was behaving in a socially responsible manner while retaining ultimate control of its large corporations.

Because large corporations dominated the NCF, a number of groups were wary of the organization's intentions. Unionists, in particular, were deeply suspicious of business attempts to draft legislation aimed at helping labor. For example, in 1913, the President of the NCF, Seth Low, established a new Minimum Wage Commission while the labor representatives opposed minimum wage laws except for women (Weinstein, 1968: 32). Labor organizations feared that socially responsible corporations might undermine their own organizing efforts. Outside of the NCF, socialists and small businesspeople generally opposed the organization's activities. Socialists were convinced that the NCF represented a plot to undermine more radical efforts to alter the basic structure of society. Small businesses were fearful that they no longer competed on an equal basis with other businesses. The National Association of Manufacturers (NAM) thus clung to the philosophy of individualism in a hopeless attempt to restore the liberal institutional structure of the late nineteenth century.

Corporate leaders in the NCF used their relationship with organized labor to protect and enforce the ideology of social responsibility against critics from outside the organization. The very structure of the organization allowed the NCF to dominate the labor representatives within the organization for this purpose. The principle of tripartite representation was inherently biased towards large corporations in part because "business was doubly represented, once on the business side and again on the 'public' side" (Weinstein, 1968: 252).[7] Nevertheless, cooperation between corporations and the AFL in the early years of the twentieth century helped defeat industrial unionists and socialists. In fact, many trade unions adopted business unionism, including the United Mine Workers and the United Brotherhood of Carpenters (Gordon et al., 1982: 144). This compromise between business unionists and large corporations weakened during the 1920s (1982: 160), however, thus suggesting the creation of a LIS.

The NCF was the clearest symbol of the corporate effort to stabilize the new contradictions of the progressive era capitalist order and the organization most responsible for the development of the ideology of corporate social responsibility. It is reasonable to believe that business leaders in the NCF were consciously committed to the construction of a new institutional structure rather than simply to the drafting of specific legislation with a new ideology to support it. According to George Perkins, "the proper sort of cooperation between our statesmen and our businessmen [would help] lay the foundation for a commercial development that would put the United States to the front both at home and abroad and keep her there" (Weinstein, 1968: 153). Perkins's comment demonstrates an awareness of the fact that capital in the progressive era had the potential to reshape the basic economic and social structure of American society.

The transformation of America's dominant economic ideology seems to present a paradox. In a 1905 essay, the English observer James Bryce wrote the following after reflecting on American political and economic developments over the course of the nineteenth century:

> The example of the United States, the land in which individualism has been most conspicuously vigorous, may seem to suggest that the world is passing out of the stage of individualism and returning to that earlier stage in which groups of men formed the units of society . . . Is it a paradox to observe that it is because the Americans have been the most individualistic of people that they are now the people among whom the art of combination has reached its maximum? (Henretta et al., 2000: 660)

It is reasonable to answer Bryce's question in the negative so long as American institutions during the progressive era are interpreted as serving capital under different historical conditions than had previously existed. The ideological shift from individualism to social responsibility provided the intellectual foundation necessary to rationalize the dominance of capital in the new regulationist institutional structure of the progressive era.

A number of groups in American society realized that the new corporate ideology provided a rationalization for the growing power of large corporations and threatened their goal of establishing a political and industrial democracy in the United States. The 1848 revolutions in Europe brought Marxism to the United States as German refugees fled Europe (Henretta et al., 2000: 571). A series of radical movements then followed in the late nineteenth and early twentieth centuries. The Socialist Labor Party was formed in 1877, the Socialist Party of America was formed in 1901, and the Western Federation of Miners created the Industrial Workers of the World (IWW) in 1905 (2000: 571). From 1905 to 1913, the socialist and syndicalist movements gained ground as the Socialist Party grew and the Industrial Workers of the World emerged (Gordon et al., 1982: 160). In the 1904 presidential election, Eugene Debs enjoyed a quadrupling of his votes (Weinstein, 1968: 118). Although Debs did not experience any substantial increase in his votes from 1904 to 1908, Debs won 6% of the votes in the 1912 election with 900,000 votes (2000: 666). Furthermore, the Socialist Party was growing rapidly by 1911 when socialists were elected mayors in 73 U.S. cities (1968: 119–120). The Socialist Party was posing a serious threat to the politics of social responsibility.

After 1905, NCF leaders understood that providing limited support for trade unions would help prevent the growth of socialism (Weinstein, 1968: 16–18). The shift of the AFL towards nonpartisan politics in 1906 also led the NCF to fear that a closer relationship would form between unions and socialists as it had in Europe.[8] Organizations, such as the Catholic Church's

Militia of Christ, joined the NCF in the battle against socialism (122–123). By 1908, under Seth Low's leadership, the NCF began to anticipate radical demands by advocating moderate reforms, further defining the limits of reform, and seeking to inhibit the growth of socialism (38). The NCF considered socialism to be the only serious ideological alternative to its politics of social responsibility (117), and it needed to be stopped.

From 1912 to 1917, the power of the Socialist Party remained roughly constant, but they experienced a substantial rise in votes in 1917 and 1918 despite the anti-radical efforts of the federal government.[9] Anti-war sentiment was strong in August of 1917 when approximately 1,000 farmers protested violently against the war in Oklahoma's Green Corn Rebellion. Many socialist anti-war meetings also took place in the North during the summer of 1917 (Weinstein, 1968: 234). After the war, however, the Socialist Party was broken up, and its significance faded (137).[10] The stagnation of the Socialist Party in the prewar period and its subsequent decline after the war parallel the decline of the American labor movement as the section on capital-labor relations demonstrates below. The corporate attack on radical ideology was thus part of a larger program to force labor into submission and the American public into accepting the domination of corporations. Although the NCF was not directly responsible for the fate of the Socialist Party, it helped contain it insofar as its philosophy of social responsibility undermined the perception that a radical solution was necessary.

The growth of the Industrial Workers of the World (IWW) resembled that of the Socialist Party during the progressive era. The IWW was founded on June 27, 1905 when seventy delegates attended the Industrial Union Congress in Chicago. According to Patrick Renshaw, the IWW's effective life span was from 1905 to 1924 (1967: 22). The organization was very small during its first year with a total membership of only 7,800 in November. When the Western Federation of Miners officially joined the IWW in June of the following year, however, the organization's membership rose by 22,000 (Thompson, 1976: 23–24). The IWW offered workers an extreme form of workers' radicalism by its endorsement of the overthrow of the capitalist mode of production.

The IWW scored many early victories in both the eastern and western United States. A sawmill strike in Portland, Oregon that began on March 1, 1907 and involved 3,000 workers represented the first west coast progress of the IWW (Thompson, 1976: 34–35). In May 1908, the IWW's General Executive Board (GEB) founded the organization's first industrial union in Paterson, New Jersey called the National Industrial Union of Textile Workers (1976: 36). From 1909 to 1912, the IWW concentrated on the free speech fights of the West (Renshaw, 1967: 116). Also, the McKees Rocks rebellion in Pennsylvania and other battles from 1909 to 1911 laid the foundation for the IWW's "substantial growth and bigger battles of 1912" (1976: 51). From 1912 to 1913, the IWW "won widespread recognition as the most forward thrust of the American labor movement" with victories in Lawrence, Lowell, New Bedford, Little Falls, and other textile centers (1976: 53). According to Renshaw, the textile workers' successful strike in Lawrence, Massachusetts was the crest of the IWW's power (1967: 133). A strike of silk weavers against the four-loom system in Paterson, New Jersey in 1913, however, ended in failure when the IWW failed to generate strike support outside of Paterson (1976: 61). The Paterson strike severely damaged the IWW in a financial sense. According to Fred Thompson, the loss at Paterson "almost did for the IWW as the Pullman strike of 1894 had done to Debs' [American Railway Union]" (1976: 61).

At least two problems arose with the manner in which the IWW handled the strikes in McKees Rocks, Lawrence, and Paterson. First, the IWW did not organize the effort in such a way that the gains won would be maintained in the aftermath of the strikes (Renshaw, 1967: 149). The strikes were also conducted without a clear leader (155). The collective form of leadership characteristic of that organization understandably created organizational problems and was the subject of many internal disputes for the IWW.

Internal disputes divided the IWW very early in its life. One such debate centered on the choice of strategy for achieving working class objectives. Specifically, "the controversy over direct vs. political action led to major cleavages in the IWW which came to a head . . . at the 1908 convention" (Kornbluh, 1998: 3). This debate about the relative importance of industrial and political action for achieving revolution had its roots in the Marxist-Lassallean conflict of the 1880s (Renshaw, 1967: 52). By 1907, the Western Federation of Miners (WFM) voted to withdraw from the IWW due to ideological differences and personality disputes within the organization's leadership (1998: 4), and in July 1908 the WFM officially severed all ties with the IWW (1967: 95). This loss greatly weakened the IWW in its early years.

A key outcome of the 1908 convention was the elimination of all reference to political activity from the Preamble so as to exclude the influence of the Socialist Party of America or De Leon's Socialist Labor Party (Kornbluh, 1998: 6). Because he contributed greatly to this internal dispute, the GEB expelled Daniel De Leon and his followers at the 1908 IWW convention (Thompson, 1976: 39). The IWW then committed itself to the use of direct action and industrial unionism with the goal of overthrowing capitalism and establishing an industrial democracy. According to Renshaw, "[a]fter three years of flirting with politics, the IWW had returned to its basically antipolitical attitude of direct action on the industrial front" (1967: 102). Much was lost, however, in the organization's struggle to formulate clear policies and objectives.

Another dispute within the IWW dealt with the organization's relationship to the rest of the labor movement. Many radicals during the period favored a policy of "boring from within" the larger, more established, and more conservative unions like the AFL to achieve radical objectives. In 1911, the IWW went on record against "boring from within" (Thompson, 1976: 76). Unlike their French counterparts who favored boring from within, the Wobblies wanted to establish a dual union to compete with the AFL (Renshaw, 1967: 68). The policy of dual unionism was thus controversial and led many radicals to reject the methods of the IWW. The problem of organization and leadership led to a debate between the east and the west within the ranks of the IWW as well. Easterners generally favored the centralization of power among the IWW leadership while westerners generally favored decentralization and local autonomy (1967: 163). These internal disputes no doubt led to the decline of the radical movement over the course of the progressive era.

The decline of the IWW also resulted from the tense relations between it and the American Federation of Labor during the progressive era. Relations were strained from the founding of the IWW. In fact, part of the reason the IWW came into existence was to "oppose the conservative orientation of the American Federation of Labor" (Kornbluh, 1998: 1). The AFL also contributed to the conflict when it publicly denounced the IWW during the 1907 sawmill strike in Portland (Thompson, 1976: 34–35). During the 1912 textile strike in Lawrence, Massachusetts, the AFL Central Labor Council would not recognize the 25,000 workers on strike for the IWW (1976: 56). After the Lawrence strike, the IWW's National Industrial Union of Textile Workers began a rapid decline (1976: 62). The AFL also condemned the IWW during the 1913 Akron rubber strike (1976: 73). Sometimes the AFL even sent in scabs during IWW strikes (1976: 24). As a dual union with few resources, the IWW faced insurmountable obstacles.

A brief examination of the size of the IWW and its fluctuations throughout the progressive era is enough to demonstrate that it was strong early in the progressive era and then began to weaken before the onset of World War I. This prewar stagnation together with its rapid decline after the war parallels the prewar stagnation and decline of the Socialist Party as explained above. For the purpose of comparison, the total number of union members in 1905 was about two million, about half of which belonged to the AFL (Renshaw, 1967: 33). IWW membership rose from about 4,000 members during its first six years to an average membership of 18,387 for 1912 and 14,851 for 1913 (Thompson, 1976: 79). Similarly, whereas in 1912 the IWW almost consistently won its fights, it was "progressively less successful" in 1913 and when hard times hit in the fall of that year the union was in "bad shape" (1976: 79). The hard times led to unemployment and persisted throughout 1914 and 1915. The prewar decline thus parallels the stagnation of the Socialist Party as well during the same period.

With the onset of war in Europe, the future of the IWW appeared even grimmer. From the summer of 1916 to the summer of 1920, an unparalleled campaign of terror was launched against IWW organizing efforts (Thompson, 1976: 111). In September 1917, federal authorities seized IWW documents in a series of raids across the nation. The simultaneous raids on forty-eight IWW Local halls led to the seizure of five tons of documents (Renshaw, 1967: 220). Approximately 2,000 Wobblies were arrested during the period, and in October 1917 the IWW formed the General Defense Committee to coordinate defense work at the national level (1976: 125). By August 1918, dozens of IWW members were given long prison sentences in the great Chicago trial. With the prison sentences the IWW had lost nearly its entire leadership (1967: 237). California and twenty-three other states enacted criminal syndicalism laws in 1919 (1967: 238). By May 1919, the IWW was in serious financial trouble with legal fees it could not pay (1967: 240). The antiradical hysteria following the 1917 revolution in Russia thus hastened the demise of the IWW.

The IWW, nevertheless, grew from the war years until 1924 when it "split wide open" due to internal faction fighting (Thompson, 1976: 150). Average membership from 1916 to 1919 was about 33,500 and had reached 35,000 by 1919 (1976: 129). It then probably reached its peak membership in 1923 with 40,000 members (1976: 111). According to Renshaw, the IWW's membership went into a steep decline after the split in 1924 that was rapid and irrecoverable (1967: 262–264). His evaluation of the IWW is rather negative. He explains that with few exceptions, the IWW "did little to improve the lot of American wage earners" and that it "must be regarded as a failure" (1967: 23, 25). However one characterizes the successes and failures of the IWW, it certainly demonstrates that strong challenges were being made to the ideology of social responsibility and that the defenders of that ideology had much to gain from the suppression of radical alternatives.

2.5   THE DECENTRALIZATION OF THE FINANCIAL SYSTEM: STATE-FINANCE CAPITAL RELATIONS

Prior to the Civil War, the nation's money supply was determined largely by the banknotes issued by thousands of state banks. The Banking Act of 1863, however, reduced the freedom of the state banks to create money by requiring the backing of U.S. government bonds (Henretta et al., 2000: 589). The national banking system that then dominated suffered from a problem of "perverse elasticity." This problem arose because the national banks would decrease their note issues when more money was needed in circulation by selling bonds to obtain money, which temporarily withdrew it from circulation, and increase their note issues when less money was needed in circulation by buying bonds to invest the surplus funds thus adding to the total circulating money (Tuttle and Perry, 1970: 327–328). The circulation of greenbacks, which had been issued to finance the war, was finally brought to an end in 1875 as well. Together, these changes in the monetary system led to the Great Deflation of the late nineteenth century (2000: 589) and carried serious consequences for American farmers whose incomes plummeted.

The system of national banks suffered from a number of other defects as well that encouraged rather than discouraged financial panics and inefficiencies in banking. One such problem involved pyramiding bank deposits, which resulted in entirely inadequate bank reserves and led to financial disaster when bank runs occurred (Tuttle and Perry, 1970: 331). Furthermore, as independent unit banks, the national banks lacked a centralized monetary authority to determine monetary policy for the system as a whole (332). When the banking system was in special need of liquidity, therefore, no lender of last resort existed to stabilize the system. The agricultural sector of the economy suffered especially during the reign of the national banks. Loans granted by national banks were restricted to commercial loans that were self-liquidating in relatively short amounts of time (332). Finally, the inefficiencies were severe as well during the period. The system of correspondent banks that the national banks adopted led to a costly and lengthy process of check clearing (332). All of these defects paved the way for the currency reform that would follow in the progressive era.

Other changes that were occurring in the U.S. financial system in the late nineteenth century had to do with the commodity basis of the nation's currency. The 1873 Currency Act marked the demonetization of silver by not naming the silver dollar as one of the coins that would continue in use. With the decline in the value of silver relative to gold in the years that followed, this legislation later was dubbed "the Crime of '73." According to Tuttle and Perry, a number of factors combined to force down the value of silver in terms of gold, including Germany's adoption of the gold standard, with France also abandoning its bimetallic standard soon afterwards, as well as the discovery of vast new silver deposits in the United States (1970: 346). These factors caused a great deal more silver to find its way to the American market, harming the holders of silver, and leading to a political confrontation in the years that followed.

The Populist Party became a powerful political force during the 1890s as farmers in the West and the South formed the Farmers' Alliance of the Northwest and the National (or Southern) Farmers' Alliance (Henretta et al., 2000: 587). The class conscious Populists viewed farmers and workers as members of a single producer class that was opposed to monopoly and financial capitalists (588). They strongly supported the unlimited coinage of silver to help cotton, wheat, and corn growers who were suffering from falling prices during the 1890s. The Party's stance on the silver issue ultimately undermined its challenge to the status quo by bringing it into the center of mainstream politics. When the silver issue died with the discovery of gold in the late 1890s, so did the Populist Party (588–589, 593).

The political struggle for currency reform was primarily an agrarian and working class movement during the late nineteenth century. The Republican Party prevented currency reform that would have alleviated many of the harsh effects of the late nineteenth century economic crisis. For example, President Grant vetoed a bill favored by the Democrats in 1874 that would have increased the quantity of currency in circulation (Henretta et al., 2000: 500). The proponents of a return to the bimetallic standard of the pre-Civil War era did score a number of victories. The pro-silver coalition in Congress managed to pass the Bland-Allison Act of 1878 and the Sherman Silver Purchase Act of 1890, both of which required the U.S. Treasury to buy silver (2000: 590–591). Under the Sherman Silver Purchase Act, the silver was paid for with Treasury notes that were redeemable in either silver or gold (Tuttle and Perry, 1970: 347). When U.S. gold reserves were being steadily drained during the 1890s, President Cleveland persuaded Congress to repeal the Sherman Silver Purchase Act in 1893 and secretly cooperated with J.P. Morgan and a group of private bankers in 1895 to purchase large quantities of gold (2000: 591). His betrayal of the pro-silver Democrats set the stage for the rise of the Republican Party in Presidential politics in 1896 that would persist well into the progressive era. The passage of the Gold Standard Act in 1900 by the U.S. Congress officially established gold as the basis of the U.S. monetary system for the first time (1970: 348). The debate about the commodity basis of the monetary system reached its end as the progressive era was commencing.

Contrary to the popular perception among historians that the U.S. financial structure was highly centralized and tightly controlled by the early twentieth century, Kolko argues that the dominant trend was the relative decrease in New York's financial significance and the rise of alternative sources of considerable financial power (1967: 139–140). Prior to 1873, the tax on state bank notes had a very repressing effect on the number of such banks

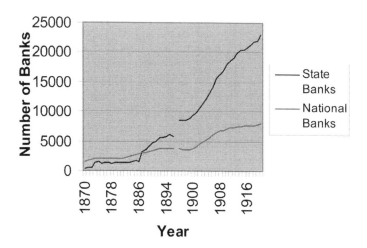

Figure 2.4: The changing composition of the U.S. banking structure: 1870–1920.
SOURCE: U.S. Bureau of the Census, 1960: 626, 628.
NOTE: The discontinuity indicates that the data before 1896 are not directly comparable with the data after 1896.

(Tuttle and Perry, 1970: 334). Since state bank notes were taxed at 10% annually and most state banks probably earned 5% or 6% on that privilege, it was not profitable to issue them and they disappeared from usage (1970: 345). After 1873, however, a small upsurge in the number of state banks can be seen in Figure 2.4 with the trend continuing afterwards. In 1887, the number of state banks in the United States surpassed the number of national banks for the first time in the post-Civil War era. Reinforcing this trend was the fact that many state banking laws were more liberal with regard to legal reserves than those of the national banking system (1970: 333). By 1896, a shift was occurring throughout the nation from national banks to state banks, and the banking structure was becoming highly decentralized (1967: 140–141). As Figure 2.4 clearly shows, from that point onward, the number of state banks far outstripped the number of national banks, suggesting a tendency towards a decentralized banking system.

Beginning in the 1890s and well into the progressive era, bankers favored financial reform with a special emphasis on creating a more elastic currency (Kolko, 1967: 146). The inability of the New York financial community to manage the nation's increasingly complex banking structure manifested itself in the 1907 financial panic. The decentralized banking structure undermined the power of the nation's key financial leaders and forced them to turn to the federal government for a relief package in excess of $37 million (1967: 155). The failure of the Knickerbocker Trust Company that led to the financial panic of 1907 made currency reform an important topic for NCF business leaders in particular. Although business leaders came into conflict with non-business leaders over the issue of state versus private control of the currency and NCF action on the issue ceased after 1908, many NCF proposals were later embodied in the Federal Reserve Act of 1913 (Weinstein, 1968: 29). NCF action in the area of currency reform thus conforms to the pattern of NCF action in the areas of trust regulation and the establishment of an interstate trade commission.

One legislative proposal, in particular, demonstrates that banking reform became a necessity after the panic from the perspective of the financial community. The Aldrich Plan, submitted to Congress as the Aldrich bill in 1912 (Kolko, 1967: 189), shared many similarities with the Federal Reserve Act (1967: 244). The bill died, however, because it attempted to leave control of the banking system in the hands of the private bankers (1967: 189). The earlier Aldrich-Vreeland Act, however, contained a number of measures that moved the nation towards a more elastic currency in line with business interests. The 1908 Act called for the formation of voluntary associations of private bankers, authorized national banks to issue notes backed by sound commercial paper as well as state and local government securities, and created the National Monetary Commission to study alternatives for a permanent solution (Dobson, 1988: 211). Because a purely private solution to the problem would not prove to be politically feasible, a more subtle solution would need to be found.

In 1912, division within the National Citizens' League for Sound Banking and loss of support for the Aldrich bill made the prospects for banking reform appear poor (Kolko, 1967: 217). Nevertheless, the ranking member of the Committee on Banking and Currency in the U.S. House of Representatives, Carter Glass of Virginia, was able to win the support of the banking community for the Federal Reserve bill by exploiting their fears of a more radical solution. He reminded them that "there was a worse possible fate than the one being offered to them" (1967: 240). According to Kolko, the Federal Reserve Act was the outcome of bankers' search for rationalization and their hopes of offsetting the decentralization of banking toward small banks and state banks (1967: 243). Reminiscent of the Aldrich Plan was the provision in the Federal Reserve Act for a Federal Advisory Council composed of bankers and businessmen. Rather than the complete private control of the Aldrich Plan, however, the Federal Advisory Council limited private interests to representation within the new Federal Reserve System. Furthermore, the legislation included a compromise to appease progressives with the creation of a Federal Reserve Board in Washington, D.C. that would oversee the operations of the whole system (Dobson, 1988: 211). The banking community had reached a strong consensus in favor of the proposed law before its passage in 1913 (1967: 242). Although the Act created twelve district reserve banks to be controlled by member banks and a Federal Reserve Board, it went a long way towards restoring New York City as the powerful center of the U.S. banking system. As governor of the New York Federal Reserve Bank, Benjamin Strong restored the relative power of New York in national banking to a level not achieved since the 1890s and one that would persist from 1914 until 1935 (1967: 251–252). The meaningful currency reform of the progressive era thus serves as a primary example of the way in which business needed to reorient itself towards an appreciation of the benefits of federal regulation.

2.6   THE TRANSFORMATION OF THE LABOR PROCESS AND THE REPRESSION OF ORGANIZED LABOR: CAPITAL-LABOR RELATIONS AND INTER-WORKER RELATIONS

A key contradiction in capitalist society and in the progressive era institutional structure in particular, is the relationship between capital and labor. To understand the nature of this relationship, it is first necessary to realize that a basic transformation of the production process was underway by the late nineteenth century. One of Andrew Carnegie's innovations, for example, was the introduction of the "line production" system in his plants. The system involved the arrangement of machines and workers into a sequence that permitted jobs to be broken down into their component parts (Micklethwait et al., 2003: 64). In the twentieth century, Henry Ford perfected this system with the use of conveyor belts to move parts past workers on the assembly line (2003: 65). Radical political economists identify this transformation of the production process and the American labor force in terms of a homogenizing tendency. Gordon, Edwards, and Reich define the homogenization of labor as "a spreading tendency toward the reduction of jobs in the economy to a common, semiskilled denominator" (1982: 100). Working conditions thus became more uniform and work tasks required only a minimum level of skill.

It is more common for historians to emphasize the application of scientific principles to the production process during this period. In 1911, Frederick Taylor's *Principles of Scientific Management* was published. Taylor "had been a steel company foreman who closely analyzed every job in the mill, and worked out a system of finely detailed division of labor" (Zinn, 2003: 324). Scientific management was an engineering approach to managing workers that involved the elimination of mental work from manual labor and the deprivation of workers' authority on the shop floor (Henretta et al., 2000: 563). It captured the attention of the public when Louis Brandeis argued in court that the nation's railroads were undeserving of a freight rate increase that the ICC was considering because they were ignoring Taylor's scientific management principles which could save them at least $1 million per day (McCraw, 1984: 92–93). Gordon, Edwards, and Reich are skeptical of the claim that Taylorism served as the primary method of controlling the labor process during the progressive era (Gordon et al., 1982: 146).[11] Instead, they describe the employer-dominated production process during the progressive era in terms of the simple "drive system." The drive system involved three main elements, including the reorganization of work due to mechanization and job restructuring, the rapid increase in plant size, and a continuing expansion of the foreman's role (1982: 128). The transformation of the production process was thus a relatively simple method of cost reduction and labor control.

Michel Aglietta's (2000) view is different in that he attributes the mechanization drive mainly to Taylorism. He defines the term "Taylorism" as the sum total of the relations of production internal to the labor process that tend to accelerate the completion of the mechanical cycle of movement on the job and to fill the gaps in the working day (2000: 114). The aim of the process then was to combat the control over working conditions that the relative autonomy of jobs in the old system could leave the workers (115). Another aspect of Taylorism that Aglietta discusses at length is the crucial role of piecework. That is, by creating far more opportunities for individual wages to be differentiated, Taylorism allowed American capitalists to take advantage of these differences to link remuneration to a stimulation of labor intensity (142). Furthermore, piecework made possible the lowering of the basic wage to the extent that the productivity of partial tasks increased, and it individualized wages in such a way as to sharpen competition among workers to a maximum. It was ideologically advantageous to the capitalist class as well insofar as it induced the illusion that wages as an economic category are tied to work performed (143). Whether one interprets the new system of labor control as a simple drive system or as the application of Taylor's scientific management principles, the effect was to raise labor intensity and deepen the competitive divisions within an increasingly homogeneous workforce.

Identifying the causes of labor homogenization is not a simple task. Gordon, Edwards, and Reich argue that the merger movement alone cannot explain the changing course of American capitalist development in the early twentieth century (Gordon et al., 1982: 112). Although the centralization of capital is not a sufficient explanation for the homogenization of labor, it certainly plays a key role in the transformation of the production process as Marx emphasized:

> Everywhere the increased scale of industrial establishments is the starting-point for a more comprehensive organization of the collective labour of many people, for a broader development of their material motive forces, i.e. for the progressive transformation of isolated processes of production carried on by customary methods, into socially combined and scientifically arranged processes of production (1990: 780).

A theoretical perspective constructed for the purpose of comprehending the history of American capitalism, in particular, permits us to move beyond Marx's general, causal statement. Social structure of accumulation theory thus provides the expanded analytical framework necessary to grasp the structural changes of the period and the causal forces that gave rise to them.

The theory of long swings in capitalist development suggests that the homogenization of labor was a capitalist reaction to the economic crisis of the late nineteenth century. The mechanized production process and the consequent homogenization of the labor force were necessary to prevent the rising labor costs that contributed to the growth slowdown during those years. In the early 1880s, employers began to experiment with the mechanization of the production process by eliminating skilled workers, reducing skill requirements, and increasing the pace of production (Gordon et al., 1982: 113). The homogenization of the workforce thus started long before the progressive era began.

Beyond the quest for lower labor costs, other factors may have been involved in the transformation of the workforce. Gordon, Edwards, and Reich claim that employers wanted to gain control over the production process in general rather than simply wanting to cut unit labor costs (Gordon et al., 1982: 115). Through skill reduction, businesses could treat workers as mere inputs to the production process with little power to influence the conditions under which they worked. By maintaining occupational segregation by ethnicity among departments and job categories, employers took advantage of racial and ethnic differences among workers (1982: 141) to prevent a harsh reaction from workers to the new system of labor control.

For example, in the Jones and Laughlin steelworks in Pittsburgh, the carpentry shop was German, the hammer shop was Polish, and the blooming mill was Serbian (Henretta et al., 2000: 557). These tactics helped employers maintain control in the new progressive era RIS that was designed to overcome the flaws of the previous institutional structure.

Neither Coase nor Chandler, discussed earlier in this chapter, recognize that the modern corporation was born in the aftermath of the economic crisis of the late nineteenth century. Chandler admits that his study of the modern business enterprise is not an investigation of the political and social arrangements existing during its inception (1977: 6). Placing its origin in this wider historical context would reveal that only large corporations could obtain the large amounts of capital necessary to take advantage of large-scale mechanization of the production process and prevent rising labor costs from eroding profits.[12]

To take full advantage of mechanized production, employers needed access to a large supply of labor capable of operating machines for long hours with few skills. According to Henretta et al., the demand for labor was so large that American industry could not rely entirely on the U.S. population for its workforce (2000: 556). From 1870 to 1900, a large number of (unskilled) immigrants entered the United States causing the labor force to nearly triple over the same time period. Although some southern blacks migrated northward and westward from 1870 to 1910, European immigrants provided northern employers with their chief supply of labor (556). In the 1880s, in particular, immigrants from southern and eastern Europe began to increase while immigrants from northern Europe began to fall until the former surpassed the latter in 1895. By 1905, the number of southeastern European immigrants entering the United States every year exceeded the number of northern European immigrants by the hundreds of thousands (557). After 1900, immigrants constituted over half the labor force of the primary manufacturing and mining industries in the United States (558). By contributing to the growth of a semiskilled class of laborers, this inflow of cheap labor reinforced the tendency towards homogenization throughout the progressive era.[13]

Even with the massive inflow of immigrant labor, the relative demand for unskilled workers increased even more rapidly than the supply. The homogenization of labor thus helped foster the growth of a national labor market (Gordon et al., 1982: 119). The massive growth of the demand for unskilled workers caused the ratio of unskilled workers' wages to skilled workers' wages to increase by roughly 5% (119). The influence of homogenization thus had real effects for skilled workers insofar as it eliminated their jobs and reduced their relative wages.

A number of other economic consequences flowed from homogenization during the progressive era. One important consequence of mechanization was the dramatic growth of plant size that followed. This change transformed social relations in the workplace from the relatively personal relations of small shops to the highly impersonal relations of large plants and factories (Gordon et al., 1982: 117). The number of foremen in manufacturing also rose from 90,000 in 1900 to 296,000 in 1920 (1982: 135). Although comprehensive data on industrial accidents do not exist before 1920, accident rates also soared and death rates reached an historic peak according to Commons between 1903 and 1907 (1982: 148). When the Triangle Shirtwaist Company fire occurred in downtown New York City in 1911, over one hundred young immigrant women perished (Henretta et al., 2000: 651). The employers were fined a mere $75 after the fire (2000: 652).

As the forces of homogenization transformed the conditions of labor, workers refused to watch in silence. In their otherwise mainstream history of "the company," Micklethwait and Wooldridge admit that "the company was a political creation" and "the product of a political battle" (2003: 53). Workers turned to labor organizations as an outlet for their frustration with the growth of large corporations and the system of labor control.[14]

Trade unionism grew rapidly after the Civil War. The National Labor Union, an umbrella organization for trade unions, was formed in 1866 to combat "wage slavery" (Henretta et al., 2000: 495). The Knights of Labor, founded in 1869, became a truly national movement in 1878. In 1886, the Knights of Labor reached its peak membership with 700,000 members (Micklethwait et al., 2003: 72). The American labor movement in the post-Civil War era, however, faced significant obstacles from the very beginning. The National Labor Union's advocacy of the eight-hour workday eventually led to its expulsion from the Republican Party (2000: 499). The Knights of Labor also began a rapid decline in the aftermath of the Haymarket Square Riot in Chicago and the founding of the American Federation of Labor in 1886 after having challenged the trade unions for the allegiance of workers during the 1880s (2000: 565–567). With Samuel Gompers as president, the AFL firmly rejected a political party for workers (2000: 567). The American labor movement was thus internally divided during the late nineteenth century and had difficulty forming an effective opposition to the forces of homogenization.

The federal government did little to help labor resist the transformation of the American workforce. When workers at the Baltimore and Ohio Railroad went on strike to protest wage cuts in 1877, President Hayes ordered the National Guard to force an end to the strike (Henretta et al., 2000: 541). During the 1890s, efforts to homogenize the labor force led to violent confrontations between capital and labor. The Homestead steel strike of 1892 and the Pullman Boycott of 1894 both ended with government intervention and the use of military force.

The recession of 1893–1897 was a turning point in the history of the American labor movement. According to Gordon, Edwards, and Reich, the recession marked the first time in U.S. history that the trade unions maintained their organizational integrity in the face of growing unemployment

(Gordon et al., 1982: 122). Union membership was also growing rapidly by the early twentieth century as Figure 2.5 shows.

The number of union members in the workforce increased fourfold between 1880 and 1900. This trend reflects growing unrest due to the intrinsic contradictions of homogenization (Gordon et al., 1982: 121). Union membership rose 300% between 1897 and 1904 but was nearly constant between 1904 and 1910. It then grew slowly between 1910 and 1916. During World War I, union membership soared from 2.8 million in 1916 to a peak of 5.0 million in 1920 (154). By 1924, union membership had fallen to 3.5 million where it remained and working class protest had moderated by the end of the 1920s (154–155).

Another measure of working class protest shows a similar pattern. The total number of work stoppages (i.e., due to strikes and lockouts) rose significantly in the early part of the progressive era as Figure 2.6 shows. The number of work stoppages soared during the merger wave, more than tripling from 1898 to 1903. After the initial surge, however, the number of work stoppages began to fall in 1904 and reached pre-merger wave levels in 1914 (U.S. Census Bureau, 1960: 99). The great reduction in the number of work stoppages provides the most direct evidence of the moderation of working class protest that occurred during the progressive era and again in the late 1920s after the postwar surge in strike activity.[15]

It is not clear why the growth of union membership or the number of strikes appear to slow down during the progressive era. The trend towards worker unrest should have continued well into the twentieth century as the homogenization of labor became more firmly established. One possibility

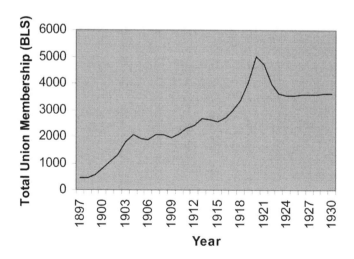

Figure 2.5: Labor union membership in the U.S.: 1897–1930.
SOURCE: U.S. Census Bureau, 1960: 97.

is that workers were relatively satisfied with the incomes they received and the conditions in which they worked. The next section demonstrates that workers had little reason to be satisfied with the levels of real income or job security they were granted. Gordon, Edwards, and Reich explain the slowdown in worker unrest as a consequence of the new system of labor control and the use of corporate power to stifle worker discontent (Gordon et al., 1982: 136). According to the authors, a "militant anti-unionism" grew after 1902 (143). The *form* of this anti-union activity, however, is the key to understanding capital-labor relations in the progressive era RIS.

The corporate policies aimed at eliminating worker unrest were varied. After the merger movement, corporations installed centralized personnel offices headed by central "employment managers" who broke down worker solidarity and weeded out troublemakers (Gordon et al., 1982: 137). Corporations also used artificial distinctions and divisions among jobs in an effort to reduce workers' unity (e.g., varied job titles, new job ladders) (138). Plant location was often selected as part of a divide-and-conquer strategy to discipline labor by moving factories out of central-city factory districts and into "industrial satellite suburbs" (138). Also, by the mid-1890s, piece-wages and more sophisticated incentive schemes were used to pay wage earners and stimulate competition among workers (140). Worker dissatisfaction with this approach to capital-labor relations is evident from the evidence presented in this section.

The poor reception to these tactics led corporate leaders to adopt new methods of labor control over the course of the progressive era. Until 1905,

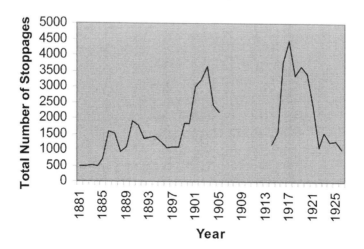

Figure 2.6: Number of work stoppages in the U.S.: 1881–1926.
SOURCE: U.S. Census Bureau, 1960: 99.
NOTE: Unfortunately, the data for the years 1906 to 1913 are not available.

the NCF viewed its main role to be a direct mediator in labor disputes as in the anthracite coal strike of 1902 (Weinstein, 1968: 9). According to Weinstein, during Mark Hanna's presidency from 1900 to 1905, the NCF concentrated on mediation and conciliation with labor to achieve the stabilization of capital-labor relations (37). "Many NCF leaders accepted the necessity of conservative unionism as an abstract principle, but opposed unions in their shops" (11). Examples of such hypocrisy were widespread among directors at U.S. Steel and International Harvester and include Cyrus McCormick, George Perkins, Elbert Gary, Henry Phipps, and Henry Davidson (11). The treatment of labor within the NCF also tended towards paternalism and lacked a spirit of true cooperation. According to the NCF's internal correspondence, the business leaders were referred to as the "important members" of the Executive Committee whereas the labor members were labeled "our friends" (30). Large corporations would need to modify their approach to capital-labor relations even further if they wished to receive labor's passive acceptance of the reality of the new institutional structure.

After 1905 the business leaders changed their approach to capital-labor relations. In January 1904, the Welfare Department of the NCF was formed, and welfare work became a significant part of NCF philosophy after 1905. During the progressive era, such welfare work generally consisted of social reforms that large corporations imposed upon themselves. According to Weinstein, the second phase of the NCF from 1905 to 1908, during which August Belmont served as NCF president, the organization in general turned away from unionism and towards welfare work (1968: 38). Specifically, "welfare work was increasingly seen as a substitute for the recognition of unions" (18). The paternalistic nature of welfare work necessarily excluded the union members of the NCF from participating (18). The growth of corporate welfare programs was enormous during the progressive era. In 1904, 50 employers had welfare programs; in 1911, 500 employers had welfare programs; and in 1914, 2500 employers had welfare programs (18–19). The NCF thus served as a means of popularizing corporate welfare policies during the progressive era.

The welfare policies implemented during the progressive era were numerous and varied widely on particulars. They included pension plans for employees, profit-sharing plans, and safety campaigns. According to the chairman of the board for U.S. Steel, the $10 million per year that it spent on employee welfare programs was intended "to disarm the prejudice against trusts." International Harvester also adopted a profit-sharing plan (Micklethwait et al., 2003: 75). The House of Morgan ultimately controlled both corporations. According to Weinstein, these two firms increasingly took the lead in paternalistic welfare measures (1968: 20). In 1916 as well, the skilled administrator for Sears, Roebuck, Julius Rosenwald, added a pension fund for employees (2003: 58). Rosenwald's welfare policies were the most extensive and consciously paternalistic according to Weinstein

(1968: 20). Corporate welfare policies were so successful that by the 1920s, "paternalistic labor relations [had] undermined union strength and successfully forestalled the organization of new unions" (1968: 20). It was this approach to capital-labor relations that ultimately undermined the resistance of unions to the new system.

On the one hand, the welfare policies of corporations are perfectly consistent with the theoretical framework that is being used to interpret the events of the progressive era. Corporations embarked on a program of self-regulation to help create an institutional structure that did not suffer from the defects of the late nineteenth century LIS. As the next section demonstrates, workers had little to celebrate during the progressive era despite the welfare policies aimed at pacifying them. This fact became painfully obvious when a series of great strikes took place in the United States throughout 1919. Over four million workers went on strike that year as well as the highest proportion in U.S. history with one out of every five workers on strike (Henretta et al., 2000: 731). The next section reveals much of the reality against which workers were protesting after the end of World War I and how much capitalists had gained at their expense.

2.7 THE PERFORMANCE OF THE PROGRESSIVE ERA REGULATIONIST INSTITUTIONAL STRUCTURE

Thus far this chapter has demonstrated that a fair amount of regulation, in one form or another, characterized the progressive era institutional structure. Business enterprises attempted to regulate their own competitive interaction through consolidation and merger. Business also encouraged regulatory reforms in their industries and in the banking system in an effort to ensure more stable profit margins and product prices. Public policy thus became a means by which capital could obtain a measure of control in an increasingly complex economic system. To provide an intellectual rationale for the centralization of corporate power, business leaders also constructed a new ideology of social responsibility to replace the outmoded ideology of individualism. Finally, the transformation of the American working class into a homogenous workforce was only accomplished after corporations implemented a variety of welfare programs to discourage unionization and pacify opponents of the new system of labor control. Even though capital was the source of the regulated labor-management relations, the dominant role of capital in placing restrictions on the operation of the labor market (as well as other input and output markets) confirms rather than undermines the regulated nature of the period. The regulated character of the period thus revealed itself in all of the main institutional features of the progressive era.

Having demonstrated the regulationist nature of the progressive era institutional structure, an evaluation of the structure's performance is in order. Capitalists evaluate their individual performance in terms of the rate of profit their businesses generate. The performance of the capitalist class as whole then depends on the aggregate rate of profit in the U.S. economy. Their desire to establish a more predictable business environment led the business class to seek a relatively stable profit rate during the progressive era. Therefore, they may have been willing to accept a lower, relatively stable rate of profit than one that was potentially higher, yet more volatile.

Gordon, Edwards, and Reich suggest that no reliable aggregate data on profit rates exist for the progressive era. They substitute an indirect measure for the aggregate rate of profit that they call the "gross surplus," which might alternatively be referred to as the rate of gross surplus. They define it as "the share of revenue from value added that manufacturers were able to retain after covering their production workers' wages" (Gordon et al., 1982: 147). Using the same definition (1982: 257), Figure 2.7 shows the movement in this variable over a sixty-year period including the economic crisis of the late nineteenth century, the progressive era, and the 1920s.[16]

The rate of gross surplus appears to be falling and relatively unstable during the late nineteenth century and higher and relatively stable during the progressive era, reaching a local maximum of almost 61% in 1909. Although the rate of gross surplus reached higher levels in the LIS following the progressive era RIS, it remained at a lower level during much of the 1920s. Hence, this evidence suggests that capitalists were successful in

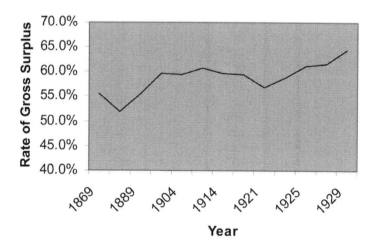

Figure 2.7: Rate of gross surplus in manufacturing in the U.S.: 1869–1929.
SOURCE: U.S. Census Bureau, 1960: 409.
NOTE: See p. 401, paragraph 3 for a defense of the continuity of the data.

maintaining a relatively stable positive rate of profit during the progressive era RIS. This finding supports the hypothesis that regulationist institutional structures are generally more favorable environments for capital accumulation and economic growth. Kolko argues, to the contrary, that "profits, if anything, declined" during the progressive era (1967: 24). The approximate measure of the aggregate rate of profit presented here, however, suggests relative stability, and it is the rate of profit rather than the magnitude of profits that concerns us.

The benefits of the regulated structure of the progressive era are also evident in other measures of business performance provided earlier in this chapter. The failure rate for U.S. business enterprises in 1906 reached its lowest level in twenty-five years (U.S. Census Bureau, 1960: 570). The average liability per failure reached its lowest point in the sixty years from 1870 to 1930 at just under $9000 (570). The capitalist class also largely achieved its goal of price stability during the progressive era. From 1903 to 1915, wholesale prices for all commodities only increased 1.4% (116–117). The deflation of the late nineteenth century was, therefore, eliminated and replaced with a very low rate of inflation. In terms of the performance of the overall economy, the progressive era RIS enjoyed relatively higher rates of economic growth and capital accumulation as shown in chapter 1.

Stable profit rates, low bankruptcy rates, and high rates of economic growth do not matter much to a working class that is unemployed or poorly paid. Business access to the large, national labor supply that followed the influx of southern and eastern European immigrants to the U.S. greatly reduced the likelihood of enhanced working class welfare. The unemployment rate reached high levels during the progressive era. Although the unemployment rate fell initially after the merger movement ended, by 1908 it had reached 8.5% and nearly 10% by 1915 (U.S. Census Bureau, 1960: 73). As Figure 2.8 shows clearly, the rate of unemployment was much higher during the progressive era (i.e., 1900–1916) than after the postwar recession in the 1920s.

A high rate of unemployment may seem tolerable if the real incomes of workers are rising throughout the period. Exactly the opposite occurred during the progressive era, however, as real wages in the manufacturing sector remained relatively stagnant during the early years of the twentieth century. Real average hourly earnings in manufacturing then fell by approximately 12.7% from 1906 to 1910 (U.S. Census Bureau, 1960: 91). Hourly earnings fell even more near the end of the war as a coal shortage developed without a compensating wage increase. As Figure 2.9 indicates, real average annual earnings in manufacturing followed a similar pattern, falling by roughly 21.5% from its pre-war peak in 1905 to its lowest level in 1917 (91).

A pattern of wage stagnation and a steep decline in earnings that followed were thus characteristic of the progressive era. The negative economic and

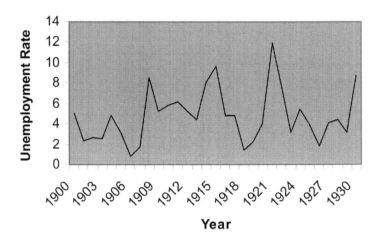

Figure 2.8: U.S. unemployment rate: 1900–1930.
SOURCE: U.S. Census Bureau, 1960: 73.

social consequences of progressive era regulation for the working class were thus inconsistent with the enhanced profitability of capitalist enterprises during that period.

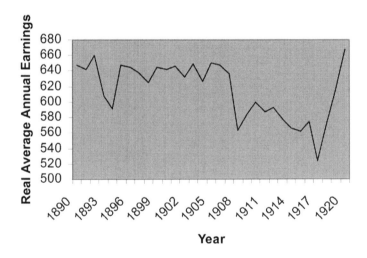

Figure 2.9: Real average annual earnings in manufacturing in the U.S.: 1890–1920.
SOURCE: U.S. Census Bureau, 1960: 91.

2.8 CHAPTER SUMMARY

This chapter has demonstrated that the economic crisis of the late nineteenth century liberal institutional structure gave rise to a new regulationist institutional structure that served to restrain many of the excesses of free market capitalism. The empirical evidence clearly shows how the centralization of capital, as manifested in the merger wave of the 1890s, provided capitalist enterprises with the economic might to cope with the contradictions of capitalist competition by implementing a regulatory program during the early twentieth century. The discussion of the economic role of the federal government also suggests that capital did not act alone in its attempt to rationalize and stabilize industry during the progressive era. President Roosevelt and President Wilson, in particular, established and maintained cooperative relations with big business. This measure of cooperation allowed large corporations to influence regulatory legislation through the National Civic Federation in such areas as currency reform and antitrust law.

Rationalizing the objectives and methods of big business during the progressive era required the new political and economic ideology of social responsibility. This ideology, which achieved its most precise formulation through the NCF, also had the responsibility of combating rival ideological positions including socialism and syndicalism. Early in the progressive era, such radical reform groups grew rapidly. The capitalist attack against socialists and syndicalists, however, led to the prewar stagnation and later decline of the Socialist Party of America and the Industrial Workers of the World. These attacks became especially potent when business enlisted the help of the federal government for enforcing wartime criminal syndicalism laws.

The new regulatory program of big business also involved a new system of cost cutting and labor control known as the drive system. In an effort to overcome the rising labor costs of the late nineteenth century, businesses rapidly mechanized production processes in manufacturing and mining, thus creating a large class of semi-skilled workers. The massive inflow of southeastern European immigrants provided a huge, cheap source of labor power that was necessary for the complete implementation of the homogenization drive. The high rate of industrial accidents and other negative consequences that followed for the working class led to an early surge in union membership that declined as the business class attacked organized labor, the Socialist Party, and the IWW. Part of this attack took the more subtle form of a paternalistic welfare program, which became a preoccupation of the NCF after the early years of the progressive era.

The section on the aggregate economic performance of the progressive era RIS has demonstrated that it possesses the essential characteristics of a RIS. It achieved high rates of economic growth and capital accumulation as well as stable prices and profit rates for capitalists. At the same time, it does not appear to have significantly diminished the negative consequences for the working class that Polanyi's double movement would imply. The harmful effects on workers included declining real earnings in an economy with high unemployment, corporate policies to discourage the organization of labor, and a production process that led to job dissatisfaction. The reason for the apparent inconsistency is simple yet easy to overlook: just as the institutions of the progressive era RIS were primarily the creation of the capitalist class, the benefits of its stability were intended for corporations alone. It is true that a RIS may be characterized by regulated labor-management relations in which organized labor has considerable power to influence the conditions and terms of exploitation, but in the progressive era RIS, the opposite was the case. Historians' traditional interpretation of the progressive period—as one in which reformers from below achieved victories in the battle against the giant trusts—is reflective of how successful corporations were at subtly shaping the regulatory measures of the state, designing welfare programs to appease labor, and hiding behind the veil of corporate social responsibility in an effort to achieve their own business objectives. To gain greater insight into the means corporations used to achieve their economic goals in particular industries during the progressive era and the extent to which they were successful, chapters 3 and 4 investigate the historical development of the iron and steel industry.

3 Regulation in the Era of Big Steel

The previous chapter explored at length the manner in which the economic crisis of the late nineteenth century led to the growth of the regulated economic structure that persisted throughout the progressive era. This chapter investigates the rise of regulation in the American iron and steel industry so as to encourage a more concrete understanding of the manner in which capitalists attempted to regulate markets and production through government channels and their own devices during the early twentieth century. The first section of the chapter explores the special conditions in the iron and steel industry that facilitated consolidation around the turn of the century and the unique pattern of combination to which they gave rise. The second and third sections then explore, respectively, the degree to which U.S. Steel succeeded in stabilizing product prices during the progressive era and the role of the federal government in stabilizing conditions in the industry. The final section presents the empirical evidence necessary to evaluate the degree to which regulation in the industry managed to increase the growth rate of industrial output, the rate of profit, and the amount of capital invested in the industry.

3.1 THE IRON AND STEEL INDUSTRY IN THE COMPETITIVE ERA

As is true of liberal institutional structures generally, the American iron and steel industry in the late nineteenth century was highly competitive. The intense competition of the period and widespread economic crisis pressured iron and steel companies to seek methods of regulating their own behavior in a manner that would alleviate the harmful economic consequences of the unpredictable business environment in which they operated. During the 1870s and early 1880s, for example, many steel companies entered into agreements based on oral promises to fix prices or divide markets. These "Gentlemen's Agreements" gave way to written agreements in the mid-1880s known as "pools" through which competitors would agree to respect each other's sales territories (Hessen, 1975: 61). The pools included the steel-rail pool of 1887, the wire-nail pool of 1895, the steel-billet pool of 1896, and the ore pool of the early 1890s (Gulick, 1924: 13). These agreements marked the first step towards the regulated structure that would characterize the industry during the progressive era.

Although many pools and gentlemen's agreements were formed, they often fell apart quickly under the pressure of industrial competition. In the 1880s, for example, the Western Pig Iron Association tried unsuccessfully to restrict output (Hogan, 1971: 236). Efforts within pools to enforce monetary penalties for noncompliance mostly proved futile as the temptation to cut prices during recessions proved too great for many companies (1971: 238). Furthermore, participants in a pool sometimes had ulterior motives. Carnegie, for example, entered pools only to gain access to the sales records and cost information of competitors (Hessen, 1975: 62). He had little interest in eliminating the competitive environment in which he thrived. According to Gulick, "until 1898 the steel industry was substantially one of competition" (1924: 13). The first regulation scheme in the iron and steel industry thus failed to stabilize conditions.

In both the late nineteenth century LIS and the progressive era RIS, a single steel company served as the industry's leader in terms of sheer market power. Whereas in the progressive era the leading steel company was firmly established practically from the outset, during the late nineteenth century the industry's leader strove continuously to establish its dominance. The success of the Carnegie Steel Company in the late nineteenth century LIS can be attributed to Andrew Carnegie's ability to master all the conditions in his industry. According to Brody, Carnegie's search for ever-lower production costs was part of the "economizing drive" that grew out of the unrestrained competition in the industry (1960: 2). His willingness to embrace new technology allowed him to push production costs lower than competitors. Although Carnegie managed to undersell competitors during the 1870s using Bessemer technology, it was his decision to adopt the recently perfected open-hearth technology in the 1880s that gave him the edge for the remainder of the decade. Carnegie had hundreds of thousands of dollars invested in Bessemer converters and yet he opted to phase out Bessemer production at his Homestead steel works in 1885 to make room for open-hearth furnaces (Hessen, 1975: 26).[1] He could then undersell them even during recessions and thus earn profits in the most unfavorable business conditions.

Before considering an additional factor leading to the industrial dominance of the Carnegie Steel Company, it is necessary to recognize that companies in the iron and steel trade during the late nineteenth century operated in a very unstable business environment. The shift from iron to steel was an early sign of this instability. Steelmaking gradually replaced iron production after the invention of the Bessemer process in 1856—an independent discovery of Henry Bessemer in England and William Kelly in America (Hessen, 1975: 23). The booming railroad industry further spurred the transition from iron to steel that took place during the last twenty years of the nineteenth century (Hogan, 1971: 303). By the 1890s "the widespread dismantling of iron mills" was underway (Brody, 1960: 8). Demand factors in the industry also contributed to the unstable and unpredictable business environment facing steel companies. During the late nineteenth century, "the demand for iron and steel came principally from the railroads as more steel went into the manufacture of rails than any other single product" (1971: 303). Because many industries transported their commodities using the nation's new railroad system, an economic slowdown could lead to a contraction in the railroad industry and a decline in the demand for steel. Hence, the demand for steel was very unstable prior to 1890 (1960: 2). Carnegie's willingness to embrace the latest technology for the production of steel only provides a partial explanation for his unparalleled success in an environment that was so menacing to new businesses.

Carnegie Steel also established a limited measure of control over the product and factor markets in which it was involved. This element of control may have been the essential ingredient in the company's success. For example, Carnegie obtained a privileged access to cheap raw materials that made him the envy of competitors. He possessed a minority interest in the H.C. Frick Coke Company and obtained low-cost iron ore through a lease on John D. Rockefeller's ore fields in Minnesota's Mesabi Range. Carnegie also anticipated the demand shift from steel rails for the railroads to structural steel for bridges and skyscrapers (Hessen, 1975: 64). This foresight led him to convert the Homestead plant from the production of rails to the production of structural steel while his Edgar Thompson plant in Braddock, Pennsylvania continued to produce steel rails. Carnegie's ability to assert a measure of control in both the product and factor markets was an early indicator that success in the iron and steel industry would only be won by evading the unpredictable forces of the market.

The Carnegie Steel Company grew primarily through the reinvestment of profits and internal expansion. Nevertheless, Carnegie did not hesitate to partake in the industry's consolidation movement when he felt threatened by competitors. His acquisition of the Homestead mill in 1882 and the Duquesne mill in 1890 were both undertaken for the purpose of eliminating competitors from the industry. All of these policies taken together allowed Carnegie Steel to become the dominant firm in the industry so that when business collapsed in 1893, Carnegie left the rail pool and went on to dominate the market (Brody, 1960: 4). By 1894, Carnegie's steel capacity had reached a quarter of national output, and he could monopolize a depressed market (5). He also managed to earn profits during every year of the recession of the 1890s by becoming a fully integrated steel company. The company's dominance was not to last, however, as other steel companies sought to partake in its competitive advantage and ultimately spread the benefits of its ruthless efficiency amongst the capitalists in the industry.

It has been noted above that the iron and steel industry in the late nineteenth century was highly competitive. Yet it is possible to be more specific about the composition of the industry during the final decades of the nineteenth century. Throughout the 1880s, the iron and steel industry consisted of hundreds of small companies capable of producing between 3,000 and 15,000 net tons of iron and steel annually. About a dozen medium-sized companies had capacities from 15,000 to 75,000 net tons and a small number of large companies could produce more than 75,000 net tons (Hogan, 1971: 235). Over time the gap between the largest and smallest companies grew until the structure of the market was substantially different from the late nineteenth century competitive structure.

Bankruptcies were common in the iron and steel industry as in the economy generally at the time. For example, there were thirty-two reported failures in the iron trade in the first six months of 1893 (Hogan, 1971: 237). Businesses were eager to protect themselves against the harsh whims of the market. The movement towards consolidation in the iron and steel industry began as early as 1889 with the formation of the Illinois Steel Company (236). By 1892, Illinois Steel and Carnegie Steel were the two largest companies in the industry with steelmaking capacities in excess of one million tons (235). As the end of the century grew near, the tendency towards consolidation in the steel industry became even more pronounced.

The merger movement in the steel industry can be separated into two distinct phases. During the first phase "from 1898 to 1900, eleven mergers which involved nearly two hundred previously independent companies were carried out" (Hogan, 1971: 239). This pattern of consolidation and incorporation in the iron and steel industry was representative of the more general movement of capital to New Jersey in the late nineteenth century. Companies incorporated under the laws of New Jersey at this time include the Lake Superior Consolidated Iron Mines Company (1893), the American Steel and Wire Company (1899), the Federal Steel Company (1898), the American Bridge Company (1900), the National Tube Company (1899), the Shelby Steel Tube Company (1900), the National Steel Company (1899), the American Tin Plate Company (1898), the American Sheet Steel Company (1899), the American Steel Hoop Company (1899), and the Carnegie Company (1900). This first phase of the merger movement created a significant number of giant corporations with competing interests that were unable to establish anything but an uneasy equilibrium.

Although many steel companies grew through merger from 1898 to 1901, others opted to expand on the basis of reinvested profits and thus retained a measure of independence during part of the progressive era. Included in this category are the Pennsylvania Steel Company, the Cambria Steel Company, the Lackawanna Iron and Steel Company, the Jones and Laughlin Steel Company, the Colorado Iron and Fuel Company, and the Tennessee Coal, Iron, and Railroad Company (Gulick, 1924: 16). The pattern of consolidation in the iron and steel industry thus exemplifies Marx's two forms of capitalist growth that he refers to as the centralization of capital (i.e., through merger) and the concentration of capital (i.e., through accumulation).[2]

The primary causes of the first phase of the merger movement in the iron and steel industry mirror those in many other industries at the turn of the century. It is generally agreed that the most important factor responsible for the consolidation movement in the iron and steel industry was the desire of steel companies to fortify themselves against the instability of the market (Hogan, 1971: 236). Other causes of the merger movement in the iron and steel industry have less to do with stabilizing industrial conditions. For example, the search for greater efficiency through integration, the desire for personal profit (i.e., through promotion), and the basic need for self-protection and survival were other key reasons for the consolidation of steel companies (239). Another significant reason is too easily overlooked. Reflecting on the formation of the Illinois Steel Company in 1889, the American Iron and Steel Association noted that "[o]ne of the consequences which may follow the consolidation at Chicago is the adoption of a similar policy by some of our Eastern Bessemer steel companies" (240). Hence, merger begot merger. The notion that smaller companies could more effectively compete with larger companies through consolidation became critically important during the second phase of consolidation in the iron and steel industry after the turn of the century.

The economic consequences of the first phase of the merger movement in the iron and steel industry appear contradictory. On the one hand, the consolidation of capital that took place encouraged the growth of monopoly power in the industry.[3] For example, the American Bridge Company would eventually control about 90% of the bridge tonnage erected throughout the country (Hogan, 1971: 273). The American Steel and Wire Company, formed in direct response to the collapse of the wire-nail pool in 1896, also gave John Gates a virtual monopoly over the American wire industry (261). Other examples of how consolidation in the iron and steel industry led to increased monopoly power are easily found. With the acquisition of the McCove Tube Company plant at Beaver Falls, Pennsylvania, the Shelby Steel Tube Company produced nearly all the seamless steel tubing in the country, obtaining a virtual monopoly in the tube business (283). Severe competition in the tin plate business in the late 1890s also led to the formation of the American Tin Plate Company: a consolidation that included practically all of the producers of tin plate in the nation (289–290). The American Tin Plate Company enjoyed high profits as a result of its monopoly position (292). Hence, the first wave of mergers in the iron and steel industry greatly enhanced monopoly power.

At the same time, the contradictory claim may be made that the first phase of consolidation greatly intensified the competitive nature of the industry. Consolidation created a small number of very large steel companies that were unable to coexist peacefully for any length of time. Although the formation of Morgan's Federal Steel Company led Carnegie to work out a pooling arrangement in rails with the president of Federal Steel, Judge Elbert Gary, the formation of other large companies at the time led to increasing competition and tension in the industry (Hogan, 1971: 272). Gulick captures perfectly the altered nature of competition in the iron and steel industry at the beginning of the progressive era:

> It had been supposed that competition would be reduced to a negligible factor, but as a matter of fact the combinations recounted above had the paradoxical outcome of increasing competition. The cause is not far to seek. Instead of competition between individual firms, none of which was particularly dominant, the stage was now set for a battle between giants, each provided with financial resources which only a few years ago had not been dreamed of. (Gulick, 1924: 17)

The real threat that the new consolidations posed to one another was not the threat of price competition. They threatened each other most of all by expanding on their product lines so that they came into direct competition for market share with each other. Therefore, the contradictory consequence of the merger movement (i.e., enhancing both competition and monopoly) is resolved as soon as it is realized that monopoly power grew in various product areas while the new industrial giants strove to break down the barriers to entry that protected the monopoly profits in each area. The inability of each consolidation to defend its monopoly position signaled that the first wave of mergers had not ended the competitive instability so feared by capitalists in the iron and steel industry.

To understand how the conditions created after the first phase of the merger movement gave rise to a second phase, it is necessary to first consider another aspect of the relationship between the newly created consolidations. Gulick explains that the new combinations can be divided into primary and secondary groups with a considerable amount of interdependence between the two (1924: 17). The primary group, which included the Carnegie Company, Federal Steel, and National Steel, produced crude steel and depended on the secondary group to purchase its semi-finished products. These producers of crude steel received financial backing from three separate interests. The Moore brothers provided the financial backing for National Steel, J.P. Morgan provided the financial backing for Federal Steel, and Carnegie himself provided the financial resources for the Carnegie Company (18–19). The secondary group, on the other hand, depended on the primary producers for its raw materials and included the American Steel and Wire Company, the National Tube Company, the American Tin Plate Company, the American Sheet Steel Company, and the American Steel Hoop Company.

The situation of interdependence created through this arrangement of steel companies intensified competition in the industry as each company strove to become self-sufficient. According to Hogan, the interdependence between the producers of basic steel and the companies that process it into finished products encouraged integration (1971: 465). Integration, of course, meant that each company began producing a wider range of steel products in an effort to become more independent of its rivals.[4] Around 1900, the American Steel and Wire Company began to shed its dependence on the crude steel of the Federal Steel Company by preparing to produce its own pig iron and steel. Similarly, the National Tube Company planned to erect additional furnaces and steel works thus eliminating a market for the Carnegie Company (Gulick, 1924: 17). Although the Shelby Steel Tube Company had a near monopoly, its position was vulnerable because it too was dependent on other steel companies for its supply of crude steel, and its virtual monopoly of the nation's seamless tube production was seriously threatened when the National Tube Company began manufacturing seamless tubing in 1901 (1971: 284). The situation became increasingly unstable as time passed.

From 1900 to 1901, the failure of the first merger wave to eliminate competition in the industry had become painfully obvious. The two largest steel companies at the time, the Carnegie Company and the Federal Steel Company, were not even combinations of previously competing concerns (Hogan, 1971: 285). Furthermore, as steel companies began to reduce their dependence on Carnegie, Carnegie fought back by branching out into other areas. Like other entrepreneurs in the steel industry, Gates wanted to reduce his dependence on Carnegie for raw materials (263). In May 1900, therefore, Carnegie Steel announced that it would enter the wire business to compete with the American Steel and Wire Company. Similarly, Carnegie announced later that year that his company would build a giant tube plant at Conneaut Harbor in Ohio to compete with J.P. Morgan's National Tube Company (465). Perhaps most threatening to Morgan were Carnegie's negotiations with George Gould to build a railroad that would compete with the Pennsylvania Railroad and threaten Morgan's dominant position in the railroad industry (Kolko, 1967: 32). The situation had reached a volatile peak and would require a more drastic solution to restrict competition than any previously considered.

The second phase of the merger movement in the iron and steel industry was much simpler than the first phase. After intense negotiations between Charles Schwab, John Gates, J.P. Morgan, and Andrew Carnegie, Morgan announced the organization of the United States Steel Corporation on March 2, 1901. The new combination consisted of the Carnegie Company of New Jersey, the Federal Steel Company, the American Steel and Wire Company, the National Tube Company, the National Steel Company, the American Tin Plate Company, the American Steel Hoop Company, and the American Sheet Steel Company (Gulick, 1924: 19–20). Once formed, U.S. Steel controlled 43% of pig iron production and 66% of steel ingot and castings production in the U.S. (20). Although not a pure monopoly, the creation of U.S. Steel ended the potentially explosive conflict among the industry's giants that followed the first merger wave in the industry.

The complete integration of U.S. Steel eliminated the interdependence of competing steel companies, which was needed to stabilize the industry during the progressive era RIS. That competition had changed in the industry is reflected in the words of Joseph G. Butler, Jr., Vice-President of the Brier Hill Steel Company in Youngstown, Ohio at a meeting of the American Iron and Steel Institute (AISI) in 1912. According to Butler, the word "competition" should be understood in a broader sense than simply price competition. Instead, it should refer to "rivalry at all points," including the development of new markets (Butler, 1912: 41). This competitive form is precisely that which followed the first wave of consolidations in the iron and steel industry and the new form of competition that U.S. Steel intended to restrain and manage throughout the progressive era. By stabilizing prices and ensuring profitability in particular product areas, the Steel Corporation reduced the incentive for competition across product areas.

3.2   CAPITALIST COMPETITION IN THE IRON AND STEEL INDUSTRY DURING THE PROGRESSIVE ERA

The United States Steel Corporation served as the key regulatory force in the iron and steel industry during the progressive era and for many years after the close of that period in American history. Its major accomplishment in this regard was a great reduction in price competition on a wide range of steel products throughout the industry. As the previous section explained, steel prices in the late nineteenth century fluctuated greatly with the unpredictable demand shifts for steel. In 1912, the industrial trade journal, *Iron Age*, expressed its fear that the iron and steel industry might return to the calamitous prices of 1897 and 1898 and that the consumers of iron and steel wanted no return of them (Berglund, 1923: 3). This section thus explores the motivation of the Steel Corporation, the means it used, and the degree to which it succeeded in the enormous task of stabilizing product prices during the progressive era.

Robert Allen's examination of steel prices seems to discount the importance of regulation in the stabilization of product prices after 1901, placing heavier emphasis on strictly economic factors as a stabilizing force. According to Allen, the American steel industry became internationally competitive between the 1880s and the early 1900s as the price of steel in the U.S. fell sharply due to falling steel-making costs. Costs then stabilized between 1902 and 1910 (Allen, 1981: 521). Allen attributes the falling costs of steel manufacture between 1879 and 1889 to falling input prices whereas the decline in costs between 1889 and 1902 were primarily the result of rapid productivity growth. Both factors ceased to put downward pressure on steel prices after 1902 (521). This interpretation suggests that the pricing policy of U.S. Steel was not the most direct factor responsible for the stabilization of product prices in the steel industry in the early twentieth century.

Accusations that the industry was engaged in illegal pricing arrangements were common during the progressive era. The leaders of the iron and steel industry were frequently challenged to provide a suitable explanation for the stable prices of steel. Testifying before a U.S. Congressional committee in 1908, Schwab offered this explanation for the fixed price of rails that persisted among American rail producers:

> I, for example, as a rail manufacturer, feel that if I were to vary that price of $28 for rails, which seems to have been recognized by all rails manufacturers as a fair price, and giving a fair profit,—if I were to vary that 10 cents a ton to-day, I would precipitate a steel war, to use such a word or expression, that would result in running my works without any profit. Everybody, by tacit and mutual understanding, feels the same thing about that. I would not vary the price of my rails under any circumstances, not if I knew it was to get 100,000 tons in orders, for the reason that my competitor next door would put the price down . . . and we would be a in a position where we would be running without any profit at all. (Hessen, 1975: 193)

Schwab's defense of the industry against conspiracy theorists sounds very much like the neoclassical kinked demand curve model of oligopolistic markets. The statement ignores, however, the fact that not all rail producers are on an equal footing in the industry as well as the fact that a formal relationship binds them in a manner not captured in the model.

This sort of reasoning was used again in 1915 when the Federal District Court of New Jersey exonerated U.S Steel in the antitrust case against that corporation. According to the court, "a single large concern, by lowering the price of any substantial steel product it sells, can depress the obtainable price." At the same time, "no single large concern, by raising or even maintaining the price of any substantial steel product, can raise the obtainable price" (McCraw and Reinhardt, 1989: 600). This reasoning is exactly the same as that employed to theoretically derive the kinked demand curve. Unfortunately, it ignores the institutional mechanism U.S. Steel devised to stabilize prices in the steel industry in the early twentieth century. Stocking identifies this tension between the two explanations as part of an ongoing debate as to whether conspiracy or independent decision-making gave rise to the basing point pricing system in the steel industry (1954: 13). To evaluate the merits of the various explanations for product price stabilization, it is necessary to investigate the Steel Corporation's policies in greater detail.

It is natural that U.S. Steel would value price stabilization during the progressive era. The demand for steel was as unstable in the early twentieth century as it was in the late nineteenth century. As Stocking pointed out in 1954, the demand for steel is a "derived demand" (1954: 27)—a statement that held true in the late nineteenth century as well as the twentieth century. Whereas in the competitive era the demand for steel was unstable due to the fluctuating requirements of the railroads, in the regulated structure of the early twentieth century, the demand for steel varied "according to changes in the development of new enterprises" (Berglund, 1923: 4). The close relationship between the demand for steel and the spirit of investment thus rendered the industry vulnerable to alternating periods of depression and prosperity and made some form of stabilization desirable (Berglund, 1924: 4). The Steel Corporation thus considered the stabilization of product markets to be one of its primary responsibilities.

It is also necessary to realize that consolidation alone was not sufficient for the stabilization of product prices in the steel industry. In the first section of this chapter, the first phase of the merger movement was described as a series of consolidations, each specializing in the production of a particular product and having a substantial degree of market power. According to Berglund, "[t]he violent fluctuations in prices during these years show that no definite price policy prevailed in the industry generally" (1924: 613). Only since the formation of U.S. Steel "has the steel trade generally felt the effect of a definite price policy" (613). Thus it was the Steel Corporation, in particular, that established a general price policy for the industry. Berglund explains the willingness of the independent steel companies to adopt the pricing policy of U.S. Steel as arising from the corporation's "prestige and generosity" (1923: 29). Whatever the reason for the consolidation's success as a regulator of prices, the Steel Corporation served as the leader of the industry in the sphere of pricing policy during the progressive era.

The means by which U.S. Steel established price stability in the iron and steel industry included a host of measures of questionable legality. Pooling arrangements, for example, continued well after the formation of U.S. Steel despite Urofsky's claim that "the subsidiary companies withdrew from all pools and other illegal or questionable activities" in the early years of the corporation (1969: 3). As noted above, U.S. Steel was an active member of the Steel Rail Association. It was also a member of the Bessemer Steel Association, which fixed the price of steel billets (Stocking, 1954: 43). One of U.S. Steel's subsidiaries, the American Steel and Wire Company, continued to participate in illegal pools formed as late as 1908 (1954: 43). Due to the threat of antitrust prosecution, however, the role of pooling arrangements in the stabilization of steel prices diminished greatly during the progressive era.

Another popular method of stabilizing steel prices during the progressive era was a series of informal dinners hosted by Judge Gary to provide a forum for the steel men to exchange information regarding commodity prices. The "Gary dinners" were held at the Waldorf Hotel from 1907 to 1911 and led to the creation of a five-member committee of steel executives to which anyone interested in the iron and steel trade could appeal for advice (Stocking, 1954: 44). The problem with this method of stabilizing prices in the steel industry was that it was a rather blatant violation of U.S.

antitrust law. The dinners thus ended when the government began legal action in 1911 (Barnett, 1994b: 353). Although a federal district court later ruled that the Gary dinners were illegal, no penalties were imposed because the practice had been discontinued.

In an effort to avoid the public suspicions raised by the informal Gary dinners, the leaders of the steel industry required a formal organization that was capable of institutionalizing the cooperative inter-capitalist relations of the progressive era. The American Iron and Steel Institute (AISI) was such an organization created by Judge Gary of the United States Steel Corporation in 1908. The organization held its first meeting in 1910. Initially, the AISI was "the focal point of industry efforts to coordinate steel pricing and to deal with the government on matters affecting pricing" (Barnett, 1994a: 14). Gary intended the AISI to "institutionalize cooperation, information exchange, and, if not price-fixing, certainly price stabilization" (Cutcliffe, 1994: 155). The steel industry thus codified the cooperative practices of the progressive era RIS in an effort to make permanent the regulatory structure that fostered corporate profitability.

The specific institutional arrangement that the Steel Corporation used to pursue its program of product price stabilization is known as basing point pricing. To understand the origin of basing point pricing in the steel industry, it is necessary to understand that the location of steel plants depends heavily on the location of raw materials, such as iron ore and coke, as well as on the location of markets for steel (Stocking, 1954: 33). The system that developed was essentially a pricing formula that eliminated the relative advantages that geography created for steel companies operating on the southern shore of Lake Michigan rather than in Pittsburgh and Youngstown (Seely, 1994: xviii). These geographic considerations led to a basing point pricing system that consolidated the power of the Steel Corporation in Pittsburgh as well as the corporation's construction of the massive Gary steelworks in Gary, Indiana during the first decade of the corporation's existence.

To understand the mechanics of basing point pricing, it is necessary to distinguish between the price where a good originates (i.e., the f.o.b. or free on board price) and the delivered price (i.e., the f.o.b. price plus the freight charges associated with its transportation to the buyer). A basing point pricing system is established when an industrial leader selects the base price (i.e., the f.o.b. price) for its commodity as well as a particular location that will serve as the basing point for all sellers in the industry. The sellers then use that location to calculate the freight charges to be included in the delivered price regardless of their own location (Stocking, 1954: 3–4). If all producers in the industry follow the leader, then a uniform set of prices will be established so that any buyer in any location will pay the same price for the commodity purchased.

During the first quarter of the twentieth century, U.S. Steel treated Pittsburgh as the basing point in a pricing system known as "Pittsburgh

Plus." Although the practice existed prior to the U.S. Steel merger, it was not until after the Steel Corporation's formation that the Pittsburgh Plus system became general and persistent throughout the industry (Stocking, 1954: 50). One way in which U.S. Steel administered the Pittsburgh Plus system was through the publication of freight rate books. After 1901, U.S. Steel led the iron and steel industry in the stabilization of prices by fixing its product prices and announcing them in steel trade journals (Hessen, 1975: 186). For example, one U.S. Steel subsidiary, the American Sheet and Tin Plate Company, published such books, constantly revising them and distributing them to competitors (1954: 52). According to McCraw and Reinhardt, the method of publishing steel prices "remained a lasting force for stabilization" (1989: 604). Thus the ideal of information exchange embodied in the philosophy of the American Iron and Steel Institute was implemented in a practical way to further the Steel Corporation's goal of price stability.

It is generally recognized that the basing point pricing system in the steel industry served to stabilize the prices of steel products. According to George Stocking, basing point pricing systems in general tend to stabilize prices and the Pittsburgh Plus system in particular helped stabilize prices in the steel industry (1954: 5–7). Donald Barnett also asserts that "[f]rom 1907 until 1919 the Pittsburgh Plus Pricing formula largely created price stability" (1994b: 353). The difficulties of maintaining the basing point system during difficult economic times manifested itself, however, in the periodic formation of Chicago Plus pricing in 1908, 1911–1912, and 1917–1918 (1994b: 353). The extent to which these disruptions influenced the growth of the major steel companies is explored briefly in the section on industrial performance below.

U.S. Steel certainly succeeded in stabilizing steel prices during the progressive era RIS. Abraham Berglund (1923) compares price fluctuations in the iron and steel industry in the periods before and after the formation of the Steel Corporation and obtains the following results as presented in Table 3.1.

Table 3.1 Extreme annual and monthly price variations for finished steel in the United States: 1898–1922.

Period	Greatest Variation from Periodic Mean Using the Highest/Lowest Annual Average	Greatest Variation from the Periodic Mean Using the Highest/Lowest Monthly Average
1898-1901	31.3%	37.0%
1902-1914	19.3%	23.9%
1915-1922	47.7%	81.8%

SOURCE: Berglund, 1923: 14.

This evidence suggests that U.S. Steel succeeded in reducing price fluctuations during the progressive era RIS and thus achieved a measure of price stability relative to other periods. Due to data limitations, Berglund is subject to the criticism that he has selected a period that is too brief to measure price fluctuations prior to the formation of U.S. Steel. He obtains equally impressive results, however, when he broadens the time span but limits the range of products to steel rails and steel billets (19). At the same time, Berglund argues that U.S. Steel's power to control prices did not change radically in any of the important branches of steel manufacture (7). Hence, this fairly general analysis of steel prices in the late nineteenth and early twentieth centuries suggests that price stability was achieved during the progressive era in a relative sense.

The stabilization of steel prices that followed the formation of U.S. Steel was most pronounced in the case of Bessemer steel rails. Having fluctuated frequently prior to 1901, the price of steel rails was then set at $28 per ton and remained unchanged until the First World War. "Such stability was unprecedented in the industry and indicates some power to control the price" (Allen, 1981: 513). The fixed price of steel rails during the progressive era is not a trivial case. As Berglund has pointed out, "[e]ven as late as the opening years of the present century the manufacture of rails was characterized as the backbone of the steel industry" (1924: 610). Rail prices are thus worthy of attention in any examination of price stability during the progressive era.

The stability of rail prices had been a goal of rail producers for many years. A moderately successful steel rail pool was formed in 1887 and worked to control rail prices until it disbanded in 1897. In 1899 the pool was reorganized and continued for a number of years after the formation of U.S. Steel as the Steel Rail Association (Berglund, 1923: 22). Rail producers were primarily interested in preventing a future collapse of the rail market (23). The small number of rail producers helped make the price stabilization program a success for many years (30). Figure 3.1 shows clearly how rail prices were stabilized after the formation of the Steel Corporation and before World War I.

According to McCraw and Reinhardt (1989), U.S. Steel managed to stabilize the prices of many steel products after 1901, which even showed little fluctuation during the 1907 panic. This price pattern held for wire and nails as well as beams and bars throughout the progressive era (1989: 601–602). Tin plate provides an excellent example of a product in the iron and steel industry whose price clearly expressed U.S. Steel's commitment to price stability. The price of tin plate was remarkably stable during the progressive era, while the price of tin (a key input for the production of tin plate) fluctuated considerably (603). Even when the pursuit of maximum profits suggested a variable price of tin plate, the Steel Corporation opted to maintain stable prices.

Efforts to control market conditions in the iron and steel industry go beyond the stabilization of prices in product markets and for good reason. A highly competitive market for coke contributed to fluctuating raw material costs with the price of coke ranging from $1 per ton to $8 per ton (Smith, 1908: 265). The price range for limestone, another key raw material for steel manufacture, also varied considerably (267). To the extent that the steel companies could stabilize the prices of raw materials, it strove to do so. Various methods, for instance, were used in the early twentieth century to protect the industry against fluctuating iron ore prices. For example, because long-term contracts at fixed prices were difficult to make, steel companies developed a sliding scale, "whereby high prices in iron cause[d] the payment of high prices for ore and *vice versa*" (264). To the best of this author's knowledge, no attempts have been made to systematically analyze the extent to which the United States Steel Corporation used its influence to stabilize input markets.

Given the Steel Corporation's dominant role in establishing steel prices throughout the industry, it is easy to assume that its primary goal was to use its market power to set the highest prices consistent with its individual pursuit of profits. Berglund (1923) has evaluated the pricing policies of U.S. Steel in considerable detail with this common perception in mind. One of Berglund's goals is to undermine the widespread belief held by the American public in the early twentieth century that U.S. Steel instigated a general rise in steel prices using its substantial market power. Elmer Hartzell also has attacked the common view that U.S. Steel charged excessive prices for

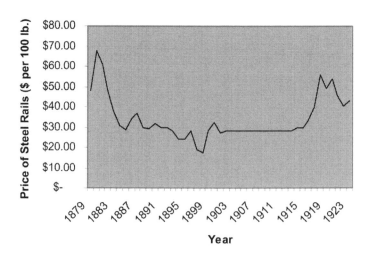

Figure 3.1: The wholesale price of steel rails in the U.S.: 1879–1923.
SOURCE: U.S. Census Bureau, 1960: 123.
NOTE: See p. 108 for clarification of the data changes that occur in 1891 and 1913.

steel (1934: 330). Of course, the charge of monopoly power may be construed as an empirical question if the price changes are examined before and after the formation of U.S. Steel.

Berglund provides a variety of empirical evidence to support his case that the Steel Trust did not charge monopolistic prices during the progressive era. He advises, however, that any comparison of steel prices before and after the formation of U.S. Steel must be made with caution because special factors (e.g., the first phase of the merger movement, WWI) considerably altered prices (1923: 9). Berglund's evidence suggests that "there was no general and pronounced upward movement in steel quotations such as had characterized the formation of the steel consolidations of the late nineties" (2). Furthermore, price levels in the first two years of the corporation's existence were "considerably below" those set during the first phase of the merger movement in the years 1899 and 1900. Steel prices then remained relatively stable during the recession of 1903–1904 (2). During U.S. Steel's existence prior to World War I, for example, moderate or even falling prices for ordinary steel products existed (10). The average price of finished steel, for instance, was 1.92¢ per pound in the period 1898–1901 whereas in the period 1902–1914 it was 1.724¢ per pound (10). Also, after 1901, steel prices lagged behind commodity prices generally (12). The Steel Corporation thus refused to exercise the full extent of its market power for reasons that are explored in detail below.

It is important to consider what U.S. Steel hoped to gain from the stabilization of product prices if not the monopolistic domination of the market for steel products. According to Berglund, the Steel Corporation wanted to limit trade fluctuations by "rendering less hasty the purchases of material on a rising market and reducing the tendency to postpone purchases on a falling market" (1923: 5). Hence, by eliminating the incentives for speculative purchases, stable prices would help stabilize trade. Unfortunately, Berglund does not emphasize in his 1923 article the way in which price stability may exacerbate trade fluctuations as he discusses in his 1924 article. The potential problems that price stability may have carried for output and employment fluctuations are discussed in the next chapter.

Although the basing point pricing system that prevailed in the steel industry during the progressive era may have made it more difficult for steel companies outside of Pittsburgh to attract buyers by cutting prices, the system certainly did not stop the growth of large firms to rival the market power of the Steel Corporation. The limited return to competitive intercapitalist relations that followed the formation of U.S. Steel in 1901 arose from the contradictory leadership structure of the Steel Corporation. The corporation's leadership was divided from the very beginning.[5] Men like Charles Schwab, William Ellis Corey, and Henry Clay Frick had contributed significantly to the rise of the Carnegie Steel Company. They were now the leaders of a corporation that participated in an institutional structure considerably different from the competitive era that made them famous.

At the same time, the financial managers that had orchestrated the largest consolidation in U.S. history were determined to remain in control of its vast concentration of wealth. This group of lawyers and financiers included primarily men like J.P. Morgan, Judge Elbert Gary, and George Perkins. A serious conflict between the two groups was inevitable.

The division among the corporation's leadership actually encouraged the formation of dominant rivals in the iron and steel industry. The most notable example is the rise of the Bethlehem Steel Corporation. Less than two months after becoming the president of U.S. Steel in 1901, Schwab purchased the Bethlehem Steel Company as an independent investment (Hessen, 1975: 147–148). Feeling obligated as president of U.S. Steel to sell the company to the J.P. Morgan syndicate that had underwritten the U.S. Steel merger, Schwab would soon negotiate its further sale to the United States Shipbuilding Company: a 1902 merger of seven shipyards on the Atlantic and Pacific Coasts (145, 149). When the U.S. Shipbuilding Company approached bankruptcy in 1903, Schwab used his favorable bargaining position to wrestle the Bethlehem Steel Company back for himself despite the legal protests of a group of U.S. Shipbuilding's bondholders. Having suffered the bad publicity from the U.S. Shipbuilding controversy, Schwab resigned as president of U.S. Steel on August 4, 1903. He thus proceeded to make Bethlehem Steel the second largest steel producer in the world after having served as president of the world's largest steel corporation.

In December 1904, Bethlehem Steel was incorporated in New Jersey as a holding company with a capitalization of $30 million. It operated the Bethlehem Steel Company as well as the seven shipyards and one manufacturing company from the shipbuilding merger with Schwab as president (Hessen, 1975: 167). Although its original capitalization was far below that of U.S. Steel at its inception, "[b]y failing to match Schwab's aggressive policies, Gary contributed to Bethlehem's growing strength" (1975: 185). "U.S. Steel under Gary did little to rationalize production facilities, innovate product lines, or consolidate management structure" (McCraw and Reinhardt, 1989: 595). The failure of U.S. Steel to consolidate its management structure is most evident when considering the stark contrast between the management structures of U.S. Steel and Bethlehem Steel.[6]

The Steel Corporation's failure to innovate is best captured with the history of a new form of structural steel in 1897 called the Grey beam. While president of U.S. Steel, Schwab encouraged the corporation's Finance Committee to purchase the rights to the invention but was rejected. In 1905, after Schwab had become president of Bethlehem Steel, he decided to undertake the production of Grey beams. Feeling obligated, Schwab informed U.S. Steel that he planned to pursue the production of the new product in 1906. After consulting a committee of experts, Gary replied to Schwab that U.S. Steel had no interest in the new process (Hessen, 1975: 173). By 1926, Schwab discovered that U.S. Steel was secretly constructing a mill to produce the patented Bethlehem (Grey) beam given its enormous commercial success. The discovery led to a legal conflict between U.S. Steel and Bethlehem Steel until U.S. Steel finally agreed to pay royalties for permission to produce the Bethlehem beam in 1929 (267–269). This brand of competition was far from common in the steel industry during the early twentieth century as "[t]here was a tacit live-and-let live agreement between Schwab and Gary, and the largest steel companies were rarely in direct competition" (267). The Bethlehem beam case is thus an example of how the Steel Corporation refused to prevent the growth of rival firms even while their relations were sometimes strained.

Inter-capitalist relations in the steel industry were generally cooperative during the progressive era RIS. The pricing policies of the United States Steel Corporation and its willingness to permit the growth of large rival firms suggest that capital in the industry was more unified than ever before even when it was spread across a number of distinct business enterprises. The steel companies thus stood united with Gary as their undisputed leader when they were forced to cope with two other key power blocs in progressive America: the federal government and organized labor.

3.3   STATE INVOLVEMENT IN THE IRON AND STEEL INDUSTRY DURING THE PROGRESSIVE ERA

Given the immense size of the United States Steel Corporation, it is no surprise that the federal government took an active interest in the corporation throughout the progressive era. The relationship between the federal government and the steel industry varied considerably throughout the period as conditions changed. Beginning with a phase of significant cooperation between the Roosevelt administration and the Steel Corporation, cooperation then waned as Taft replaced Roosevelt and U.S. Steel's economic behavior spurred criticism of the corporation. Efforts to reestablish cooperative state-capital relations during WWI were only temporarily successful. Nevertheless, the U.S. government ultimately recognized the Steel Corporation's right to remain intact as the acknowledged leader of the iron and steel industry. This section reviews these broad developments to provide an overall assessment of the nature of state-capital relations in the iron and steel industry during the progressive era.

Cooperative state-capital relations were readily achieved during the first few years of the Steel Corporation's existence. The relative ease with which this cooperative arrangement was achieved depended heavily on the personal relationship between Judge Gary and President Roosevelt. Possibly aware of a similar arrangement with International Harvester, Gary approached Roosevelt on behalf of U.S. Steel in late 1904 to establish an informal understanding between the corporation and the executive branch of the federal government. Gary offered to open all of the books and financial records of the Steel Corporation to the President in return for the opportunity to defend any of its actions or correct any wrongdoing prior to the initiation of an antitrust suit against the corporation (Kolko, 1967: 79). In late 1905, Gary, Frick, Roosevelt, and Roosevelt's Commissioner of Corporations, James R. Garfield, met at the White House. At that time, Garfield assured Gary that the information gathered by the Bureau of Corporations would not be used publicly unless the government had a clear duty to expose the corporation (80). The cooperative relations that Gary and Roosevelt established were thus based on mutual respect and responsibility.

The decline of cooperative relations between the Steel Cooperation and the federal government began soon after the corporation undertook a key acquisition in late 1907. U.S. Steel's interest in acquiring the Tennessee Coal, Iron, and Railroad Company (TCI&RR) arose when Morgan approached Gary in 1907 and asked him if U.S. Steel would be willing to purchase the company. Morgan was concerned that Moore and Schley, a New York brokerage firm that had used a large quantity of TCI&RR stock as collateral on about $25 million in loans falling due, was about to fail (Cutcliffe, 1994: 155). Morgan convinced Gary and the U.S Steel finance committee to acquire the company, but first Gary and Frick traveled to Washington to obtain the express permission of President Roosevelt and Secretary of State, Elihu Root (156). The steel executives' willingness to approach the President is perfectly consistent with the détente arrangement that had governed their relationship since 1904.

The general economic conditions during the time of the acquisition should not be ignored. During the 1907 financial panic, the U.S. Treasury was pumping millions of dollars into the financial markets at the request of New York bankers as discussed in chapter 2. It was in the midst of this financial chaos that Morgan coolly acquired TCI&RR (Kolko, 1967: 156). U.S. Steel's absorption of the Tennessee Coal, Iron, & Railroad Company occurred on November 6, 1907 (Smith, 1908: 273). According to McCraw and Reinhardt, the acquisition was "motivated primarily by a desire to avert financial panic rather than to obtain assets at bargain prices" (1989: 604). The perception that U.S. Steel was fulfilling its sense of social responsibility with the acquisition is one that the corporation hoped to encourage.

Despite Gary's claim that U.S. Steel acquired TCI&RR to stabilize the financial markets, U.S. Steel gained considerably from the deal. TCI&RR was the major steel producer in the South in the early twentieth century, and its low production costs had the potential to give it control over the entire Southern market (Kolko, 1967: 114). The purchase greatly enhanced U.S. Steel's access to raw materials given TCI&RR's 352,548 acres of coal- and ore-rich properties in Alabama and Tennessee (Sholes and Leary, 1994: 427). Specifically, the acquisition increased the Steel Corporation's ore reserves by 40% and gave it control of a company worth at least four times its purchase price (1967: 117). Furthermore, the acquisition allowed U.S. Steel to conquer a competitor that was selling rails to western railroads at prices that were much lower than those charged by U.S. Steel (1994: 427). The Steel Corporation undoubtedly benefited economically from the Tennessee acquisition.

Other circumstances surrounding the acquisition of TCI&RR demonstrate how unreasonable it is to argue that U.S. Steel was solely concerned with averting a financial panic. When Moore & Schley approached U.S. Steel requesting millions of dollars worth of loans, the brokerage firm offered U.S. Steel a list of stock to serve as collateral. In addition to Tennessee stock, the firm possessed large holdings of American Tobacco, Guggenheim Copper, and others. The Steel Corporation selected Tennessee stock as collateral for its loans to the firm of sufficient size to give it control of the entire company (Kolko, 1967: 115). Although U.S. Steel claimed that it was driven to the acquisition by a sense of public duty, Roosevelt was never informed that Moore & Schley possessed considerable alternate collateral or that the firm only needed $6 million in loans rather than the $45 million that U.S. Steel loaned the company to obtain the Tennessee stock (116). In any case, the Tennessee affair occurred within the détente system that governed relations between the U.S. government and U.S. Steel.[7] The demise of that system was later reflected in the attention paid to the Tennessee acquisition as the Justice Department prepared its antitrust suit against U.S. Steel.

Gary was well aware of the importance of establishing cooperative relations with the federal government from the very beginning. In 1901, Gary informed J.P. Morgan that U.S Steel needed to prove that its intentions were good if it was to avoid antitrust prosecution (McCraw and Reinhardt, 1989: 611). Although Gary managed to maintain a cooperative relationship with President Roosevelt, signs that the détente system was beginning to erode were evident before the end of Roosevelt's presidency. In 1905, for example, the U.S. House of Representatives endorsed a resolution calling upon the newly created Bureau of Corporations to investigate U.S. Steel (Tiffany, 1994: 438). Even so, McCraw and Reinhardt claim that U.S. Steel did not act as though it was seriously concerned with antitrust prosecution until about 1908 as indicated by its rapid expansion of capacity. The same authors attribute the Steel Corporation's eventual behavioral shift to the antitrust suits initiated against American Tobacco and Standard Oil in 1906, the corporation's concerns about the acquisition of TCI&RR, and the 1908 election of William Howard Taft (1989: 611–612). By that time, however, the Steel Trust could not revive the détente system or bring the federal government's antitrust machinery to a halt.

In 1910, Congress again passed a resolution calling for another investigation, which led to the formation of the Stanley committee to examine the corporation's history in detail. The Stanley Committee investigation of U.S. Steel, initiated by the U.S. House of Representatives in 1911, drew attention to Roosevelt's role in the TCI&RR acquisition and raised the question of the fate of the government's détente with U.S. Steel (Kolko, 1967: 170).

The final split between Taft and Roosevelt occurred when Taft's Attorney General, George Wickersham, declared political war against Roosevelt by initiating an antitrust suit against U.S. Steel in 1911 that made the TCI&RR acquisition a key point in the complaint (1967: 171). The main charge against the Steel Corporation, of course, is that it was an unlawful monopoly (Tiffany, 1994: 438). The fate of the Steel Corporation would take an unexpected turn, however, when the First World War began. That dramatic episode in world history provided U.S. Steel with the opportunity to revive the détente system it so desired.

Melvin Urofsky's detailed analysis of the relationship between the steel industry and the federal government during WWI emphasizes the manner in which the war provided an opening for the steel industry to reestablish the détente system (or *entente cordiale*) of the Roosevelt years. When Woodrow Wilson became President of the United States, however, the possibility of a renewal of cooperative relations appeared rather dim. Woodrow Wilson's 1912 political program, dubbed the "New Freedom," made it difficult for the industry to achieve a cooperative arrangement with the federal government given that Wilson's program was inherently opposed to such favorable treatment for the powerful units within American society. According to Urofsky, there seemed little chance in the winter of 1912 that the détente would be reestablished under the Democrats (1969: 35). Nevertheless, the demands of the war made increased cooperation between the government and the steel industry essential to an Allied victory.

The steel industry was greatly affected by the outbreak of World War I. The demand for steel during the war was enormous in comparison with anything the industry had ever experienced. After Schwab returned from England in 1914, he had obtained over $50 million in contracts from the Allies for field gun ammunition and submarines (Urofsky, 1969: 90). The war also gave an impetus to further consolidation in the steel industry as the largest corporations struggled to expand to fill war orders. For example, Bethlehem Steel acquired the Pennsylvania and Maryland Steel Companies in 1916. Another consolidation, the Midvale Steel & Ordnance Company, was formed in 1915 by a group of Carnegie veterans. In 1916, Big Steel thus included Bethlehem Steel and Midvale Steel, in addition to U.S. Steel (97). As the steel industry changed in response to the demands of war, the relationship between the federal government and the industry was also transformed.

On many occasions during the war, it seemed as though the U.S. government was firmly opposed to the revival of the détente system with respect to the steel industry. For example, on one occasion the State Department interfered with the industry's war business in a case involving the sale of submarines to Great Britain by Bethlehem Steel prior to America's entry into the war (Urofsky, 1969: 98–103). In his biography of Charles Schwab, Robert Hessen provides an interesting account of the way in which Schwab circumvented the State Department's roadblocks

to the sale of Bethlehem's submarines (1975: 211–216). When cooperative relations did exist between the industry and the federal government,
they became the subject of numerous attacks by anti-war critics in Congress and elsewhere. In 1915, for example, steel companies were accused
of fomenting a war fever, and the industry's leaders were attacked for
their financial support of the Navy League of the United States (1969:
111). When steel companies began to profit from the sale of war-related
goods, the federal government was especially cautious in its support for
the industry. The difficulties of reviving the détente system appear to have
had their own special characteristics in wartime.

One incident, in particular, that involved the steel industry and the U.S.
Navy appeared to permanently squash any hope for the reestablishment
of cooperative state-capital relations during the war. Relations between
the United States military and the iron and steel industry had been far
from smooth even during the late nineteenth century as demonstrated by a
dispute between the Carnegie Steel Company and the U.S. Navy over the
production of armor plate during the early 1890s (Hessen, 1975: 31–58).
During World War I, a new conflict occurred between the "armor trust,"
which included U.S. Steel, Midvale, and Bethlehem, and Secretary of the
Navy Josephus Daniels over the price of armor plate (Urofsky, 1969: 116).
The intensely Democratic Daniels wanted competition to determine the
price the Navy paid for its armor plate rather than the cooperative arrangement among the big three producers that consistently resulted in identical
bids. According to Urofsky, the charge that "prices were ridiculously out of
line with costs was probably true" (1969: 132). Daniels proposed the construction of a government-owned armor plant to put competitive pressure
on the steel companies (1969: 123). The government's attempt to resurrect
market competition was inevitably met with resistance.

The steel industry immediately expressed its opposition to the proposal
of a government-owned armor plant. The main objection of the major steel
companies to the government's plan is that it would disrupt the market
(Urofsky, 1969: 134). Despite Schwab's many efforts to convince the President, Congress, and the American public that the armor plant was unneces-
sary, he ultimately failed (Hessen, 1975: 223–225). When the armor makers
finally offered to agree to *any* price set by the FTC, it was clear how much
the industry believed that the FTC supported its views of "proper profits, rationalization, and stability" (1969: 145). Although the government
finally abandoned the armor plant project, the passage of the armor plate
bill in August 1916, providing for the construction of a government-owned
armor plant, strongly represents the tension between the industry and the
federal government during the war years.

State-capital relations may have been strained early in the war, but the
war eventually encouraged a certain degree of cooperation between the
steel industry and the U.S. government. According to Urofsky, the key word
to describe relations between the steel industry and the government from

1917 to 1918 is "co-operation," which is ironic given that Wilson's New Freedom favored a small-unit highly competitive economy, with limited and decentralized government (1969: 152–153). Kevin Dwyer also agrees that relations between the steel industry and the U.S. government returned to "a state of peaceful coexistence" during World War I (1994a: 487). The increased cooperation between the government and the steel industry manifested itself in a variety of ways as the end of the war grew near.

One way in which the government helped reestablish a limited détente between the Steel Corporation and the federal government was in the area of antitrust law. Prosecution of big business under the antitrust laws virtually ceased during the war as Wilson agreed to an FTC request that it be relieved of the responsibility of antitrust investigation (Urofsky, 1969: 180). In May 1917, the United States Supreme Court agreed with the Attorney General and President Wilson that prosecution of the antitrust suit against U.S. Steel should be postponed until after the war so as not to disrupt the production of steel that was badly needed for the war effort (182). This willingness to allow U.S. Steel to proceed without government interference during the war is reminiscent of the way in which Roosevelt refused to meddle in the corporation's affairs so long as he believed that it was fulfilling its social responsibilities.

Cooperative relations between the government and the steel industry were not limited to antitrust activity. If the détente system was reestablished during WWI, it showed its smoothest operation when the government cooperated with the steel industry to fix prices so that the industry could pursue its goal of stabilizing the market (Urofsky, 1969: 192, 203). The government, of course, desired stable prices for the purposes of war planning.[8] On the other hand, relations between the U.S. government and the steel industry did not always proceed smoothly even in the area of price stabilization. For example, the two power blocs disagreed as to whether the fixed prices would apply to the American government alone or also include the Allies and the American public (215). Nevertheless, they managed to compromise in a manner that suggested cooperation was the goal of both participants. The creation of the Price Fixing Committee led by Robert Brookings in 1918 was "the final step in the development of the wartime entente" (235). As this section and the previous section show clearly, the stability of steel prices reflected cooperative inter-capitalist relations as well as cooperative state-capital relations during the early twentieth century.

The cooperative relationship between the steel industry and the federal government was perceived in a positive light by the industry. "*Iron Age* spoke glowingly of the benefits of the war in rationalization, stability, co-operation, and even government control" (Urofsky, 1969: 191). Steel officials were eager to maintain cooperative state-capital relations after the war ended given the safety from antitrust prosecution that government involvement seemed to imply. They especially welcomed government involvement in the sphere of price fixing (292). Although the steel industry worked with Commerce Secretary William Redfield and a special postwar Industrial Board to maintain the détente system beyond the war's end, ultimately President Wilson could not support such a flagrant disregard for the nation's antitrust laws (308–324). Even the war proved to be incapable of reviving the détente system to the degree it had been established at the height of the progressive era.

Although the Steel Corporation could not maintain the détente system it favored after the war's end, it did enjoy victory in the even greater battle for its survival. Ever since the formation of U.S. Steel, Gary's program of industrial stabilization forced him to continuously strive to maintain an uneasy balance of conflicting forces. As George Stocking described Gary's dilemma, "[h]ow the industry could safely steer between the Scylla of the Sherman Law and the Charybdis of chaotic competition perplexed and disturbed him" (1954: 39). The shareholders of the Steel Corporation ultimately reaped huge rewards thanks to Gary's cautious approach. In 1915, a federal district court ruled that U.S. Steel was not guilty of the charges brought against it in the Justice Department's antitrust suit of 1911. After the Justice Department's appeal to the U.S. Supreme Court, the Court ruled in March 1920 to uphold the lower court's decision (Tiffany, 1994: 438). The Supreme Court decision of 1920 that exonerated U.S. Steel once and for all was very close and depended heavily on the fact that the corporation's market share had declined considerably (McCraw and Reinhardt, 1989: 612–613). The emphasis was thus placed on the consequences of the U.S. Steel merger, not the intentions of its managers and directors. Whatever the reason, the United States Steel Corporation succeeded in maintaining a level of cooperation with the federal government necessary to withstand an antitrust suit and a significant number of congressional investigations in an era when trust busting was most fashionable.

3.4 THE PERFORMANCE OF THE IRON AND STEEL INDUSTRY DURING THE PROGRESSIVE ERA

This chapter has explored the manner in which the United States Steel Corporation used regulatory measures to stabilize conditions in the steel industry during the progressive era. An investigation of the labor policy of the Steel Corporation has been reserved for the next chapter because this manner of proceeding helps clarify how the corporation's efforts to stabilize inter-capitalist and state-capital relations as discussed in this chapter contributed to increasingly unstable capital-labor relations. Before exploring this connection, however, this section examines the extent to which the Steel Corporation's stabilization program enhanced the relative economic performance of the iron and steel industry within the context of the progressive era RIS.

Social structure of accumulation analysis involves an analysis of the institutions and industrial performance for a particular institutional structure. As chapters 1 and 2 demonstrate, economic performance may be measured at the aggregate level in terms of the rate of economic growth, the rate of capital accumulation, and the rate of profit. At the industry level, the same measures may be employed to evaluate the performance of the industry relative to the preceding and succeeding institutional structures. This attempt to apply SSA theory to a particular industry may provide a model for radical political economists who wish to conduct microeconomic analyses within the SSA tradition.

The steel industry exhibited tremendous growth during the late nineteenth and early twentieth centuries. In 1924, Abraham Berglund could boast on behalf of the industry that "[t]he growth of the steel industry in the United States during the past forty or fifty years has been phenomenal" (1924: 611). The industry's leaders were also very confident that the Steel Corporation would continue the rapid growth and profitability of steel production in the United States. "In Schwab's view, the company's dominant position in the industry was merely the base for limitless growth and profits" (Hessen, 1975: 114). The theoretical framework applied here requires an empirical test to evaluate these claims.

Measuring the rate of economic growth at the aggregate level implies that some method must be used to aggregate the many different commodities produced in the economy. In chapter 1, the average annual percentage change of real gross domestic product served this function. At the level of industry, it is possible to use the growth rate of physical production for a single commodity to gain insight into the relative performance of the industry during a specific time period. Table 3.2 provides the average annual growth rates of two distinct intermediate commodities produced in the iron and steel industry. The industry's physical output of crude steel and physical pig iron have been selected because they avoid the problem of aggregating many different forms of finished steel products. At the same

Table 3.2   Physical growth rates of iron and steel output in the United States: 1879–1929.

Period	Growth Rate of Physical Pig Iron Output (%)*	Growth Rate of Physical Crude Steel Output (%)†
1879-1896	9.1	13.4
1897-1916	10.3	14.0
1917-1929	4.9	6.5

SOURCE: U.S. Census Bureau, 1960: 365–366, 416.

* Pig iron figures prior to 1910 refer to pig iron production whereas figures after 1910 refer to pig iron shipments.

† Crude Steel refers to total steel ingots and castings produced.

time, they are necessary for the production of all finished steel commodities and so accurately capture the relative growth of the industry. Table 3.2 clearly shows that the industry achieved its fastest average annual growth in the late nineteenth and early twentieth centuries. The average growth rates of both commodities were highest during the progressive era RIS although only slightly above the growth rates of the late nineteenth century LIS. The industry showed the slowest growth during the 1920s LIS. These results provide support for the general hypothesis presented in chapter 1 that regulationist institutional structures are more favorable to rapid economic growth than liberal institutional structures.

The trend of capital accumulation in the iron and steel industry also supports the hypothesis that regulationist institutional structures offer a more suitable environment for the rapid accumulation of capital than liberal institutional structures. Figure 3.2 traces the movement of the total capital invested in the manufacture of iron and steel products from 1879 to 1929.

As Figure 3.2 clearly shows, the total capital invested in the iron and steel industry rose at relatively low levels during the late nineteenth century. It then increased greatly in absolute terms during the progressive era until it reached a period of stagnation that persisted throughout the 1920s. Contributing factors to the rise in capitalization during the progressive era include the growth of the automobile industry and the impact of war production, leading to a rising demand for steel. Nonetheless, the trend is

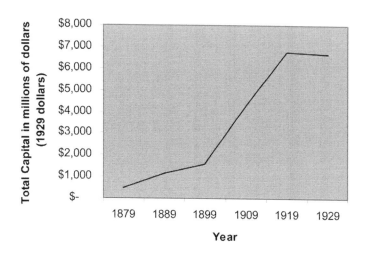

Figure 3.2: Total capital invested in the U.S. iron and steel industry: 1879–1929.
SOURCE: U.S. Census Bureau, 1960: 412.
NOTE: The figures have been converted to 1929 dollars and presented in millions of dollars. The figures for 1879 and 1889 include custom and neighborhood shops; the remaining figures cover factories having annual production of $500 or more.

consistent with the modified SSA framework presented in chapter 1 that leads us to expect faster capital accumulation in regulationist institutional structures than in liberal institutional structures.

Turning to the relative profitability of the steel industry during the progressive era, it is important to remember that the rate of profit is the key measure of profitability for capitalist corporations. As in chapter 2, reliable data on the aggregate rate of profit for the iron and steel industry is not available for the time periods being examined. An investigation of the profit rate of the United States Steel Corporation is possible, however, and provides a sense of the extent to which the regulatory features of the progressive era contributed to heightened profitability for the steel industry.

Most scholars agree that the Steel Corporation was a highly profitable enterprise during the first two decades following its formation. The promoter's profits earned when the Steel Corporation was formed were being at least partly realized in 1908. Smith was able to confidently remark that the "company is apparently getting the future profits that were counted upon by the promoters when they so tremendously over-capitalized it at its formation" (1908: 272). According to McCraw and Reinhardt's assessment of the corporation, "the founders of U.S. Steel succeeded brilliantly in their aims" by returning respectable dividends to shareholders and stabilizing prices (1989: 617). Price stability was thus perceived to play a significant role in the profitability of the corporation.

George Stocking directly relates the Steel Corporation's price stabilization program to the profitability of the corporation in a manner that is consistent with the SSA approach of relating institutional features directly to economic performance. To the extent that the Pittsburgh Plus pricing system prevented the forces of unrestrained competition from eroding the steel price structure, Stocking explains, "it probably made the steel industry as a whole more profitable than it would otherwise have been" (1954: 60). Stable prices were thus entirely consistent with high profits for U.S. Steel. In terms of the steel rails discussed at some length in the second section of this chapter, their total cost of production in Pittsburgh was about $14 or $15 per ton. It is thus easy to comprehend how the Steel Corporation could afford to maintain a steady price of $28 per ton during the progressive era (Smith, 1908: 272). To use Smith's words, if U.S. Steel could maintain such conditions, "its future [would be] more assured than that of autocrats who command what they will from a diligent and servile populace (272). The Steel Corporation's regulatory efforts thus helped reinforce its ability to reap huge profits.

Scholars have also attempted to quantify the magnitude of U.S. Steel's profitability during the progressive era. According to Robert Allen, the U.S. Steel merger allowed the corporation to raise markups to the 30% range for at least the first decade after the merger. Markups had been much lower in 1879 and 1889 (Allen, 1981: 523). Between 1902 and 1910, the markup over unit costs could be maintained because the steel industry was "sufficiently collusive" (523). In the case of steel rails, costs declined 19% but rail prices declined only 4% between 1889 and 1902 as markups rose 18% (523). Allen argues that steel rail prices in the early twentieth century were fixed at about 1890 levels and steel producers enjoyed all of the decline in costs due to technical progress as excess profits (523). Allen further argues that the evidence suggests that markups on the industry's products (e.g., most rolled products) were generally high (527). Allen's study is important because it links stable prices to falling costs and excess profits, thus offering a clear motive for the Steel Corporation's preoccupation with price stabilization.

The Steel Corporation's profits may have been even higher than many studies indicate. Smith explains that its subsidiaries made U.S. Steel appear to have much higher costs than it actually had because its subsidiaries maintained separate books even though all profits were ultimately collected at the top (1908: 270). At the various stages of the corporation's integrated process, the book cost of its activities should be understood as actual cost plus profit (270). For the Steel Trust then, the consolidation of capital made possible the consolidation of profit.

An honest evaluation of the profitability of the Steel Corporation during the progressive era RIS demands the selection of relatively conservative estimates of the corporation's rate of profit. This way of proceeding is intended to remove any doubt that the estimates provided have been selected with the intention of overstating U.S. Steel's rate of profit so as to cast the corporation in a negative light. Elmer Hartzell (1934) offers a rather sympathetic discussion of the Steel Corporation's dominant position in the iron and steel industry during the early twentieth century. Hartzell opts to track the trend of profits as a percentage of the corporation's assets, excluding intangibles (1934: 327). Using this measure of the rate of profit rather than profits as a percentage of the book value of the corporation's assets allows Hartzell to demonstrate that the Steel Corporation's profit rate actually declined during the first three decades of the twentieth century. By excluding goodwill items,[9] Hartzell proceeds to calculate the earnings of U.S. Steel available for interest and dividends as a percentage of total assets (328–329). It is possible to graphically represent Hartzell's estimates of U.S. Steel's rate of profit from 1901 to 1932.

As Figure 3.3 shows, the rate of profit was consistently higher during the progressive era RIS than during the LIS of the 1920s although it fluctuated considerably in both periods. The average annual rate of profit from 1901 to 1916 was 11.14% and only 5.5% from 1920–1932. It was highest early in the progressive era while Roosevelt and Gary had reached their informal understanding about the role of government in relation to business. McCraw and Reinhardt attribute the Steel Corporation's success during these years to Gary's strategy because it led to strong profits for shareholders, stability for the iron and steel industry, and freedom from dissolution under the Sherman Act (1989: 596). The high rate of profit that the Steel Corporation enjoyed during the progressive era, however, was far from secure.

The corporation's profit rate began to decline late in the progressive era once the independent steel concerns became serious competitors for U.S. Steel and the federal government began to take a more aggressive stance towards the corporation. The fact that the profit rate declined in 1908 following the 1907 financial panic is not surprising, but it is worth noting that it remained at a lower level for a number of years until it was revived during WWI. The presidential shift from Roosevelt to Taft and the consequences it carried for the attitude of the federal government towards the steel industry may have contributed significantly to the reduced profitability of the corporation in the latter half of the progressive era. The outbreak of World War I clearly raised the rate of profit to its highest level in the corporation's history, but it fell to very low levels thereafter as the temporary détente of the war years came to an end.

The fact that the United States Steel Corporation began a steady decline in the latter part of the progressive era is also reflected in the trend of the corporation's market share of steel output. Although U.S. Steel sought to control market conditions, it never possessed absolute control of the country's output of iron and steel (Berglund, 1923: 5). Neither did the corporation's possession of iron ore, coke, and pig iron ever constitute anything like monopoly control (6). The percentage of the nation's output of crude steel produced by U.S. Steel was highest in the first few years of the corporation's existence at over 60% (7). McCraw and Reinhardt have shown that in many product categories, including steel ingots and castings, steel rails, and heavy structural shapes, the proportion of output produced by the United States Steel Corporation fell steadily from 1901 to 1927. Their average of nine

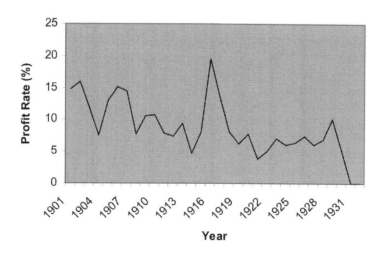

Figure 3.3: The profit rate of the United States Steel Corporation: 1901–1932.
SOURCE: Hartzell, 1934: 329.

product categories (not weighted) indicates that U.S. Steel's market share fell from 61.9% in 1901 to 51.7% in 1913 to 42.1% in 1927 (1989: 597). Hence, from a peak of nearly two-thirds of the nation's steel production, the Steel Corporation's high market share fell significantly throughout the progressive era and well into the 1920s as shown in Figure 3.4.

In the rest of the industry, many independent steel companies enjoyed a relative increase in the amount of business they conducted. The growth of U.S. Steel, in particular, did not prevent the growth of the independent steel companies during the first two decades of the twentieth century, whose share in the nation's production of steel increased rather than diminished (Berglund, 1924: 612). The growth of the independent companies relative to U.S. Steel is startling, particularly in the case of Bethlehem Steel. While U.S. Steel increased its production by 40% between 1901 and 1911, Bethlehem Steel increased its production a phenomenal 3779.7% (Urofsky, 1969: 79). The evidence indicates that the independent steel companies enjoyed high rates of profit as well. Whereas the annual average rate of profit for U.S. Steel between 1901 and 1930 was 12.6%, Bethlehem Steel earned 10.3%, Republic Steel earned 10.1%, Youngstown Sheet & Tube earned 16.3%, and Inland Steel earned 16.9% (McCraw and Reinhardt, 1989: 599). The available evidence also suggests that the American steel industry made extraordinary profits during WWI despite the price controls and high taxes. All steel companies performed at the highest profit level in their history during the years 1917 and 1918, averaging a return of 28.9% in 1917 and 20.1% in 1918 (1969: 228). Furthermore, the independent steel companies frequently performed better than the largest steel companies (1969:

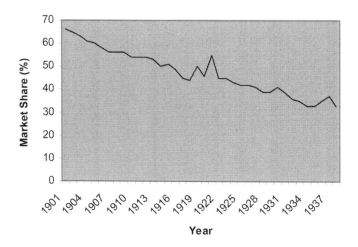

Figure 3.4: U.S. Steel's percentage share of steel ingot production: 1901–1938.
SOURCE: McCraw and Reinhardt, 1989: 598.

230). In summary, high rates of profit in the steel trade were not restricted to the United States Steel Corporation during the early twentieth century.

How to interpret the Steel Corporation's decline is the final question that needs to be addressed before concluding this chapter. According to Kolko's analysis of the iron and steel industry, the House of Morgan failed to establish stability and control over the industry, which remained competitive prior to World War I (1967: 39). This interpretation of the Steel Corporation's early history suggests that its decline was undoubtedly harmful to the corporation. The problem with this interpretation is that it only makes sense in the context of a liberal institutional structure. Given the regulated character of the progressive era, however, it is reasonable to believe that the Steel Corporation sacrificed immediate, short-term gain to help its competitors, thereby safeguarding its own position as the leader within the industry.

Many scholars indicate that the latter interpretation is the more accurate one. According to Berglund, for example, the Steel Corporation avoided destructive competition with its independent competitors and allowed its market share to steadily decline (1923: 29). The opportunity for the independent steel companies to grab a greater share of the market arose partly because U.S. Steel fixed its prices annually and left it susceptible to undercutting by competitors (McCraw and Reinhardt, 1989: 603). According to William B. Dickson, who was a Carnegie veteran and the second vice president of U.S. Steel, the corporation's "rigid adherence to stable prices in the face of price-cutting by its rivals simply built up the competition" (Hessen, 1975: 187). One might even say that U.S. Steel essentially gave away its markets to competitors (1989: 605). To some extent, the declining market share of U.S. Steel must have been voluntary. During the 1920s, Gary claimed to have voluntarily restricted U.S Steel's market share in all product lines to a 50% maximum to avoid a radical backlash (1989: 612). The leaders of the Steel Corporation thus appear to have been well aware of its policy of "voluntary decline."

The Steel Corporation's treatment of Bethlehem Steel is perhaps the best indicator that the corporation was willing to tolerate the growth of rivals as a matter of corporation policy. It is not likely, for example, that Bethlehem Steel would have weathered the economic downturn of 1907–1909 if U.S. Steel had cut prices aggressively to maintain high output levels (Cutcliffe, 1994: 154). More generally, Hessen argues that "[i]f, during the depression of 1907, U.S. Steel had cut prices . . . , smaller firms such as Bethlehem would probably not have been able to survive" (1975: 187). Furthermore, when smaller firms were unable to resist the temptation to undercut U.S. Steel during the same depression, U.S. Steel responded by disciplining, rather than destroying, its competitors.[10]

It is of interest that Smith identified the Steel Corporation in 1908 as a "loser" due to its declining market share but not as a "sufferer" due to its profitable operations (1908: 273). Its label as a loser suggests that it found an intermediate position between "sufferer" and "winner." Perhaps Gary's greatest success as the leader of the Steel Trust was in recognizing that it simply could not pursue the path of a winner given the political climate created by progressive era politics.

This chapter has explored a number of key regulated features of the iron and steel industry within the context of the progressive era RIS. The need for regulation in the steel industry arose in the late nineteenth century when severe competition and falling steel prices led to numerous bankruptcies and an unpredictable business environment. The first phase of the merger movement led to increasing tension in the industry rather than greater stability. Fearing the worst, the leaders of industry and corporate finance formed the United States Steel Corporation in 1901. The Steel Corporation succeeded in stabilizing prices and creating a strong, albeit temporary, agreement with the federal government that allowed it to pursue its business objectives while fulfilling its greater social responsibility as interpreted by the Roosevelt administration. When this cooperative arrangement began to crumble, the Steel Corporation strove in vain to reestablish a similar understanding with the Taft and Wilson administrations. Nevertheless, U.S. Steel's policy of self-regulation stabilized steel prices, maintained high rates of industrial growth and capital accumulation, ensured a high profit rate for itself and its competitors, and protected it from dissolution by the federal government. Regulation in the era of Big Steel was thus an unmistakable success for the leaders of the United States Steel Corporation and its key competitors. The next chapter examines the manner in which the steelworkers were affected by the industry's strategy of regulation.

4 The Consequences of Progressive Era Regulation for the Steelworkers

4.1 THE BATTLE FOR REGULATORY CONTROL OF THE IRON AND STEEL INDUSTRY

The passage from one institutional structure to the next is a gradual process that reveals the manner in which past social relations are transformed into new relations. Capital-labor relations in the iron and steel industry during the progressive era are no exception to the general rule. It is thus necessary to consider the special character of capital-labor relations in the iron and steel industry within the context of the late nineteenth century LIS before one may correctly comprehend the nature of the same relations within the progressive era RIS. This section thus provides the historical background that is essential to a proper understanding of the capital-labor confrontation that occurred in the steel industry with the formation of U.S. Steel.

In the early 1880s, capital-labor relations in the iron and steel industry were in many ways more cooperative than they were during the progressive era. For example, employers during the 1880s were accustomed to shutting down the mills for the annual picnic of the Amalgamated Association and legal holidays in general. By 1907, however, the annual picnic was gone and workmen (aside from blast furnace crews who worked without end) were only allowed Christmas and the Fourth of July (Fitch, 1969: 177). That cooperation may have been greater within the late nineteenth century LIS than within the progressive era RIS creates a puzzle given that liberal institutional structures are expected to be less cooperative than regulationist institutional structures. This chapter demonstrates how our modified SSA framework may address this difficulty.

A considerable part of the solution to this puzzle may be found in the fact that labor in the iron and steel industry was better organized during the late nineteenth century than during the early twentieth. The skilled and semi-skilled workmen in the iron and steel industry were organized into three national unions by 1873. They were the Sons of Vulcan, the Associated Brotherhood of Iron and Steel Heaters, Rollers, and Roughers, and the Iron and Steel Roll Hands. In 1876 they formed the National Amalgamated Association of Iron and Steel Workers. As chapter 3 explains, iron and steel companies were very much preoccupied with the fierce inter-capitalist competition of the free market structure and thus did not undertake a large-scale unification of capital in the industry until the late 1890s. Therefore, the workmen were able to combat the power of their employers much more effectively in the latter part of the nineteenth century than in the last decade of the nineteenth century and the early twentieth century.[1]

Organized labor in the iron and steel industry during the late nineteenth century preceded capital in its reaction against the free market. It began to develop and implement its own program of regulation on a small scale in the post-Civil War era. According to Katherine Stone, the workers' power over production in the iron and steel industry during the late nineteenth century is reflected in a number of institutions, including the skilled workers' union, the sliding scale of wages, the contract system, and the apprenticeship-helper system (1975: 27). These institutions are ingenious in the way they worked together to transform free market institutions into weapons to bolster the power of labor against capital.

Before investigating the manner in which these institutions restrained the excesses of the free market, it is necessary to briefly discuss the nature of these excesses from the perspective of the workmen. Wage rate fluctuations in the iron and steel industry during the nineteenth century were a key problem arising from the free market structure of the period. Prior to 1860, the open competition between iron producers resulted in severe price fluctuations and ultimately fluctuations in wage rates. Fluctuations in wage rates of 20% to 40% were common from one year to the next, and ironworkers in the late 1850s found their wages cut to less than half of what they were in the late 1830s (Hogan, 1971: 85–86). Wages continued to fluctuate considerably after the Civil War as well. In the blast furnace departments, for example, wages rose between 1860 and 1873 but then declined during the depressed economic conditions of the 1870s (77). Once organized, the workmen were able to form a rational response to the hardships that wage movements imposed upon them.

The sliding scale of wages was one institution, in particular, that the Amalgamated Association used to resist wage rate fluctuations in the late nineteenth century. The Sons of Vulcan had been formed as early as 1858 by iron puddlers in response to the wage rate fluctuations. The union considered its greatest achievement to be the "sliding-scale" wage rate system, whereby wages varied in direct relation to the price manufacturers charged for iron (Hogan, 1971: 86). It was first introduced in the Pittsburgh iron works in 1865 and spread throughout the industry over the next twenty-five years (Stone, 1975: 31). When the Amalgamated Association was formed, it established and maintained the sliding scale of wages based on fluctuations in the market price of iron so that by 1890 nearly all iron mills signed its scale and the closed union shop prevailed (Hoagland, 1917: 675). The Amalgamated Association was strong in its advocacy of the sliding scale during the first fifteen years of its life, and it continued to be endorsed by the majority of the members of the association in 1901 (Wright, 1901: 42). Organized labor thus used the system to overcome the negative consequences of free and unfettered markets.

The sliding scale system was also beneficial in eroding the power of employers in wage rate determination. It eliminated the opportunity for the employer to determine wages because tonnage rates were tied directly to market prices (Stone, 1975: 31). The institution thus prevented employers from regulating wages as they would during the progressive era. For a time, Carnegie also favored the sliding wage scale but abolished it in 1894 when it was no longer advantageous to him (Eggert, 1981: 13). Carnegie's opposition to the system arose because Amalgamated contracts typically included a minimum wage below which wages could not fall even if the price of iron or steel fell considerably. When Carnegie's steel prices plummeted, his wages could only fall so far.

The Amalgamated Association, on the other hand, was pleased with the results of the innovation. Proud of the fact that the collapse of the 1879 iron boom did not result in serious strikes throughout the iron industry, President John Jarrett of the Amalgamated Association noted the event as "clear proof of the advisability and utility of the scale of prices system of *regulating* wages" (Hogan, 1971: 88; emphasis added). The skilled iron-workers thus were attempting to impose a regulatory program in the late nineteenth century. A battle between capital and labor for regulatory control of the iron and steel industry would intensify, however, as the end of the nineteenth century grew near.

The other key institution through which organized labor attempted to harness the power of the free market for its own regulatory control of the iron and steel industry was the contract system. Subcontracting on certain jobs was an important feature of the wage structure in the iron and steel industry during the late nineteenth century. For example, a Pittsburgh puddler in 1878 would be paid a tonnage rate out of which he would pay his helper (Hogan, 1971: 85). The helpers would be assigned the heavy parts of the work and usually earned between one-sixth and one-half of the wages of skilled workers (Stone, 1975: 30). Skilled workers often had the opportunity to hire additional helpers as well. Hence, the market determined wage rates and the workers themselves determined the division of labor and the pace of work (1975: 32).

Workmen were very much involved in the determination of wages and the nature of the production process in the late nineteenth century. Although the markets of the late nineteenth century LIS were competitive, the skilled ironworkers used the free market elements to their advantage. They managed to claim many of the benefits of that institutional structure because the iron companies were too poorly organized to more effectively exploit their workers. Even in the late nineteenth century, the companies made some efforts to resist this worker control over production. The result was a hybrid system, rather than a pure contract system, in which the company would pay a small fraction of a helper's pay (Stone, 1975: 30). Ultimately, however, the skilled workers succeeded the most in using the reality of the free market to influence the labor markets in the iron and steel trade during the late nineteenth century.

Although Stone acknowledges the contract system as one of the institutions protecting the power of the skilled workers over production, it is also true that the Amalgamated Association's failure to adequately regulate the behavior of its members contributed to the demise of the contract system in the iron and steel industry. Throughout the 1870s, the Amalgamated Association attempted to enforce a rule defining "a job" and prohibiting members from holding two or more. By 1887, the union had stigmatized as a "black sheep" any workman who received income from more than one job. When the union failed to modify the behavior of its members, it began to turn against the contract system itself and even deemed its presence a sufficient cause for initiating a strike (Fitch, 1969: 100). Furthermore, the union had failed to stop the custom through which one workman received and distributed the pay of an entire crew (100). The union's difficulty of regulating its members' behavior thus hastened the demise of the system and shifted the balance of power away from labor and towards capital.

The sliding wage scale and contract system are two key examples that have been used to illustrate the manner in which organized labor used the free market conditions of the late nineteenth century to establish a limited measure of control over the industry. The sliding wage scale allowed the Amalgamated Association to link wage rates to the prices determined in a highly competitive iron market. The contract system enhanced competition in the labor market by multiplying the number of buyers of labor power. At the same time, it helped skilled workmen maintain control over the production process and the distribution of its gains to the less skilled helpers. A proposal put forward by President John Jarrett of the Amalgamated Association in 1884 illustrates well the mindset of the top officials of the union during this period in its history. Jarrett proposed the building or purchase of an iron mill to be managed for profit by the Amalgamated Association so that it could "know the market and so could understand the position of the employer as well as that of the wage-earner" (Fitch, 1969: 106–107). Although the plan was never implemented, it demonstrates how union officials respected knowledge of the free market for its potential to improve the union's position in wage negotiations.

Irrespective of its efforts at regulation, the power of organized labor in the iron and steel industry began to crumble by the end of the nineteenth century as capitalists in the industry realized that consolidation and mechanization were necessary to overcome the economic crisis that inter-capitalist competition precipitated. As commodity prices fell, labor costs needed to be cut through the introduction of labor-saving machinery. Andrew Carnegie (and U.S. Steel after him), for example, demanded careful analysis of cost data (Brody, 1960: 19), and the mechanization associated with the homogenization of the workforce was the best way to force costs down further. The mechanization drive was already underway in Carnegie's steel mills in the 1880s. For example, 1600 men were laid off in December 1884 while new machinery was being installed at Carnegie's Edgar Thomson steelworks in Braddock.[2] Automatic roll tables for the blooming mill and improved equipment for drawing and charging at the heating furnaces were among the extensive changes in the mill (Fitch, 1969: 112).

It was not until the 1890s, however, that the mechanization drive began to take effect generally throughout the industry. The technological changes during this decade included electric trolleys, the pig casting machine, the Jones mixer, mechanical ladle cars, electric traveling cranes, the Wellman charger, electric cars, and rising-and-falling tables (Stone, 1975: 35). According to Allen (1981: 521), the invention of the mixer in 1889 made it possible to directly transport molten iron from the blast furnaces to the Bessemer converters and thus led to an impressive saving in fuel. For the period 1892 to 1908, Fitch adds ingot manipulation, larger and more powerful engines, and the substitution of electric power for steam to this list of technological changes (1969: 140). The instability of the late nineteenth century LIS thus forced capitalists in the iron and steel industry to respond in a manner that carried real consequences for the workmen.

One consequence of mechanization for the workmen was a drastic increase in productivity. The highest period of productivity growth in the steel industry occurred between 1889 and 1902 as the average products of fuel and metallic inputs rose considerably (Allen, 1981: 521). As labor productivity rose, costs per unit of output fell significantly. According to Brody, "[t]he proportional reduction of labor cost was the principal achievement of the economizing drive" (1960: 28). At the same time, a class of semi-skilled workmen emerged as the power of the skilled workmen began to decline. The steelworkers were thus transformed from manipulators of raw materials and molten metal to the operators of machinery (Brody, 1960: 31).[3] This erosion of the power of the skilled workers was an essential factor that contributed to the eventual implementation of a capitalist regulatory program and the disappearance of the regulatory program of organized labor in the steel industry.

The Amalgamated Association contributed to its own demise as the homogenization drive began to undermine its power. Hoagland labels the policies of the Amalgamated Association as "suicidal" during the final decades of the nineteenth century. The union always demanded the full advantage of new machinery and refused to organize the unskilled workmen (1917: 676). The trade union thus failed to realize how mechanized production would eventually undermine its bargaining power. Furthermore, the Amalgamated's policy of exclusion weakened the union when it most needed to create unity among the workmen. During the nineteenth century, skilled laborers had a right to become members of the union while unskilled laborers could join only at the discretion of the skilled members (Wright, 1901: 38). When the Knights of Labor attempted to organize the unskilled workmen at the Edgar Thomson Works in Braddock, Pennsylvania in 1888, a conflict between that labor organization and the Amalgamated Association for the allegiance of the workmen weakened rather than strengthened the organizing effort in the steel industry. Hence, when the showdown between capital and labor finally occurred, labor was poorly organized in relation to capital.

At the same time, capitalists in the industry were well aware of the need to attack the Amalgamated Association and thus break the power that the skilled workers possessed over the production process. This power shift would further permit the companies to mechanize steel production and reduce per unit labor costs. In Stone's words, "[t]he social relations of cooperation and partnership had to go if capitalist steel production was to progress" (1975: 34). It was by means of two bitter strikes in the steel industry that capital came to dominate labor during the progressive era and established its regulatory program of price and wage rate stabilization for the industry.

The shift from iron to steel production towards the end of the nineteenth century coincides with the way in which capital-labor disputes also shifted from iron to steel mills at that time. Specifically, the 1882 general strike in the Pittsburgh iron mills over wages was the last great strike in the iron business after which the steel mills occupied center stage in terms of commercial importance and labor conflict (Fitch, 1969: 110). Organized labor achieved some success as the decisive battles grew near. After a strike of Homestead steelworkers in 1889, a contract was won at Homestead that "gave the skilled workers authority over every aspect of steel production there" (Stone, 1975: 32). In fact, the famous 1892 strike emerged from the capital-labor conflict that really began in 1889.

The main points of contention in the 1892 strike at Homestead include the company's proposals to reduce the minimum wage permitted under the sliding scale, change the expiration date of the contract from June to December, and reduce tonnage rates (Wright, 1901: 47). Given the falling steel prices of Carnegie Steel, a reduction in the minimum wage could be disastrous for the steelworkers. The proposal to change the expiration date of the contract from June to December would also restrict the union's ability to protest the demands of management due to the higher cost of living in the winter months. According to Wright, however, the Homestead contest "was waged really more largely for the purpose of securing recognition than for any other reason" (59). The steel company's attempts to change the sliding wage scale for its own advantage and to refuse recognition of the Amalgamated Association as the steelworkers' bargaining agent both marked direct challenges to the regulatory program of organized labor that had achieved a measure of success throughout the late nineteenth century LIS.

As is well known, the fierce battle at Homestead between the steelworkers and the Pinkerton guards ultimately led to defeat for the union when the Pennsylvania state guard was ordered to restore order in the town. The significance of the strike in changing relations in the industry is beyond dispute as it was definitely a turning point for the industry. Prior to that year, the Amalgamated Association had been "remarkably free from disastrous strikes" (Wright, 1901: 38). Hoagland refers to the Homestead strike of 1892 as "the first blow to the union from which it did not fully recover" (1917: 676) and according to John Fitch, "the death knell of unionism was struck for the steel mills of the United States" (1969: 132). After the strike, Frick wrote to Carnegie, "We had to teach our employees a lesson, and we have taught them one that they will never forget" (Brody, 1960: 84). Both the participants in the strike and scholars were thus keenly aware of the strike's significance and the role it had played in reshaping capital-labor relations.

It is clear that Carnegie Steel pursued the Homestead strike to its tragic conclusion to establish control over wages and break the power of the Amalgamated Association. The destruction of the union was, in turn, necessary for the company to reestablish control of the production process. The strike thus allowed for the rapid mechanization of production and the consequent homogenization of the steel workforce that occurred throughout the 1890s. According to Fitch, after "the strikes of the nineties, the steel manufacturers carried to new lengths their internal policy of reducing cost by increasing output and lessening dependence on human labor" (1969: 139). The failure of the Amalgamated Association also allowed for the maximum extension of the working day. According to Hogan, the year 1892 marked the beginning of a new era as Carnegie Steel attempted to introduce the twelve-hour day wherever possible (1971: 448). The strike thus stripped the Amalgamated of its regulatory agenda and any control of the production process it had previously possessed.

The Homestead strike was financially very difficult for the Amalgamated as well. In 1892, the union's strike disbursements reached $115,504—an amount greater than the sum total for the remaining decade (Wright, 1901: 43). Furthermore, the union's expenditures exceeded its receipts in 1892 by $39,787.84, and the organization's financial resources continued to fall from 1892 to 1898 (43–44). Chairman Henry Clay Frick of the Carnegie Steel Company estimated that the strike cost the workmen approximately $1 million (58). Contributing to the decline in its financial resources is the drastic decline in union membership throughout the 1890s as Figure 4.1 illustrates. The decline in union membership of the early 1880s may be attributed to the failed iron strikes of 1882. Membership rose considerably throughout the remainder of the decade, however, reaching its peak in 1891 at 24,068 and then plummeted after the Homestead strike. The small recovery in the year 1900 represents organized labor's final attempt to challenge capital for regulatory control of the industry during the progressive era.

The consolidation movement in the iron and steel industry that began towards the end of the nineteenth century signaled the steel companies' attempt to restrain free markets for their own advantage through the unification of capital. In the aftermath of the Homestead strike, organized labor was unable to pose any serious threat to the growing power of the steel companies until the consolidation movement had been completed in the industry with the formation of U.S. Steel in 1901. In fact, aside from the 1892 and 1901 steel strikes, Wright argues that all strikes in the industry were petty from 1891 to 1901 (1901: 46). The ruthless anti-union campaign of Carnegie Steel was responsible for this fact. Carnegie Steel crushed organizing efforts in 1896 and 1899 (Brody, 1960: 56). By 1900, the policy generally throughout the industry was that any worker found secretly carrying an Amalgamated card was fired instantly (Wolff, 1965: 230). Organized labor was being swept aside so that the free market instability of the late nineteenth century could be eliminated through a regulatory program created by capital.

The weakened Amalgamated Association also encountered difficulties in its attempts to organize the steelworkers to match the power of capital during the 1890s. For example, the union became less unified during the 1890s when it released several bodies of men (e.g., rod-mill workers) without absorbing any new bodies (Wright, 1901: 41). At the same time, the union did attempt to unify the workmen to a certain degree as the definitive battle of 1901 drew near. In May 1897 the Amalgamated Association formally recognized the tin workers as a significant part of its organization

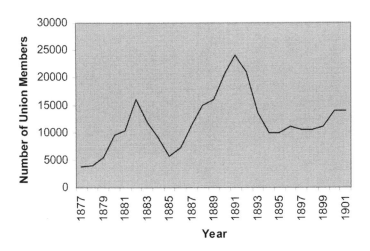

Figure 4.1: The total membership of the Amalgamated Association of Iron and Steel Workers: 1877–1901.
SOURCE: Wright, 1901: 40.

when it renamed itself the National Amalgamated Association of Iron, Steel, and Tin Workers (37). Although greatly weakened by the Homestead steel strike, the union would not and could not silently observe as its regulatory program for the industry was rejected in favor of that of the gigantic United States Steel Corporation.

The Amalgamated Association did rise to capital's challenge in 1901, but its strike against U.S. Steel was the decisive battle that ensured the victory of capital over labor in the steel industry during the progressive era. The stakes in the battle were very high. If organized labor was to have any hope of implementing or influencing the regulatory program in the industry, it first needed to secure the recognition of U.S. Steel and the large independent steel companies. According to Wright, the 1901 steel strike was the first strike conducted solely on the issue of union recognition (1901: 62). When the union finally lost, it lost big. William Foster concludes that the "failure of the 1901 strike broke the backbone of the Amalgamated Association" (1969: 12). According to Urofsky, "[t]he union suffered a serious loss of power and membership as a result of Homestead, and squandered what little it had left in a poorly timed and badly organized strike against the Steel Corporation in 1901" (1969: 252). The story of the 1901 strike against U.S. Steel shows clearly how the outcome represented a shift in the balance of power towards capital that would persist for more than three decades.

The catalyst for the 1901 strike was an Amalgamated organizing drive that began in early 1900 at a non-union mill at Wood's Sheet Mill in McKeesport, Pennsylvania. In February 1901, American Sheet Steel officials discharged some of the union men at the mill (Wright, 1901: 59–60). A general strike of the sheet steel workers was then called when the American Sheet Steel Company refused to sign the wage scale for all its mills.

The strike call was the necessary consequence of a constitutional amendment passed by the Amalgamated Association in an attempt to confront the growing power of capital in the industry. The amendment to its constitution in 1900 reads, "Should one mill in a combine or trust have a difficulty, all mills in said combine or trust shall cease work until such grievance is settled" (Hoagland, 1917: 677). This action affected about 100,000 workmen and brought the Amalgamated Association face-to-face with the newly formed Steel Corporation. "Instead, then, of having for its opponent the American Sheet Steel Company ... the association found itself the antagonist of the great and powerful United States Steel Corporation" (Wright, 1901: 60). Hence, the final battle for regulatory control of the industry during the progressive era began on July 1, 1901.

The Steel Corporation's tactics during the strike did not suggest that it hoped to rid the steel industry of unionism forever. U.S. Steel at the time was willing to recognize and bargain with the Amalgamated Association in union mills, but it generally refused to extend recognition to non-union mills. Gulick refers to the policy of the Steel Corporation in 1901 as the corporation's "go-easy" policy (1924: 99). The corporation itself referred to this policy in April 1901 as one of "temporizing" for the next six months or a year until the new trust was firmly established (99). The strike, therefore, need not have been one to eliminate unionism from the industry. Ultimately, however, the stubborn position of the Amalgamated Association led to a longer strike than the workmen could withstand.

Just as the Steel Corporation did not intend to use the 1901 strike to break the power of the Amalgamated Association once and for all, it was careful to avoid casting the appearance that it existed as a unified force confronting labor. In April, for example, a steel manufacturer, named Edenborn, recommended that U.S. Steel present itself as a mere stockholder in its subsidiary companies without any direct control over them (Eggert, 1981: 35). The idea of appearing fragmented before the public greatly appealed to the corporation executives even while control of the situation remained firmly in their hands. For example, a discussion of U.S. Steel executives on June 17, 1901 suggests that the board of directors considered having the corporation's subsidiary presidents delay for a day when approached by a union in non-union mills so that the corporation could advise them. The president rejected the idea, however, only because it would be clear to all that the Steel Corporation had used its influence (Gulick, 1924: 98). At another meeting of the U.S. Steel executive committee on July 6, 1901, the possibility of subsidiary companies sending representatives to meet with Amalgamated representatives was raised. According to the minutes of the meeting, "[t]he chairman stated that it should be clearly understood that the United States Steel Corporation has nothing whatever to do with it" (1924: 98). Hence, the reality and the appearance of capitalist combination were critical factors in the 1901 strike for industrial control.

Because the Amalgamated stubbornly insisted upon union recognition in all of the mills of the American Sheet Steel Company, it was forced to settle with the Steel Corporation on September 13, 1901 on terms that were less favorable than the corporation's original offer. In the end, the union lost nine union mills with lost wages in excess of $4 million (Wright, 1901: 67–68). In addition, the constitutional provision regarding sympathetic strikes was also withdrawn after the strike (Gulick, 1924: 101–102). The repeal of the sympathetic strike provision implied that organized labor would not function as a unified force for social change in the steel industry during the progressive era. By the time the U.S. Senate undertook its investigation of the 1919 steel strike, President Tighe of the Amalgamated Association testified that capital-labor relations in 1901 consisted of "giving way to every request that was made by the companies when they insisted upon it" (Foster, 1969: 12). Hence, the showdown between capital and labor in the steel industry ended with the victory of unified capital and the destruction of organized labor.

4.2 PART I OF BIG STEEL'S REGULATORY PROGRAM: REGULATING CIRCULATION AND PRODUCTION

After the strike of 1901, the United States Steel Corporation was free to move forward with its regulatory program without any significant interference from organized labor. Both labor and capital recognized the need to place restrictions on the market after the economic crisis of the late nineteenth century. The battle for regulatory control of the steel industry, however, had placed the power to design and implement that program firmly in the hands of the Steel Corporation. Its program may be divided into two distinct parts. The first part of the program was designed to regulate competition among the steel companies, on the one hand, and between the steel companies as a (more or less) unified group and a fragmented industrial workforce, on the other hand. Its corresponding consequences for the steelworkers are discussed in this section. The second part of the program, covered in the next section, was designed to protect the first part of the Steel Corporation's regulatory program against the criticism of the federal government and the American public.

Chapter 3 investigated at length the price stabilization program of the United States Steel Corporation, which was designed to regulate competition among the steel companies. The Steel Corporation used a variety of methods to stabilize prices during the progressive era and thus eliminated much of the business uncertainty that had plagued the industry in the previous century. With this background in mind, it is possible to investigate the consequences that the stabilization program carried for the steelworkers during the progressive era, and it is to them that we now turn.

Abraham Berglund has conducted the most thorough investigation of the relationship between the stabilization of steel prices in the early twentieth century and output fluctuations. Because output fluctuations are closely associated with employment fluctuations, a close connection between price stability and output fluctuations during the progressive era would certainly be a matter of significance to the steelworkers. According to Berglund, if the pricing policies of the United States Steel Corporation necessitated, on the average, greater variation in output and increased fluctuations in employment than in the previous competitive era, then the social significance of this fact is obvious (1924: 608). With the social significance of the matter clearly established, an investigation of the statistical evidence for increased output and employment fluctuations during the progressive era is warranted.

Berglund's analysis is particularly relevant to a comparison of the industry's trade fluctuations in the late nineteenth century LIS and the progressive era RIS because he compares the conditions in the industry preceding and following the formation of U.S. Steel. He uses a moving average based upon a five-year period to measure the approximate annual deviations from the nation's normal output for each year (1924: 612). His statistical investigation leads Berglund to conclude that "the percentages of average deviation for the years succeeding the organization of the United States Steel Corporation are materially greater than the corresponding percentages for the period from 1887 to 1901, inclusive" (615). Rather than pursuing Berglund's evidence in great detail, one graph is sufficient to give one a sense of the increase in trade fluctuations that occurred after 1901. Figure 4.2 depicts the fluctuations in the growth rate of crude steel production for a considerable span of time before and after the U.S. Steel merger. As the graph shows clearly, the extreme expansions and contractions of steel output growth were greater after U.S. Steel was formed in 1901.

Berglund also emphasizes the fact that the extreme variations between 1902 and 1922, inclusive, take place mostly in depression years and are decidedly greater than the corresponding variations in years of prosperity (1924: 616). Even the outbreak of World War I caused steel prices to rise much more in the U.S. than any boost it gave to iron and steel production because steel mills were incapable of responding quickly to the increased demands of the war (616–617). Surprisingly, Berglund finds that the output deviations for the war and postwar years from 1915 to 1922, inclusive, are actually lower than in the prewar years from 1902 to 1914. Hence, the war cannot explain the greater trade fluctuations in the 1902 to 1922 period (617). It seems then that the regulated characteristics (i.e., pricing policy) of the progressive era RIS may have actually exacerbated industrial fluctuations in the iron and steel industry.

Berglund is careful to link the fluctuations in steel production to the price stabilization program of the Steel Corporation. According to

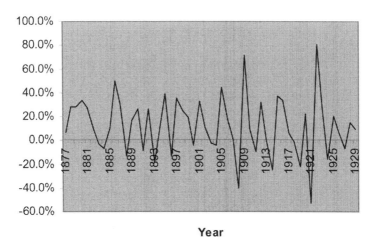

Year

Figure 4.2: Growth rate of physical primary steel output in the U.S.: 1877–1929.
SOURCE: U.S. Census Bureau, 1960: 416.
NOTE: Primary steel output or crude steel refers to the total number of steel ingots or castings produced in long tons.

Berglund, "price stabilization has required frequent and, in some cases, drastic adjustments with respect to output to meet market conditions" (1924: 618). Consistent with this general trend is the fact that fluctuations in rail production were very pronounced from 1901 to 1916 when the prices of Bessemer steel rails and open-hearth rails were rigidly fixed at $28 and $30 per gross ton, respectively (620). On the other hand, Berglund refuses to condemn the Steel Corporation even though he concedes that its price stabilization policies have probably contributed to the fluctuations in iron and steel output and in the number of workers employed in the nation's steel plants (626). He frees the Steel Trust of any blame by providing it with a long run excuse for its pricing policies. That is, price stabilization may actually encourage industrial stabilization in the long run by warding off the commercial crises usually associated with violent price movements (626–627). Furthermore, even though the extreme variations of the period after 1901 are characterized by sharp reductions in output during depressions, they are almost invariably followed by prompt recoveries to normal production, which Berglund attributes to U.S. Steel's pricing policy (627–628). Ultimately, however, he dismisses the serious consequences that even short spells of unemployment may carry for steelworkers and their families.

The trade fluctuations certainly imply that employment in the steel industry has fluctuated to greater extremes during the progressive era than in the previous competitive period. At the same time, it is possible to consider the employment fluctuations more directly. Before investigating employment fluctuations directly, however, it may be helpful to first consider the other aspect of U.S. Steel's market stabilization program during the progressive era that emphasized wage rate stability and was equally responsible for employment fluctuations in the steel industry during the progressive era.

As is the case with product prices during the progressive era, stable wage rates were a goal of the Steel Corporation that was only partially realized. When the power to control wages throughout the industry did exist, it was firmly in the hands of U.S. Steel. For example, because the wages of the American Sheet and Tin Plate Company determined union wages in the independent unionized mills, the U.S. Steel subsidiary controlled wages in the industry generally (Hoagland, 1917: 686–687). The success of the wage stabilization program, however, was mixed. Wages for skilled steelworkers fell as much as 60% and 70% from 1889 to 1908, but they comprised only 5% of the industry's workforce (Hogan, 1971: 446). Over the same period, the unskilled steelworkers, who comprised 60% of the industry's workforce, enjoyed wage increases of 18% while the 35% of the steelworkers classified as semi-skilled workers had virtually no change in wages (1971: 446–447). By creating a class of semi-skilled workmen, the homogenization of labor in the steel industry was, therefore, consistent with the overall program of wage rate stabilization.

Gary also sought to maintain wage stability during economic recessions. For example, as orders declined during the economic downturn of 1907–1909, Gary maintained present wage levels with Morgan's support but then cut labor costs by running plants below capacity or shutting them down altogether (Cutcliffe, 1994: 153–154). In 1911, U.S. Steel did not cut wages at all for the first time in a business decline, and the independent steel manufacturers generally followed U.S. Steel in setting wages and prices (Brody, 1960: 154–155). Stable wages continued to some extent for the remainder of the decade. Even immediately after WWI, the steel companies maintained wartime pay rates (Hogan, 1971: 457). Gary's wage maintenance policy was abandoned, however, during the postwar depression when all steel companies slashed wage rates, and Gary fell back on the market as the ultimate determinant of wages (1960: 270). Regardless of a number of deviations from the general policy, the wage stabilization program was a significant aspect of U.S. Steel's regulatory program during the progressive era.

The price and wage stabilization program together served to increase fluctuations in employment and thus job insecurity for the steelworkers within the progressive era RIS. Annual employment figures for the iron and steel industry as a whole are not published although the average number of workers employed by U.S. Steel each year is available (Berglund, 1924: 622). According to Berglund, however, his estimates of the fluctuations in the average number of employees may be treated as fairly typical of the steel business generally. He concludes that although employment fluctuates in the industry, it does not fluctuate as much as output because of the large amount of fixed capital in the industry (625). This fact is small comfort considering the *absolute* numbers of workmen regularly thrown out of employment. Figure 4.3 shows the extent of these fluctuations with emphasis placed on the absolute magnitude of employment fluctuations during the progressive era.

Although stable prices and high profit rates may have been achieved during the progressive era, stable employment was not achieved. Nearly a quarter of the Steel Corporation's workforce was thrown out of work at various times during the period. In absolute terms, this figure amounted to nearly 50,000 men and thus the benefits of progressive era regulation were hardly passed along to the steelworkers. The 1907 recession was especially hard on labor in the steel industry.[4] As of December 1, 1907, U.S. Steel had laid-off 20,000 men and was operating at 70–75% of its maximum capacity (Smith, 1908: 273). By December 12, the Steel Corporation had 51 blast furnaces out and six banked "as a part of its general policy of maintaining prices" (1908: 273). Gulick has noted how extreme the employment fluctuations were in the industry compared with other industries. Specifically, he notes that "[i]n 1909 the steel works and rolling mills had relatively the largest fluctuation in the size of the labor force of any of the large manufacturing industries" (Gulick, 1924: 81). One should also not assume that these fluctuations influenced a small segment of the population. From 1901 to 1924, about 1 million people in the United States relied on the Steel Corporation as their immediate source of income (1924: 20). The social significance of the Steel Corporation's price and wage maintenance policies during the progressive era was, therefore, considerable.

In terms of leadership in these matters, Judge Gary of U.S. Steel was the primary advocate of the price and wage stabilization program for the steel industry during the early twentieth century. His concern for wage rate stability has been linked to the drive to stabilize prices. According to Dwyer, "Gary's larger program for price stability in the industry hinged on standardized production costs—which, in Gary's view, meant having to find a way to standardize the wage rate" (1994c: 475). Following Gary's lead, most steel companies supported the drive system, as opposed to scientific management as Urofsky states (1969: 258), as a means of stabilizing the wage factor in cost determination and as part of their overall program of industrial rationalization. Gary thus eventually succeeded in persuading the industry to support the goal of wage stability.

Before Gary's program of market stabilization could be implemented, however, he needed to eliminate the ex-Carnegie Steel officials from the Steel Corporation's top leadership. In fact, the ex-Carnegie officials and the Gary/Morgan financial officials at U.S. Steel were in as much disagreement on the matter of wage stability as they were on the matter of price stability as discussed in chapter 3. During the 1904 and 1907 recessions, when "Gary initiated a program to stabilize the wage structure and cut back on capacity utilization, which meant laying off workers" (Dwyer, 1994c: 475),

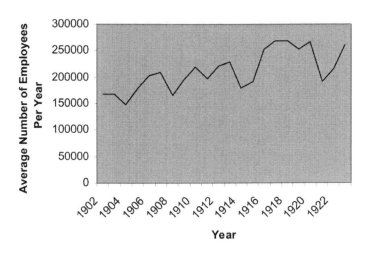

Figure 4.3: Average number of U.S. Steel employees per year: 1902–1923.
SOURCE: Berglund, 1924: 623.

an internal dispute arose between the financial executives (e.g., Gary, Perkins), who favored stabilization, and the ex-Carnegie Steel executives (e.g., Corey, Dinkey, Dickson) at U.S. Steel, who favored the product and labor market competition of the late nineteenth century.

W.B. Dickson understood well the harmful effects that U.S. Steel's regulatory program would bring for the workmen. By 1904, Dickson was beginning to criticize Gary's commercial policy. The corporation was running just above 50% of capacity, and Dickson felt that U.S. Steel should produce "full output at competitive prices than . . . half output at artificial prices" (Eggert, 1981: 58–59). When Gary insisted on maintaining stable prices during the 1907 panic, Dickson argued that instead prices should be reduced to bring in enough business "to keep intact the most valuable element in the business; namely, an experienced workforce" (59). After resigning from U.S. Steel, Dickson remained an avid proponent of cutting wages and prices to keep the mills running, and he tried to convince the workmen while at Midvale to accept wage cuts. At a meeting on February 4, 1921 Dickson tried to convince the other independent steel companies to follow Midvale's lead and thus set off a public battle between Gary and himself (144). Gary's policies clearly dominated the industry during the progressive era, however, aside from any rebellious behavior by men like Dickson.

Gary's victory over the former Carnegie Steel executives was virtually complete during the first decade of the Corporation's existence. After 1908, "steel prices, costs, and wages developed along the lines that Gary sought" (Dwyer, 1994c: 475). In October 1909, Schwab presented Gary with a "formal loving cup" at a banquet the industry hosted in Gary's honor (Cutcliffe, 1994: 154). Gary's policies had triumphed. A more formal signal of Gary's dominance in the industry was given the following year. On March 1, 1910, the board of directors at U.S. Steel adopted a resolution declaring the chairman (i.e., Gary) to be "the chief executive officer of the corporation" and "in general charge of the affairs of the Corporation" (Eggert, 1981: 69). Judge Gary and George Perkins wanted to eliminate the "ruthless cutting of costs" and "repeated slashing of wage-rates and prices" associated with the Carnegie years and succeeded in 1911 when the last of the Carnegie steel men (e.g., Corey, Dickson) finally resigned from the corporation's top leadership (1981: 30–31). The regulatory program of U.S. Steel thus required several years to gain widespread acceptance, but it ultimately prevailed.

At first glance, it seems strange that the industry would be satisfied with stable wages when cost cutting had been a near obsession of the Carnegie Steel officials. Gary's preference for wage stability appears especially odd when one considers the possibility that stable prices may be maintained even when wages are being reduced. According to Eggert, Gary's insistence on maintaining steady wage rates as long as prices remained stable stemmed from his desire to be fair to the workmen (1981: 64). A more likely reason for Gary's advocacy of stable wages is that he understood that U.S. Steel was, in many ways, at the mercy of the major power blocs in society—namely, labor, government, and the public. Judge Gary "fought as hard to maintain wage levels in bad times as he did to sustain prices [because] . . . [c]utting wages, he argued, provoked strikes" (Urofsky, 1969: 270). That is, when choosing between wage cuts, which affect most or all workmen, and layoffs, which affect a smaller number of workmen, Gary chose layoffs because a harsh response from labor was less likely. Although in a weak and passive state, organized labor was a force for the steel executive to respect and fear during the progressive era. Overall, the wage stabilization program thus served to mollify the workforce and prevent the growth of organized labor in the industry during the progressive era.

Part I of U.S. Steel's regulatory program included the regulated interaction between a rough union of steel companies and a mostly fragmented workforce. The discussion above has emphasized the explicit effort to regulate labor market competition with special attention given to wage rate stabilization. The regulation of capital-labor competition extended beyond the sphere of circulation, however, to the sphere of capitalist production. Although the steel companies were not organized in this effort to the same degree that they were concerning wage stability, the push to mechanize production possessed a dual role for the steel companies. Market forces drove the steel companies to cut labor costs by mechanizing production, but they also consciously attempted to wrestle control of the production process away from the steelworkers. A contest between capital and labor for control of the production process was thus another form of capital-labor competition whose outcome the steel companies refused to leave entirely to the whims of the free market. The homogenization drive that began in the 1890s was thus continued well into the progressive era, and it is this aspect of the regulatory program and its associated consequences for the steelworkers that must now be considered.

The drive system became more firmly entrenched throughout the steel industry during the progressive era as the class of semi-skilled workers in the industry grew. According to a survey of 28 steel plants conducted by the U.S. Commissioner of Labor in 1913, the percentage of steelworkers who might be classified as semi-skilled rose from 35% to 58% from 1900 to 1910 (Stone, 1975: 39). It was the drive system rather than scientific management that served as the primary method of labor control during the progressive era. In 1898, for example, the Bethlehem Steel Company hired Frederick Taylor to apply time-and-motion study methods to the handling of raw materials in the yards and to implement a piece-rate system. When Schwab took control of Bethlehem, he dismantled nearly all of Taylor's policies and replaced scientific management with the drive system (Hessen, 1975: 166). In addition, the new system of labor control put an end to the contract system in the iron and steel industry. Skilled workers were no longer permitted to hire and train their own helpers. The elimination of the contract system was so complete that it actually led to a shortage of skilled workers by 1905 and required employers to establish a new apprenticeship system that they controlled directly (Stone, 1975: 56–57). These facts merely help to establish that the drive system did become more firmly entrenched in the steel industry during the progressive era.

Certainly the steel companies were responding, in part, to market forces with the drive to cut costs through the introduction of labor saving machinery. The Carnegie years had made the technological changes a necessity for survival in the industry. The cost benefits continued to be important well into the progressive era. According to J. Russell Smith, for example, the labor cost of a ton of iron was very high in blast furnace departments as late as 1908 due to the variety of work required. He notes that at a relatively small blast furnace, labor charges were subdivided into fifty-two classes (Smith, 1908: 267). In the larger blast furnace departments in Pittsburgh, however, the low cost of blast furnace labor was partly a consequence of the fact that the furnaces do not make their pig iron into pigs for transportation to other works like smaller furnaces. A sizable portion of the many classes of labor mentioned above were employed in making the molds for the pig iron, pouring it into the molds, breaking it up, piling it, handling it, and loading it (268). In this way, the homogenization drive in the steel industry served to cut the labor costs that had harmed business during the economic crisis of the late nineteenth century.

At the same time, the push to stabilize wages and the technological backwardness of the Steel Corporation suggests that U.S. Steel, at least, may have had another motivation for the greater entrenchment of the drive system. In addition to cutting labor costs then, the homogenization drive may have been intended to transfer control of the production process from the workers to the employers (Gordon et al., 1982: 115). Gordon et al. (1982: 115) note one early example of the way in which employers in the iron industry attempted to wrestle control of the production process from the skilled ironworkers with an invention known as Dank's puddling machine. In the case of the steel industry, Fitch's comments on the impact of mechanization in the steel industry are especially appropriate. Fitch claims (1969: 139) that the "tendency to make processes automatic has resulted not only in a lessened cost with an increased tonnage, but it also reinforced the control of the employers over their men." Employers thus used new production methods to transfer knowledge and control of the production process from workers to managers to achieve what Stone (1975: 54) refers to as the "redivision of labor." It was this motivation for the further implementation of the drive system that brings the homogenization of the steel workforce into the capitalist program of regulation during the progressive era.

The significant role of mechanized production in transferring knowledge and control of the production process from workers to employers is particularly evident when considering the transition from iron to steel production. The shift from iron to steel production was a necessary condition for capital to break the power of the skilled workmen in the industry generally. In 1917 Hoagland reported, "the iron industry has experienced practically no change in technique in forty years" (1917: 681–682). Skilled men were thus still needed in the iron industry as much as before. For this very reason, the potential for mechanization was a primary determinant of the evolution of capital-labor relations in the steel industry. Whereas the manufacture of wrought iron, sheet steel, and tinplate resisted mechanization, steel manufacture appeared to offer unlimited opportunities for improvement (Brody, 1960: 8–9, 13). The strategy of implementing technological changes in the steel industry to undermine worker control over the production process could, therefore, not be used with equal effect in the iron industry.

The negative consequences of Part I of U.S. Steel's regulatory program for the steelworkers are many and varied. The lack of job security associated with fluctuating employment has already been linked to the price and wage stabilization program of U.S. Steel. The homogenization drive by which the steel corporations obtained control of the production process also carried negative consequences for the steelworkers. Early in the progressive era, working conditions deteriorated quickly. In 1906, for example, 405 U.S. Steel employees died from industrial accidents, 178 of which worked in the Carnegie division of U.S. Steel (Eggert, 1981: 44). The high accident and death rate led to harsh public criticism. William Hard's 1907 article, for example, "Making Steel and Killing Men," reported 46 deaths and almost 2,000 serious injuries at U.S. Steel's South Works at Chicago in 1906 (Dwyer, 1994c: 475). Hard's attack was directed against the same South Chicago steelworks Upton Sinclair so vividly described in *The Jungle* when the main character, a Lithuanian immigrant named Jurgis Rudkus, became the victim of a furnace explosion (1960: 203–208). The Amalgamated Association established a death benefit fund in 1904, making it clear that the steelworkers were forced to fend for themselves early in the progressive era.

No account of the steel industry during the progressive era would be complete without a consideration of the long working hours the steelworkers endured. By 1890, the two-turn system was firmly established in blast furnace departments, and the twelve-hour day was universal in pig iron production (Fitch, 1969: 168). The two-shift system dominated throughout the progressive era in the steel industry as well. The system required many steelworkers to work twelve hours per day, seven days per week. The transition from day to night duty required workers to work a twenty-four hour continuous shift once every two weeks (called the "long turn") with twenty-four hours off on alternating weeks (Gulick, 1924: 22–23). The steelworkers expressed their dissatisfaction with the long working hours on a number of occasions. Low wages and long working hours were a major complaint of the employees of Bethlehem Steel during a strike against the company in 1910. Because the company was approaching record profits, "the men demanded the complete elimination of Sunday work" (Hessen, 1975: 195). The failed strike did not eliminate the frustration with the two-turn system, which grew throughout the remainder of the decade.

No clear consensus exists regarding the percentage of steelworkers who worked the twelve-hour day during the progressive era. According to Hogan, 56.2% of the wage earners engaged in the manufacture of steel were employed in companies where the prevailing hours were in excess of sixty hours per week by 1909 (1971: 448). Gulick conservatively estimates that roughly 35% of U.S. Steel's workmen worked twelve hours per day in 1911 (1924: 31). Other estimates are even higher. According to Urofsky, three out of four steelworkers labored twelve hours per day in 1910 (1969: 253). The eight-hour day persisted only where tremendous physical exertion and intense heat were found, such as in the Bessemer departments (Hogan, 1971: 448). The long working hours in most departments continued even after World War I ended and the wartime labor shortage had subsided. In 1920, in particular, Foster reported that the twelve-hour day prevailed for half of the steelworkers, and a quarter of the steelworkers worked seven days per week with the long turn every two weeks (1969: 14). Whatever the precise proportion, the long working hours were general throughout the industry and applied to a substantial portion of the steelworkers.

It is reasonable to ask what relationship, if any, existed between the twelve-hour day and the regulatory program of the Steel Corporation. A traditional Marxian explanation is that the longer working day would allow the steel companies to appropriate more absolute surplus value than with a shorter working day. On the subject of the shift-system, in particular, Marx writes that the "prolongation of the working day beyond the limits of the natural day, into the night, . . . only slightly quenches the vampire thirst for the living blood of labour" (Marx, 1990: 367). Nevertheless, this interpretation may also be used to explain how a longer working day may reduce labor cost per ton. If daily wages are held constant, then the longer working day simply spreads a constant labor cost over a larger daily output thus pushing labor costs per ton down. Running full in blast furnace departments, for example, is necessary to reduce labor cost per ton. Smith explains that in a Pittsburgh furnace department, labor cost per ton was nearly 35% greater in August, the month of smallest production, than in April, the month of maximum production, when output was 28% greater (1908: 268).

In addition to constant daily wages, Marx may shed light on another reason for this problem facing the capitalist. As he explains with respect to idle means of production, the "loss becomes a positive one as soon as the interruption of employment necessitates an additional outlay when the work begins again" (1990: 367). The shutting down of blast furnaces is costly due to deterioration upon cooling and may cost as much as $1 million to

revive a furnace once it has become cold. The same follows for coke ovens
and steel furnaces (Stocking, 1954: 25). The Marxian interpretation is reasonable, but it is consistent with any institutional structure and thus lacks
the historical specificity needed to understand it within the context of the
regulatory program of Big Steel.

Another possible reason for the industry's insistence on maintaining the twelve-hour day long into the progressive era is that it fit neatly
into the capitalist program of regulation. As discussed in detail above,
industrial rationalization and stabilization were key goals of the Steel
Corporation. The emphasis thus far has been placed on product price
and wage rate stabilization. Steady employment, however, was another
of Gary's goals (Brody, 1960: 154). Although not at the top of Gary's
list of priorities, stable employment was believed to follow naturally
from the price stabilization program. In particular, Gary believed that a
cooperative effort to stabilize steel prices "would, in the long run, create a stable demand for steel and, as a result, stable employment and
wage rates" (Hogan, 1971: 445). The twelve-hour day may have been
one measure that the Steel Corporation used to stabilize employment to
a certain extent. If U.S. Steel's employees were working only eight hours
per day and the demand for steel fell considerably, for example, the Steel
Corporation would need to layoff 50% more workers to reduce production by any fixed amount than if it only employed twelve hour workers.
It is exactly this same reasoning that the led the industry to conclude that
a shift to the eight-hour workday would require a 50% increase in the
workforce (Urofsky, 1969: 259). Therefore, the long working hours in
the steel industry during the progressive era may be linked to the regulatory program designed by U.S. Steel.

A final negative consequence of the first part of Big Steel's regulatory program for the steel industry was the unequal distribution of the
benefits of productivity growth that resulted. The mechanization of steel
production led to a sharp increase in labor productivity early in the progressive era without a corresponding increase in the income of the workmen. From 1890 to 1910, the productivity of the blast furnace worker
tripled and his income only rose by half while the productivity of the
steelworker doubled and his income rose by only one-fifth (Brody, 1960:
48). Robert Allen (1981) has arrived at similar results using an accounting scheme he constructed to explain the decline in the price of steel rails
during the final decades of the nineteenth century. The scheme permits
one to separate the effects of input price changes, efficiency changes, and
changes in the deviation of price from unit cost (Allen, 1981: 514). Allen
claims that both falling input prices and increased efficiency forced rail
prices downward and that profit margins rose between 1889 and 1902
as rail producers realized almost all of the gains of technical progress as
higher profits (514).

Allen's (1981: 523) analysis conflicts with the analyses of Peter Temin (1964) and Donald McCloskey (1973) who argue that productivity growth in the iron and steel industry ceased in the 1880s and diminish the role of market power in raising the price of steel rails. According to Allen (1981: 526), their measurement of productivity growth is based on the faulty assumption that long run competitive equilibrium characterized the iron and steel industry during the late nineteenth and early twentieth centuries. It is an assumption that is "certainly not true for rails" (Allen, 1981: 527). As George Stocking (1954: 34) forcefully states, "business rivalry in making and selling steel does not—in truth, cannot—conform fully to the economist's model of perfect competition." Because the market for steel certainly cannot be characterized as perfectly competitive during the progressive era, Allen's claim that the benefits of productivity were unequally distributed in favor of the steel companies seems warranted.

The steel companies went out of their way to defend the unequal distribution of the gains from productivity growth. The steel companies believed that "increased output was not due to labor exertion but to capital investment, and so productivity gains acted to reduce labor costs and not to raise wage rates" (Hogan, 1971: 444). In an effort to strengthen the industry's case further that earnings should be divorced from productivity, Charles Schwab reported to a congressional committee in 1912 that huge amounts of capital, not human labor, were needed to raise output (Brody, 1960: 41). Hence, we should not mistake the fruits of capital for the fruits of human labor! Never mind the fact that the labor process must exist in all societies whereas it is only in the capitalist mode of production that the presence of capital transforms it into a social process of valorization.[5]

Historians of the steel industry have often agreed with the progressive era steel executives that the distribution of productivity gains was a just distribution. Robert Hessen, for example, defends Schwab's refusal to grant the requests of the workmen during the strike at the South Bethlehem plant in 1910 on the grounds that it would have required either passing along the higher labor costs to the buyers of steel in the form of higher prices or reduced profits for the corporation. In Hessen's view, "neither possibility was feasible or fair" (1975: 197). Yet at a press conference the month the strike began, Schwab boasted that he would be committing $12,000,000 for new plant and equipment in the near future (196). Schwab was reinvesting as much of the corporation's profits as possible back into the business. It was, therefore, perfectly feasible to divert some of these funds to raise the incomes of the steelworkers. The fairness of this alternative is, of course, left to the reader to decide. Faced with the negative social consequences for the steelworkers that flowed from the first part of its regulatory program, the next section explains how U.S. Steel implemented the second part of its regulatory program in an effort to safeguard its control of production and circulation.

4.3   PART II OF BIG STEEL'S REGULATORY PROGRAM: POSITIVE AND NEGATIVE DEFENSIVE MEASURES

The contradictory nature of U.S Steel's corporate policies becomes apparent when contrasting the first and second parts of its regulatory program. As the previous section explained, the first part of the Steel Corporation's regulatory program consisted of price and wage rate stabilization and led to numerous difficulties for the steelworkers, including job insecurity, high accident rates, long working hours, and an unequal distribution of the benefits of regulation. In contrast, the second part of U.S. Steel's regulatory program consisted of a variety of methods aimed at pacifying major power blocs in society (i.e., the steelworkers, the federal government, and the American public) that were responding negatively to the harmful consequences of price and wage rate stabilization. The second part of the capitalist regulatory program may also be divided into two parts consisting of positive and negative measures. The positive measures consisted of paternalistic welfare measures, company unions, and hours reform and were aimed at winning the support of the public, the government, and the steelworkers for the Steel Corporation and the industry in general. The negative measures, on the other hand, consisted of harsh anti-union tactics that persisted throughout the progressive era and beyond.[6] As is the case with the first part of the regulatory program, the rest of the industry eventually followed U.S. Steel's lead by implementing similar measures.

The positive and negative measures within its regulatory program are considered "defensive" measures insofar as the Steel Corporation was responding to potential external threats from three key power blocs in American society. According to Seely (1994: xxi), for example, the welfare measures were part of U.S. Steel's strategy to ease tensions with labor. Moreover, Stone points out that the welfare work of the Steel Corporation was partly intended to reduce labor turnover. As George Perkins, the primary designer of the welfare programs, explained, changing jobs tended to make workers identify with other workers and to see themselves as a class (Stone, 1975: 53).

On the separate matter of hours reform, Gulick argues that the two main factors that pushed U.S. Steel towards reform (e.g., the elimination of Sunday labor) were the low demand for steel due to poor business conditions and public criticism of the corporation's labor policy (1924: 55). The program of stabilization in general included a number of labor reforms to improve labor-management relations and generate public-relations benefits (Dwyer, 1994c: 474). In summary, Eggert claims that it is misleading to suggest that U.S. Steel's labor reforms were purely generous acts. Frequently, "they were hurried responses to threatened governmental investigations or muckraking exposes of conditions in the plants" (Eggert, 1981: xiv). Just as the threat of government intervention influenced U.S. Steel's pricing and production decisions as chapter

3 discussed, the Steel Corporation also responded to pressure from the government, the public, and labor in the area of labor reform. The paternalistic welfare program[7] of the United States Steel Corporation is the most beneficial aspect of its regulatory program from the standpoint of the steelworkers. It is, therefore, necessary to consider what it is and how it is be interpreted within the context of a regulatory program that generally subordinates the interests of labor to the interests of capital. In general, welfare capitalism may be defined as a "series of reforms from within carried out by a company" (Dwyer, 1994c: 474). Beginning in 1913, the Steel Corporation began publishing an "Iron and Steel Institute Monthly Bulletin" to report on the welfare work of the different steel companies (Stone, 1975: 53). Regardless of the public relations benefits the industry enjoyed from these measures, it rationalized its actions on the basis of the new corporate philosophy of social responsibility. David Brody agrees that U.S. Steel had a strong sense of social responsibility throughout the progressive era (1960: 169). The Steel Corporation's ideological position fit in nicely with that of the National Civic Federation and thus helps explain the corporation's prominent role in that organization.

U.S. Steel's welfare program began as early as 1902 when it announced that its stock subscription plan would begin in 1903.[8] The plan was open to all employees of the Steel Corporation and was thus treated as a very progressive measure for the time. The plan worked in the following way. During each of the first five years of stock ownership, if a worker maintained continuous employment and demonstrated a "proper interest in [the] welfare and progress" of the corporation, then he would receive annual checks at the rate of $5 per share. At the end of five years an additional dividend would be paid from a special fund established on the basis of the accumulation of $5 payments from workmen who discontinued service. The corporation, however, would "then by its own final determination award to each man whom it shall find deserving thereof as many parts of such accumulation fund as shall be equal to the number of shares then held by him under this plan" (Fitch, 1969: 209).

The plan is controversial for a number of reasons, not least of which is the language that explicitly penalizes steelworkers who discontinue service or hold the same shares for more than five years. That is, it is in a workman's best interest to sell the shares and purchase new ones after five years so as to begin the accumulation of $5 checks anew. As Gulick insightfully noticed, the stock subscription plan encourages the rapid turnover of shares while the opposite is true for the turnover of men (1924: 188). U.S. Steel's stock subscription plan is thus not a profit-sharing plan at all. Instead, the plan may be a method of holding the skilled and trained employees whom it would be difficult to replace (1924: 178, 180). At the same time, the plan implicitly penalizes workmen who violate the anti-union policy of the corporation by joining a union. George Perkins even admitted that the stock purchase plan would discourage unionization (Eggert, 1981: 43). The stock subscription plan is thus correctly classified here as a defensive measure of the Steel Corporation's regulatory program.

Another objection to the plan is that it often was accompanied by wage cuts as occurred in 1904. According to one workman, "When they give away one dollar they know where they are going to get another in its place" (Fitch, 1969: 212). Although the return may be high, it is based on a steel-worker's acquiescence as an employee (213). The stock subscription plan could thus be used to change the form of wage payment so as to give the steelworkers a false sense of economic power and identity. Finally, although the stock subscription plan was technically open to all corporation employees, most common laborers could not participate due to the high price of corporation shares. Hence, at the inception of the stock plan in 1903, only 10% of the corporation's employees participated, and this proportion had only risen to 15% by 1911 (Eggert, 1981: 42). The details of the plan, therefore, support an interpretation of the Steel Corporation's regulatory program as one that pursues the goals of capital at the expense of labor.

The Steel Corporation also maintained a bonus system that was supposedly designed to motivate employees to work harder and reward them for their efforts. Like the stock subscription plan, however, the bonus plan failed to include all of the corporation employees in practice and actually only applied to corporation officials and subsidiary managers. Katherine Stone describes a number of subtle ways in which the steel companies sought to discipline the homogenized workforce using reward mechanisms. By paying the semi-skilled workers piece wages (i.e., a fixed sum for each unit produced), for example, the companies played upon individual workers' ambitions and thus broke down workers' collective identity (Stone, 1975: 42–43). Artificial job ladders and employer certificates were also used to create division within an increasingly homogenous workforce (Stone, 1975: 45–49). At the same time, the steelworkers were conscious of the negative consequences of the bonus plans. For example, whereas Hessen (1975: 195) identifies low wage rates and long working hours as the primary complaint of the workmen when they struck against the Bethlehem Steel Corporation in February 1910, Stone (1975: 45) acknowledges the importance of the workers' opposition to the bonus system. By excluding common laborers and creating division among the semi-skilled workmen, the bonus plans served the interests of capital.

The Steel Corporation also designed and implemented a pension plan for employees. On January 1, 1911, U.S. Steel established its pension system with the formation of the "United States Steel and Carnegie Pension Fund." The fund was created from Carnegie's $4 million accident relief fund and another $8 million from U.S. Steel (Gulick, 1924: 141). Like the stock subscription plan, however, the pension plan reduced labor turnover. According to Fitch, pension systems, as they are dependent on the length of continuous service, provide stability for a labor force but at the expense of its mobility (1969: 197–198). The pension plan thus contributed to the appearance of a socially responsible Steel Corporation while fitting neatly into its regulatory program.

The most famous and well-publicized aspect of the Steel Corporation's welfare program was the safety program. According to Gulick, the "real center" of the U.S. Steel welfare program and "the source from which practically everything else has sprung" is the safety movement (1924: 138). Both Gulick and Foster, who offer very critical accounts of the Steel Corporation's history, acknowledge that the corporation was undoubtedly in the lead in terms of installing safety devices and creating safety committees (Foster, 1969: 14; Gulick, 1924: 150). The popularity of the safety program is captured in the fact that the United States Steel Corporation was the originator of the famous Safety First slogan (Hogan, 1971: 453). The widespread programs for accident prevention and insurance in the steel industry were also devised for the purpose of counteracting the stream of adverse publicity (1971: 453). Because the safety program was a matter of great consequence to the steelworkers given the high accident and death rates discussed in the last section, it is worth considering the structure and results of the program.

U.S. Steel first appointed a permanent committee on safety in April 1908. Each subsidiary company was required to maintain a central safety committee, plant safety committees, and workmen's safety committees consisting of three workmen (Gulick, 1924: 140). To promote safety, the Steel Corporation used everything from warning signs and movies to safety appliances to reduce its accident rate (145–146). It also maintained rescue crews, first aid rooms, dressing stations, and emergency hospitals for accidents that do occur (151–152). In October 1911, the Steel Corporation also formed a five-member sanitation committee to collect and disseminate information along with the safety committee (142). In terms of results, the safety program was successful in reducing the number of serious accidents in the industry. Serious accidents at U.S. Steel fell 43%, at Inland Steel 55%, and at Jones & Laughlin 71% (Hogan, 1971: 453). The safety program was undoubtedly the defensive measure that served the steelworkers best insofar as it reduced the likelihood of death, dismemberment, and disease and thus the worst excesses of the mechanization drive.

The final aspect of the Steel Corporation's welfare program to be considered is the housing program. Company housing has a long history in the iron and steel industry. In fact, the subsidization of company housing by steel companies predates the Steel Corporation. Carnegie favored the practice of granting low-interest loans to employees to purchase homes and repay them through paycheck deductions over long periods of time (Brody, 1960: 87). Similarly, when the Apollo Iron and Steel Company built the town of Vandergrift in 1895, it sold land and advanced loans to workers to buy houses (88). "By 1900 three-fifths of America's steelworkers lived in steel towns, often in housing rented or mortgaged from the company" (Dwyer, 1994c: 474). As with many regulatory reforms developed in the steel industry during the late nineteenth century, the Steel Corporation adopted and perfected them to ensure profitability during the progressive era.

Morgan Park, Minnesota is the town that best reflects the extent to which U.S. Steel went to provide housing for employees. The town really became a separate town with no government except that provided by the Steel Corporation (Gulick, 1924: 164). The Steel Corporation also maintained a savings department to raise the funds needed for home loans (Fitch, 1969: 193). Although company housing was an important aspect of U.S. Steel's regulatory program in the early twentieth century, it was not until September 4, 1919 that U.S. Steel's Committee on Housing was formed and its home-owning plan was not put into effect as a model for its subsidiaries until 1920 (1924: 142–143, 169). As usual, other steel companies followed the lead of the corporation. By 1920, Youngstown steel companies had invested $5 million in immigrant housing (Brody, 1960: 189). The housing program was also part of a larger plan to dominate social and political life in the mill towns. Recreational facilities such as playgrounds, athletic fields, tennis courts, and swimming pools were an important part of U.S. Steel's welfare program. In Gary, Indiana, U.S. Steel built the schools, a library, a hospital, and a YMCA building (1960: 116). The Pennsylvania Steel Company also gave Steelton a $100,000 brick school building, and the Colorado Iron and Fuel Company built and staffed Pueblo's excellent hospital (1960: 116). The steel companies were thus the dominant force in the lives of the steelworkers and their families.

The defensive character of the housing and recreational programs becomes apparent when one considers the relationship of dependence it created between the steelworkers and their employers. The use of building loan plans and company-built houses rented at comparatively low rates were used to "further extend [the steelworkers'] attachment to the company" (Hogan, 1971: 451). Eggert (1981: 46) adds that the housing program also helped discourage unionism. The truth of this claim became apparent during the 1919 steel strike when many steel companies either evicted striking steelworkers or foreclosed the mortgages on their half-paid-for houses (Foster, 1969: 184). According to Foster (184), "[n]o employer should be permitted to own or control the houses in which his men live." Once again, the positive welfare measures of the United States Steel Corporation served the interests of capital while creating the appearance of social responsibility.

In close connection with the steel industry's welfare measures was the creation of employee representation plans (ERPs). The ERPs were basically company unions set up for the purpose of giving labor a collective voice in the management of the steel companies while allowing management to maintain firm control of the subjects discussed and the election of labor representatives. As is true in the case of the welfare program generally, the ERPs were used to satisfy the major power blocs in society. John D. Rockefeller, Jr.'s employee representation plan, for example, was established in

January 1916 at the Colorado Iron and Fuel Company after the Ludlow Massacre and the negative public response that followed (Eggert, 1981: 112). After leaving U.S. Steel, Dickson became a top official for the Midvale Steel and Ordnance Company where he helped rapidly implement an ERP at Midvale in October 1918 that stemmed mainly from the company's desire to "avoid an even less desirable alternative" (1981: 105). The ERP at Midvale was a reaction to the National War Labor Board's (NWLB) critical evaluation of the company in the summer of 1918 for its refusal to bargain collectively with employees (1981: 109). Lukens and Bethlehem Steel also adopted ERPs shortly after Midvale (1981: 115). By 1919, Youngstown Sheet and Tube, Inland, and other steel companies had adopted similar plans (Brody, 1965: 83). Interestingly, Gary opposed ERPs on the grounds that only stockholders should have a voice in the management of a corporation; company unions thus were a violation of property rights (1965: 84). In general, however, the plans were useful to the steel companies insofar as they forestalled government interference in labor-management disputes.

The ERPs may have been an effective method of preventing government interference in the steel industry, but they did not serve the interests of the employees as the steel companies claimed they would. The ERPs generally were ineffective instruments for the genuine representation of employees (Dwyer, 1994c: 474). According to Eggert, the Midvale ERP had no chance of evolving into "a system of full and equal partnership between management and labor" (1981: 141). The active role of management in the plan was sufficient to squash any opportunity for workers to pursue their collective goals. The purpose of ERPs was not to give workers more bargaining power but to "create contented workers" (Brody, 1960: 227). By the end of the war, the workmen in Pueblo, CO and South Bethlehem no longer took the ERPs seriously and thus rushed to join the unions (1960: 234). Although democratic on the surface, company unions resemble company housing in that they are instruments of capital used to eliminate opportunities for independent action by workers.

The final positive measure of U.S. Steel's regulatory program to be discussed in connection with labor policy is hours reform. On April 23, 1907, the finance committee adopted a resolution to reduce Sunday labor to the minimum, but by 1909, practically all U.S. Steel plants operated with Sunday labor again and the independent companies had never followed Gary's directive to eliminate the seven-day workweek (Eggert, 1981: 47–48). W.B. Dickson, in particular, led the struggle for hours reform at U.S. Steel in 1907 and achieved the temporary and partial elimination of Sunday labor in 1910 (xv-xvi). These positive changes in the labor policy of the Steel Corporation were very real, but they would prove to be only temporary.[9]

Progress in reducing the number of steelworkers working twelve hours per day was slow at best. According to Gulick, next to nothing was accomplished in reducing the twelve-hour day during the progressive era (1924: 32). Although it had been eliminated by 1915, seven-day labor returned as the wartime labor shortage led to the restoration of long hours in the steel industry. Even after the war, the twelve-hour day persisted for many steelworkers in the Pittsburgh district (Hogan, 1971: 457). Hence, throughout the progressive era, the problem of long hours in the steel industry persisted.

When hours reform did occur in the steel industry, it was less than desirable. By 1920, for example, the permanent advance that had been achieved in reducing the seven-day workweek seems to have been made at the cost of putting more workers on the twelve-hour shift (Gulick, 1924: 37). Any gains in reducing the length of the workweek were thus offset by an extension of the twelve-hour workday to a greater number of steelworkers. From 1911 to 1920, Gulick (31, 39–40) claims that the percentage and number of twelve-hour workers were materially larger having risen from 35% to over 39% and from 45,248 to 85,000. The failure of the industry to implement the reforms it publicly supported thus requires an explanation.

The relatively poor progress made in the industry in terms of hours reform suggests that the industry was offering the appearance of reform in response to some form of external pressure. During 1907 and 1908, a group of young scholars directed by Paul Kellogg and funded by the Russell Sage Foundation began the Pittsburgh Survey (Eggert, 1981: 48). Paul Kellogg's studies helped bring an end to the twelve-hour shift, and it was he who was most directly responsible for bringing the issue to the attention of the Harding administration (152–154). Even threats from within the corporation put pressure on Gary to implement hours reform. From 1911 to 1915, a U.S. Steel stockholder from Boston, named Charles Cabot, attacked the twelve-hour day at U.S. Steel during its annual stockholder meetings (81). The threat of an external response to the long hours in the industry thus came from all directions, including muckraking journalists, the federal government, and Steel Corporation stockholders and executives.

Ultimately, governmental pressure proved to be the deciding factor in the industry's decision to eliminate the twelve-hour day.[10] The Steel Corporation was aware from the beginning that the government was a key player that could influence the corporation's labor policy. At the first annual session of the AISI in 1910, Dickson warned the steel manufacturers that the failure to voluntarily eliminate Sunday labor would lead to "radical and ill-advised legislation" (Brody, 1960: 170). Hence, self-regulation was necessary in the realm of capital-labor relations as well. When President Harding began to apply pressure on the industry in 1922 to abolish the twelve-hour day, a committee of steel officials reported that the abolition of the twelve-hour day would require 60,000 additional employees in addition to raising costs (Gulick, 1924: 44). The increased labor supply, however, more than compensated for the expected shortage the industry feared (1924: 50). Gary was thus proven wrong in his assertion that the additional workers required would be difficult to find. The cost of eliminating the twelve-hour workday at U.S. Steel also proved itself to be about a third of Gary's inflated estimate that it would increase production costs 15% (Cutcliffe, 1994: 153). As the last section suggested, however, the industry's reliance on the twelve-hour day to limit the number of employees may have served as an instrument for stabilizing employment during the progressive era and may imply a reason why the industry clung to the twelve-hour day until its abolition in 1923.

The above discussion of the positive measures of U.S. Steel's labor policy concentrated on the welfare program and hours reform. It is natural to consider why the welfare program was implemented with greater success than hours reform. Even though the cost of eliminating the twelve-hour day turned out to be lower than expected, its cost relative to the cost of the welfare program may shed light on the question raised. Eggert (1981: 94–95), for example, estimates that the added labor cost of eliminating the twelve-hour day at U.S. Steel would have reached $18.6 million whereas the total cost of its welfare program was only about $5 million. It should come as no surprise then that welfare policies remained the foundation of the industry's treatment of labor during the 1920s (Brody, 1960: 268). Hours reform was popular with the American public but too expensive for the Steel Corporation to pursue until it was forced to change.

The negative measures of the United States Steel Corporation involve primarily anti-union tactics. They are negative because they do not appeal to the public and thus are conducted without fanfare. Gulick provides a long list of methods U.S. Steel used to maintain a non-union organization, including the closing of mills after signing a scale for them, the use of convict labor, the use of labor spies, the use of strikebreakers, and the discharge and blacklisting of union men. Other alleged methods include the use of foreign over native labor, control of the press, control of public officials, and welfare programs (Gulick, 1924: 111). The inclusion of welfare programs in this list of negative measures is consistent with its above description as a positive measure because this negative motivation was never publicized. Gulick explains, "[W]ithout doubt any part of the [welfare] plan or all of it [could] be used in checking unions, if only by removing sources of dissatisfaction" (186–187). This policy is unacceptable, however, because in other important ways the corporation did not meet the legitimate expectations of its employees (187). Hence, the positive measure possessed a negative effect on the steelworkers in addition to the positive effects that followed.

Two other negative measures that the Steel Corporation and the industry in general have used to prevent the formation of unions may also be mentioned briefly for completeness. In chapter 3, the location of raw materials and markets for steel were identified as important determinants of the geographic location of steel plants. In addition to these factors, large corporations may have chosen plant location as part of a divide-and-conquer calculus with respect to labor. According to Gordon, Edwards, and Reich (1982: 138), the construction of towns like Gary, Indiana was part of a broader decentralization movement through which employers hoped to maintain labor stability by moving factories out of central-city factory districts and into "industrial satellite suburbs." Hence, the location of company towns may have been as important for defending the overall regulatory program of the Steel Corporation as the domination of the social and private lives of the steelworkers within the mill towns.

A final negative measure is the Steel Corporation's open shop doctrine that it rigidly maintained throughout the latter half of the progressive era in all of its mills. Judge Gary's official position for U.S. Steel during the progressive era was that it does not combat labor unions; it simply refuses to deal with them (Gulick, 1924: 94). Gary was fond of reminding labor leaders that the Steel Corporation is happy to deal with any individual employee on any matter of importance to him. In fact, U.S. Steel officials claimed that the policy served to protect individual freedom by permitting individual workmen to work under any conditions they might choose. The open shop policy of the Steel Corporation was thus rationalized in terms of the outmoded ideology of individualism throughout the progressive era. Given the Steel Corporation's near obsession with the social responsibility of big business, its illogical ideological position serves as the capstone of the contradictory progressive era institutional structure.

4.4   THE REVIVAL OF UNIONISM: A NEGATIVE RESPONSE TO THE CAPITALIST PROGRAM OF REGULATION

The last two sections have discussed in detail the contradictory regulatory program that the United States Steel Corporation strove to enforce throughout the progressive era. The collapse of the détente system established by Gary and Roosevelt as discussed in chapter 3 and the growing pressure from the American public for labor reform rendered uncertain the future of the capitalist program of regulation. This section explores the key role that organized labor played in challenging the regulatory program of Big Steel. It was this power bloc that suffered the most during the progressive era in terms of an unequal distribution of the benefits of regulation. The industrial structure created during the progressive era carried consequences for the steelworkers that ultimately led to one of the greatest uprisings in the history of the American labor movement.

In the aftermath of the 1901 strike against U.S. Steel, organized labor in the steel industry was left in a state of utter ruin. In 1903, the last great steel plant became non-union in Mingo Junction, Ohio (Brody, 1960: 58). One strike of significance did occur in 1904 when the Carnegie Company was merged with the American Steel Hoop Company. The temporary restoration of unionism in the Carnegie mills ended, however, with the defeat of the Amalgamated Association when it struck against the company for an unacceptable wage scale in the hoop mills (Gulick, 1924: 102). In general, the Amalgamated was gradually weakened from 1902 to 1908 as the Steel

Corporation would only grant agreements for mills that were later dismantled or kept out of use (Hoagland, 1917: 677). With the Roosevelt administration firmly behind the Steel Corporation, organized labor appeared to
have no future in the steel industry.

In other sectors of the iron and steel industry, organized labor retained
a certain degree of bargaining power with respect to employers. In the
iron industry, for example, labor was far better organized than in the steel
industry where unified capital had faced a fragmented labor force since
1901. Until 1906, the Amalgamated Association continued to make yearly
agreements with the Republic Iron and Steel Company. After 1906, the
union continued to make its agreements with the Western Bar Iron Association, which represented the twelve independent iron companies then con-
trolling the industry's output of iron (Hoagland, 1917: 678). In addition to
the better organization of labor in the iron industry, there was a notable
"absence of concentration of capital" in that industry as well (682). Conditions in the sheet and tinplate industry were even more favorable to labor
in that no definite association of manufacturers existed for the purpose of
dealing collectively with labor (687). Hence, the iron and sheet and tinplate
industries had the potential for a more equal distribution of the benefits of
regulation than was the case in the steel industry.

Real economic consequences flowed from the fact that labor possessed
more bargaining power in the iron and sheet and tinplate industries. For
example, the wrought iron mills remained on ten-hour shifts during the
progressive era while the sheet and tinplate mills stayed on eight-hour
shifts (Brody, 1960: 36). The limits to homogenization and the absence
of capitalist concentration in those industries kept labor relatively strong
and prevented the deterioration of labor conditions. Even in the iron industry, however, the exclusionary principles of the Amalgamated Association
prevented the union from organizing the 65% of workmen not covered
by agreements and were thus "a great aid to employers in keeping down
the radical element in the industry" (Hoagland, 1917: 682). Hence, while
more gains for labor were won in the iron and sheet and tinplate industries
early in the progressive era, the influence of organized labor remained
greatly limited.

It became startlingly clear to labor leaders in 1909 that soon organized
labor in the sheet and tinplate industry would lose the ground it had been
fortunate enough to retain during the first decade of the Steel Corporation's existence. Changing conditions in the industry led to a strike that
year that served as a wakeup call to organized labor in the United States.
According to Kevin Dwyer (1994b: 402), the primary cause of the 1909
steel strike was the introduction of new technology in the manufacture of
sheet steel and tin plate, which decreased the need for skilled labor. This
increase in the relative bargaining power of capital led to an announcement
by U.S. Steel on June 1, 1909 that it would be implementing an open shop
policy later that month at twelve plants of the American Sheet and Tin

Plate Company. The policy meant that U.S. Steel would no longer recognize or bargain with any organization that claimed to represent its workmen. The announcement was supported by company rhetoric that proclaimed a worker's right to personal liberty (1994b: 402). Steel officials treated the open shop principle as a means of protecting the right of men to work under their chosen conditions, and thus they transformed themselves from oppressors into protectors of liberty (Brody, 1960: 176). The contradictory ideology of the Steel Corporation is strongly apparent here. Workers are denied personal liberty if they are compelled to act collectively while steel companies have a social responsibility to act collectively to maintain stable prices and wages. The ideology of social responsibility is a convenience that U.S. Steel used selectively to rationalize its program of regulation in the spheres of circulation and production.

Coincident with U.S. Steel's open shop announcement was a strike in McKees Rocks, Pennsylvania in June 1909. The strike was an unorganized protest against a new form of wage payment at a U.S. Steel subsidiary called the Pressed Steel Car Company. The strike marked the IWW's first entrance into the steel industry and was won despite the efforts of the state police (Thompson, 1976: 42–43). Other IWW victories were won at Inland Steel and Republic Steel in East Chicago and at Standard Steel Car in East Hammond (44). It is of interest that the McKees Rocks strike and the open shop announcement occurred in the same month. Unlike the exclusive Amalgamated Association, the IWW was eager to organize the unskilled immigrant workers who played a key part in the McKees Rocks victory. This radical threat to passive unionism in the steel industry at the very least encouraged U.S. Steel to continue with its plan to enforce an open shop policy.

The 1909 steel strike against U.S. Steel marked the lowest point for organized labor in the iron and steel industry during the progressive era. The strike, having lasted fourteen long months, "was a complete failure and marked the elimination of unions from the mills of the United States Steel Corporation" (Gulick, 1924: 103). After the 1909 strike against U.S. Steel, "every trace of unionism was wiped out of the mills not only of the United States Steel Corporation, but of the big independent companies as well" (Foster, 1969: 13). To make matters worse, the company had also cut wages by an average of 3.5% to 4% (1924: 102). The outcome of the strike was the most visible sign that the Steel Corporation now possessed nearly complete control over the conditions of employment and no longer needed to even acknowledge the fact that its workmen formed a collective body with common interests.

The open shop announcement of 1909 directed the full attention of American labor leaders to the rotten conditions in the steel industry and thus breathed new life into efforts to organize the steelworkers. The 1909 strike against U.S. Steel demonstrated clearly to all that the Amalgamated Association was incapable of conducting an effective organizing campaign. The AFL thus emerged as the primary organizer of steelworkers (Dwyer, 1994b: 403). AFL support had been less than desired in the past. Although the AFL had pledged its support at the beginning of the general strike in August 1901, it failed to materialize to any great extent, and the Amalgamated Association eventually lost fourteen mills which were unionized prior to the strike (Hogan, 1971: 443). The shocking reality of the steel situation in 1909 gave the AFL a new opportunity to revive unionism in the industry.

Historian David Brody has noted that the completeness of the steel masters' achievement of ending organized labor in the industry "set in motion countervailing forces in the American labor movement" and marked "the turning point away from narrow craft unionism" towards industrial unionism (Brody, 1960: 125). In December 1909, 46 union leaders met in Pittsburgh and issued a "Plan of Action and Appeal" for "the complete organization of every wage earner in the iron, steel, and tinplate industry" (1960: 133). The Amalgamated Association also eliminated skill as a membership requirement in 1910 (Brody, 1965: 31). By 1912, the AFL had announced an organizing campaign in the steel industry but by the summer of 1913 the drive had stalled, and the Amalgamated was quietly avoiding the recruitment of the unskilled workmen (1960: 141, 144–145). Although American labor leaders had become highly conscious of the special problems facing labor in the steel industry, the outbreak of war in Europe was the catalyst that organized labor needed to initiate a major organizing drive in the steel industry.

The influence of World War I on organizing efforts in the iron and steel industry was considerable. Although the Amalgamated Association remained limited to puddling, sheet and tinplate mills, it increased its membership from 6,880 in 1913 to 19,002 by 1917 (Hogan, 1971: 456). The reason for the rise in union membership can be attributed to the high demand for steel, the conscription of steelworkers for military duty, and the interrupted flow of foreign labor into the United States. These factors worked together to create an excess demand for labor in the steel industry. The labor shortage that World War I created thus immediately improved the opportunities for union organization (Brody, 1960: 199). World War I thus gave a boost to the industry's weak union.

In addition to the growing power of organized labor during WWI, the federal government began to side with labor because it hoped to avoid interruptions in war production that might arise from labor-management disputes. That the government was a powerful wartime ally to organized labor is suggested by President Wilson's address to the AFL convention in Buffalo in 1917 (Brody, 1960: 202–203). The government's commitment to labor was tested during the war in the steel industry when two significant disputes between capital and labor took place and led to a conflict between Big Steel and the federal government. One dispute was between U.S. Steel and the War Labor Policies Board (WLPB) over the eight-hour day. In

August 1918, Gary convened a meeting of approximately 150 steel manufacturers at the Waldorf-Astoria in New York City to organize a collective
response to the government's attempt to challenge the industry's open shop
principle and general labor conditions (Urofsky, 1969: 273–274). By October 1, 1918, however, U.S. Steel and many independent steel companies had
implemented the basic eight-hour day.[11] The measure was implemented as
a result of government pressure (Eggert, 1981: 92). Specifically, U.S. Steel
agreed to adopt the basic eight-hour day at the insistence of the WLPB.[12]

The other labor-management dispute during the war was between Bethlehem Steel and the National War Labor Board (NWLB) over the issue of
collective bargaining. Although Bethlehem Steel finally agreed to negotiate
with labor representatives during the war, the "ultimate outcome of both
struggles clearly illuminated the limits of the Government's commitment,
and the depths of the industry's power" (Urofsky, 1969: 264). After the
war, the steel companies refused to abide by the decisions of the wartime
boards, which had then lost most authority to act. President Eugene Grace
of Bethlehem Steel, for example, said the company was no longer obligated
to abide by the NWLB's decision (Brody, 1965: 76). According to Eggert
(1981: 128), the end of World War I "removed the government's excuse for
'meddling' in employer-employee relations" and thus led to the dissolution
of the wartime labor boards and the end of the wartime pledges against
strikes and lockouts. The end of the war thus resulted in the government
leaving the side of labor, and the unions had to confront a united, unrestricted capitalist class rendering a conflict inevitable (Brody, 1960: 230).
The end of WWI left the steelworkers alone yet united in their frustration with the capitalist regulatory program that had been gradually implemented over the last three decades.

On August 1, 1918, the officers of fifteen international unions met in
Chicago and formed the National Committee for Organizing the Iron and
Steel Workers. The end of the war did not bring an end to the demands of
the steelworkers, which included union recognition and shorter working
hours, among others. After more than a year of organizing the industry,
the great steel strike of 1919 began on September 22, 1919. By September
30, the total number of steelworkers on strike had reached 365,600 (Foster,
1969: 100). Whereas the 1892 Homestead strike and the 1901 strike against
U.S. Steel were two battles for regulatory control of the steel industry, the
steel strike of 1919 was organized labor's battle against the entrenched
regulatory program of the United States Steel Corporation.

The strike of 1919 was a battle between unified capital and unified labor
on a scale that the steel industry had never before experienced. The extent
to which capital was united in its effort to defeat labor was surely part of
the reason for labor's ultimate defeat in the struggle. In his book on the
1919 steel strike, for example, William Foster uses the term "Steel Trust"
to refer to the collectivity of the great steel companies rather than simply
the U.S. Steel Corporation alone. He does so specifically to emphasize the

extent to which capital was organized in the industry. According to Foster, the steel companies are "organized more or less secretly into a trust" (Foster, 1969: 2). The power that the Steel Corporation wielded over the other steel companies helps explain how this unity came to be. Many companies would have preferred to settle with the unions or close their plants altogether rather than operate with the unproductive strikebreakers, but they operated anyway because they were afraid to disobey Gary's order to operate (175–176). Success in the strike would depend heavily on the ability of either side to maintain unity as the struggle continued.

Beyond the extent of organization, the reasons for the failure of organized labor in the strike are many and varied. According to Gordon, Edwards, and Reich, the steel industry was unique in the degree to which corporate policies were effective in defeating worker opposition to homogenization (1982: 159). Although the frustration of the steelworkers erupted in the industrial strike of 1919, the failure of the strike can be partly attributed to the specific labor policies of the Steel Corporation. For example, during the 1919 steel strike, the steel companies "recruited more than 30,000 black strikebreakers and brought them into the mills under armed escort" (Barrett, 1994: 405). The effect of this action was that it helped keep the mills running while it demoralized the striking steelworkers. As in the 1892 Homestead strike when Frick hired 300 Pinkerton detectives to take back the steel plant, the steel companies also enlisted the help of detective agencies such as the Sherman Service and the Corporations Auxiliary Company during the 1919 strike. The tactics of the Steel Corporation were thus partly responsible for the eventual loss of the strike.

The changing role of the federal government was a critical factor as well during the strike as it had been throughout the progressive era and during World War I. Initially, the Wilson administration supported the National Committee's good faith effort to negotiate with the Steel Corporation. At the request of the National Committee, President Wilson tried to arrange a conference with Gary from August to September of 1919, but the Judge was unwilling to budge at all on the issue of the open shop. Wilson asked Gompers to postpone the strike until the October 6th Industrial Conference in Washington, D.C., but the workmen could not be prevented from striking even if the order had been given. The National Committee thus voted unanimously to continue with the strike set for September 22.

Wilson's support for labor was not always so clear, however, even in the months prior to the strike. For example, the pressure that Wilson put on Gary to agree to a conference with members of the National Committee and his subsequent refusal were conducted privately whereas the request he made to the National Committee to postpone the strike and its refusal were announced publicly (Brody, 1965: 105–106). The poor chance that the President's Industrial Conference would resolve the dispute was also evident in the structure of the conference. The Industrial Conference was organized according to the tripartite principle of representation in organizational bodies established with the National Civic Federation nearly two decades earlier. The participants at the conference were thus organized into three groups representing the Public, Labor, and the Employers. Gary was a member of the Public Group and had been selected by Wilson (116–117). The problems with this approach to resolving the crisis are obvious, especially given that the groups needed to reach a consensus to pass any resolution, and Gary was fully committed to the principle of the open shop.

The lack of government support for organized labor during the 1919 steel strike was no more evident than in its use of military force. The request for military intervention was not a new method for the companies in the iron and steel trade. During the 1892 Homestead strike, the Pennsylvania national guard was ordered to protect the strikebreakers as they entered the plant. During the 1913–1914 coal strike at the Colorado Iron and Fuel Company, government investigators uncovered that John D. Rockefeller, Jr. had coerced the governor of Colorado into rescinding his initial decree to the militia not to aid the strikebreakers. When the order was finally given, the terrible Ludlow massacre was the result (Weinstein, 1968: 196). The situation was no different during the 1919 steel strike. The mounted police of the Pennsylvania State Constabulary harassed the steelworkers on strike in western Pennsylvania. Major civil liberties violations occurred in Pennsylvania steel towns during the strike as steelworkers were denied their rights to free speech and free assembly (Murray, 1951: 457). Civil rights violations were also appalling in the Chicago steel district. Federal troops, under the leadership of General Leonard Wood, entered Gary, Indiana on October 6, 1919 at the request of the governor of Indiana and proceeded to raid the homes of suspected radicals. Neither side ever demonstrated that a connection existed between the Gary radicals and the strike movement (1951: 459). The federal government had thus completely refused to provide the support for labor it deemed so necessary and just during World War I.

The changing role of the American public was no less important to labor's loss in the strike. Like the federal government, the public had shifted its support away from labor during the strike. It had initially been sympathetic to the strikers' demands for better working conditions (Murray, 1951: 453). Robert Murray has documented the manner in which major American newspapers encouraged the paranoid delusions of the American public that the strike was part of a Bolshevik revolution to overthrow American capitalists and undermine U.S. institutions. The *New York Times*, the *Washington Post*, and the *Wall Street Journal* all contributed to the charges of radicalism in the organizing effort in the steel industry (1951: 451–452). When public support for the strikers failed, the steel companies were given complete freedom to refuse any effort to reach a cooperative conclusion to the strike (Brody, 1960: 249). Although organized labor received some public support, it was mostly alone during the strike of 1919.

The unified nature of capital in the steel industry, the loss of public support, the disadvantages associated with the presence of the military, and the absence of presidential support all contributed to labor's failure in the steel strike of 1919. The final responsibility for the loss of an industrial strike must ultimately rest with the unions themselves because generally speaking no other power bloc can be counted on for support in a capitalist society. It is, therefore, necessary to look within the strike movement for a reason for labor's loss of the strike.

The National Committee had difficulties from the outset because it needed to rely on twenty-four distinct national unions to work together for the common interest even when it conflicted with their individual interests. This structural problem led to a lack of financial and organizational support throughout the strike. More importantly, the Amalgamated Association demonstrated its inability to participate fully in industrial unionism during the 1919 steel strike. While the national movement was quickly developing during the spring of 1919, the Amalgamated Association made a bid for separate consideration by the steel companies (Foster, 1969: 69). Gary, of course, refused to bargain with any labor organization whatsoever. The Amalgamated Association also approached the Bethlehem Steel Corporation at Sparrows' Point with an offer to settle the strike that was again separate from the general movement less than two months into the strike (250). It also was refused.

The problems for which the Amalgamated Association was responsible, however, went much further during the strike than attempted secret agreements with the steel companies. A clause in the Amalgamated agreements with the steel companies indicated that workmen who became members of the union during the scale year must work until the expiration of the contract even if management and labor could not arrive at an agreement in the meantime on the scale of wages covering the new members (Foster, 1969: 173–174). Because the union's first responsibility was to the skilled workers working in contract mills, it ordered the unskilled workers, who had recently become Amalgamated members, back to the mills. The Amalgamated Association ordered its members in its contract mills to return to work in November 1919. This action greatly weakened the strike effort. Foster is very critical of the Amalgamated Association because it also immediately withdrew from the National Committee after the great strike ended on January 8, 1920 and abandoned all efforts to organize the big steel mills (249). The behavior of the Amalgamated during the strike is a perfect example of the problems that arise when craft union principles are adhered to in an industrial strike.

The problems that the Amalgamated Association created in 1919 also demonstrate how the unions failed to maintain unity among the workmen while capital remained unified. The steel companies had been aware of the manner in which the Amalgamated policies served their interests. In fact, many employers freely admitted that they preferred to bargain with the conservative Amalgamated Association as a sort of insurance against a more democratic union (Hoagland, 1917: 685). Two insurgent movements developed within the Amalgamated Association in 1912 and 1913 in an effort to transform the union into a more democratic, industrial union, but both failed (1917: 683–684). The Amalgamated's "feeble existence was [thus] insurance against the organization of a stronger rival" (Wolff, 1965: 231). The unification of capital in the steel industry extended beyond the formation of U.S. Steel in 1901, and it was this unity that the steelworkers could not break in 1919.

The collective power of the steelworkers as it was realized in the McKees Rocks rebellion of 1909 can be attributed to the openness of the IWW to organizing all steelworkers regardless of race or ethnicity. Unfortunately, the IWW did not have a strong presence in the steel industry in 1919 in part because a leader of the organizing drive, William Foster, favored a policy of "boring from within" the AFL rather than the dual unionism the IWW favored (Thompson, 1976: 51). It was after a return from Europe that Foster concluded that the IWW's belief in dual unionism was misguided (Renshaw, 1967: 166). Shortly after the 1919 strike, Foster considered the approach of the IWW to be "idealistic," a waste of time, and a hindrance to the trade union movement (1969: 256, 261). What the IWW might have brought to the organizing effort in the steel industry in 1919 must be left to the imagination.

Once the 1919 strike had ended in failure for the steelworkers, the industry returned to its usual state of capital-labor relations. According to Brody (1960: 278), "Organized labor posed no threat in the postwar decade." The future of the steelworkers was not without hope, however, as they had set in motion events during the 1919 strike that eventually led to the elimination of the twelve-hour workday. That is, after the Industrial Conference failed to resolve the capital-labor dispute in the steel industry, the National Committee turned to an organization that represented the Protestant Church in secular affairs, called the Interchurch World Movement, to negotiate an end to the strike. Gary's refusal to recognize the organization did not eliminate its involvement in the industry's problems. The organization published a report in 1920 on the conditions leading to the steel strike and drew the public's attention to the twelve-hour issue. The report was a significant factor that ultimately led to the abolition of the twelve-hour day in 1923. Brody's interpretation of the steel strike of 1919 as a crisis for organized labor may thus be contrasted with William Foster's emphasis on the moral victory of the workers (1969: 4). The struggle of the steelworkers in 1919 gave them the motivation to strive for their right to bargain collectively with employers, which was finally obtained in the late 1930s.

This chapter began with a discussion of how the Amalgamated Association attempted to impose its regulatory program in the iron and steel industry during the late nineteenth century. In an effort to overcome the late nineteenth century economic crisis, the steel companies rapidly transformed the production process and steel workforce during the 1890s. The full imple-mentation of its solution for the industry, however, required that it break the power of the skilled steelworkers, which it did with two major battles for regulatory control of the steel industry in 1892 and 1901.

Once the Amalgamated Association was defeated, the United States Steel Corporation moved forward with a product price and wage rate sta-bilization program that formed the first part of its regulatory program. The output and employment fluctuations that flowed from the price and wage policies of the Steel Corporation imply that steelworkers during the progressive era suffered from a lack of job security. The further homog-enization of the workforce also allowed the Steel Corporation to wrestle control of the production process away from the steelworkers. It thus formed an addition to the Steel Corporation's regulatory program inso-far as it allowed the corporation to regulate its competition with the steelworkers for control of the production process. The negative con-sequences of the Steel Corporation's regulation of production included high accident and death rates, long working hours, and an unequal dis-tribution of the benefits of productivity growth.

In an effort to defend the market stabilization policies and homogeni-zation drive against the potential threats of organized labor, the federal government, and the American public, the steel companies introduced a number of positive and negative measures. The paternalistic, positive mea-sures included a stock subscription plan, a bonus plan, a pension plan, a safety plan, a housing plan, company unions, and hours reform. Because hours reform was more expensive than the welfare program, the former was carried out with less enthusiasm and success during the progressive era. The negative defensive measures included a host of anti-union tactics and the open shop policy. Although these defensive measures represented more immediate gains for labor, they fell far short of the gains the steel-workers demanded and deserved.

The steelworkers' dissatisfaction with the Steel Corporation's regulatory program led to a revival of unionism in the steel industry. The turning point occurred with U.S. Steel's open shop announcement and the McKees Rocks strike in 1909. From then forward, the AFL began an organizing drive that gained its greatest impetus with the labor shortage that occurred after the onset of World War I. The federal government's abandonment of organized labor after the war left the steelworkers alone when it finally rose to challenge the entrenched regulatory program of the United States Steel Corporation in 1919. The powerful resistance of the steel companies and the federal government, the antiradical hysteria of the postwar period, and problems within the strike movement itself resulted in the defeat of the steelworkers and the victory of the steel companies. The Steel Cor-poration's regulatory program continued without interruption throughout the 1920s, but finally came to an end when the steelworkers were granted union recognition in the 1930s.

5   Analytical Results of the Case Study

The modified SSA framework developed in chapter 1 provided an analytical framework that is capable of identifying the key developments in the iron and steel industry during the progressive era within a broad historical and institutional context. Chapter 2 described in detail how this historical and institutional context might be understood as a regulationist institutional structure that was formed as a reaction against the free market excesses of the late nineteenth century. With the basic institutional structure of the progressive era firmly established, chapters 3 and 4 then investigated at length the main institutional features of the American iron and steel industry during the progressive era and the enhanced capitalist performance to which they gave rise. This chapter presents the main results of the case study. It proceeds by considering a number of observations about the steel industry during the progressive era that appear to be at variance with the primary characteristics of a RIS. Although we should not modify our understanding of a historically specific institutional structure on the basis of one industrial case study, our theoretical framework should provide a coherent analysis of the developments in each industry. In addition to the main results of the study that pertain to the relationship between regulation in the iron and steel industry and the Progressive Era RIS, a number of minor results are discussed.

   A number of the results of the case study appear to be inconsistent with what we generally expect from regulationist institutional structures. The main inconsistency is that capital appears to have dominated labor in the iron and steel industry during the progressive era to a much greater extent than one might expect within a RIS. The Amalgamated Association was virtually driven from the industry, eliminating the opportunity for the steelworkers to have a direct role in creating the regulatory structure of the industry. In addition, many of the complaints of the steelworkers were never adequately addressed during the progressive era, including long hours and productivity growth that far outstripped real wage growth. Similarly, the federal government appears to have left the steel industry alone for the most part, especially during the Roosevelt years. The détente system thus appears to be somewhat inconsistent with the acknowledged role for government intervention to aid in restraining free market excesses that is generally anticipated in a RIS. The challenge of this case study has been to understand how these conditions prevailed within the context of an institutional structure that represents a negative reaction against the free market.

The puzzling presence of capital's domination of labor in a RIS has been repeatedly recognized in earlier chapters. Specifically, one might be tempted to argue that a key theoretical distinction between a LIS and a RIS should be that labor has the power to significantly influence the conditions of labor in a particular RIS. The relative strength of the Amalgamated Association in the late nineteenth century LIS and its relative weakness in the progressive era RIS suggest the opposite conclusion about capital-labor relations in the two structural forms. Other aspects of labor conditions in the industry during the two institutional structures, including working hours, regularity of employment, and working conditions, raise the same theoretical difficulties. That is, the steelworkers had no direct influence over labor conditions in their industry during the progressive era, and they experienced a number of negative consequences that arose from the capitalist control of those conditions. Therefore, organized labor was not a significant *source* of regulation in the steel industry during the progressive era and many of the economic *consequences* of the regulation that did exist appear to have been negative for the steelworkers.

The steel companies' domination of the steelworkers within a RIS thus raises two potential problems for our modified SSA framework. The highly regulated characteristics of the Progressive Era RIS were especially evident in the steel industry where the excesses of free market capitalism contributed to the industrial crisis conditions of the late nineteenth century, which culminated in the doubled-phased consolidation movement. Yet our modified framework suggests that labor should have played a significant role in creating the regulatory structure of the steel industry and that it should have, in turn, served to mitigate the worst consequences of free markets, which include deteriorating labor conditions and labor-management relations. The puzzle has the potential to undermine our ability to understand the steel industry's development using the modified SSA framework.

The primary result of the case study is that the United States Steel Corporation exerted its economic power through the complete and direct control of the regulatory machinery it created to govern the steel industry during the progressive era. The regulatory program it implemented to stabilize product and labor markets was intended to create a more stable industry for profitable investment. Its reorganization of the production process also allowed it to transfer control of the production process from the steelworkers to foremen and managers, thus further undermining the potential influence of the skilled workmen on the regulatory structure. It was thus the Steel Corporation that determined the nature of the reaction against the free market conditions that had prevailed in the steel industry for many years. At first glance, this key result appears to contradict the hypothesis that labor played a significant role in creating the regulatory structure of the steel industry, thus undermining the application of the modified SSA framework to that industry. Instead, capital appears to have had its own reasons for creating a regulatory structure, which included stable markets and a fragmented workforce. Specifically, the conflict between capital and labor in the steel industry that intensified towards the end of the nineteenth century could not end with capital victorious so long as highly competitive conditions persisted in the industry. The power of the skilled steelworkers needed to be broken through the large-scale mechanization of industry that was most successfully undertaken by large combinations of capital achieved through mergers. As a result, the largest steel companies strove to create a new industrial structure that eliminated the free market instability of the late nineteenth century and gave capital the advantage in capital-labor disputes.

This solution to the paradox is actually foreshadowed in chapter 1 where the possibility is raised that two forms of regulationist institutional structure might exist. On the one hand, a regulationist structure may be the outcome of a prolonged class struggle that leads to a significant role for organized labor in the shaping of the institutional structure. Alternatively, capital may dominate and suppress organized labor, imposing its own regulatory solution to the problems of unrestricted markets. According to David Harvey, the final chapter of any case study should be about how the case study has advanced the theory and with what general effects (2006: 87). In this particular instance, our case study has suggested the solution to this particular paradox. Furthermore, when the regulatory program that has been imposed for the benefit of capital begins to threaten the welfare of the working class, the deepening of that regulatory apparatus can actually engender a harsh reaction against it as occurred in the steel industry in 1919.

The most direct way in which the regulated industrial structure served the ends of the steel companies in their effort to repress the steelworkers is through the general unification of capital in the industry that it implied. In addition to the formation of U.S. Steel, the capitalist regulatory program that governed the industry encouraged the steel companies to unite in capital-labor disputes. It has been noted for example, how information sharing at AISI meetings encouraged the convergence of labor policies. The fact that the iron and sheet and tinplate companies were less successful in uniting against labor demonstrates how important the regulatory control of the steel industry was for the steel companies in capital-labor disputes. Therefore, the severe capitalist repression of labor within the context of the progressive era regulationist institutional structure seems to have eliminated any role for labor in creating the regulatory structure that governed the industry.

The fact that the steelworkers lacked the power to shape the conditions they faced in the industry within the Progressive Era RIS makes it clear why they suffered so many negative consequences as a result of the Steel Corporation's regulatory program. An equitable distribution of the benefits of regulation are not implied or guaranteed in any regulationist institutional structure. In the steel industry, this inequity was especially prevalent during the progressive era given that steelworkers' wages did not reflect the period's rising productivity. Furthermore, once the capitalist regulatory program was firmly in place in the steel industry, the negative reaction of the steelworkers, the federal government, and American public opinion to the industry's conditions ceased to be a reaction against the excesses of the free market. Instead, it was a negative reaction to the manner in which the Steel Corporation controlled those excesses through its regulatory program.

Polanyi's double movement thus acquires a new character on the basis of this case study analysis. The abstraction we know as the free market is not the only disastrous extreme the capitalist control of society may encounter in the course of the double movement. The capitalist class may actually be the dominant player in society's reaction against the free market. In that case, responsibility for the suffering of the lower classes of society becomes easier to identify because it is the direct result of the conscious control that capitalists wield over markets and the conditions of production. In the same way capitalists and bourgeois economists blame the economic crisis of a LIS on society's refusal to permit the unrestricted operation of free markets, they may also defend the economic crisis of a RIS in terms of society's refusal to permit capital's unrestricted regulation of free markets.

The capitalist regulatory program of the United States Steel Corporation should be understood in these terms. The great steel strike of 1919 was not a reaction on the part of organized labor to the excesses of free markets for steel and labor power but to the excesses of the capitalist program of regulation in the steel industry. The program of price and wage rate stabilization led to irregular employment and long working hours. The mechanization of production and the homogenization of the workforce led to deteriorating working conditions. The refusal to bargain collectively with employees represents the steel companies' refusal to allow the steelworkers to join in the regulatory effort. As a result, they avoided passing on the gains of productivity growth to the steelworkers in the form of higher wages.

The above analysis has emphasized the steel companies' domination of the progressive era regulatory structure and organized labor's exclusion from its development and benefits. Labor may have found other routes for influencing the regulatory program of the Steel Corporation, however, if only in an attenuated and less direct manner. The struggle between capital and labor in any institutional structure always involves a combination of repression and cooptation. The analysis above has concentrated exclusively on the aspect of repression, but cooptation was also an important part of the capital-labor relation in the steel industry during the progressive era.

Because the federal government, the American public, and organized labor would, and ultimately did, react negatively to the capitalist control of production and circulation, the Steel Corporation implemented a variety of positive defensive measures. Many of these measures were arguably implemented in response to the *potential* strength of the steelworkers. For example, the Steel Corporation's safety program helped pacify the steelworkers after the mechanization of production had caused conditions in the steel mills to deteriorate. The mechanization drive had also created a large class of semi-skilled steelworkers. The enhanced class-consciousness that generally accompanies the homogenization of the workforce may have served as a major source of the steelworkers' power to indirectly influence the capitalist program of regulation in the steel industry. Given the strength of the radical movement during the progressive era, steel executives may also have implemented their defensive measures to discourage radical organizers from entering their industry as occurred at McKees Rocks in 1909.

The paternalistic welfare program and limited hours reform were relatively cheap methods of satisfying the federal government and the American public during the progressive era as well, but their failure to transfer a sufficient share of the benefits of regulation to the steelworkers ultimately led to a more serious negative reaction on the part of organized labor and radical organizations. The negative reaction was not carried out with the intention of restoring free market conditions in the iron and steel industry but rather to give labor the opportunity to participate in the shaping of the industrial regulatory program and thus to obtain a significant share of its social benefits. Our modified SSA theory may then provide a cogent framework for understanding capital-labor relations in the steel industry during the progressive era so long as the role of labor in the regulatory process is understood broadly to include both direct and indirect influences.

The relative stability of the steel industry within the context of the Progressive Era RIS was achieved because the Steel Corporation found ways to repress and pacify the steel workforce as it implemented its regulatory program for the steel industry. Despite the character of the Progressive Era RIS as a relatively settled institutional structure, the struggle between capital and labor persisted throughout the progressive era. The form of that struggle in the steel industry did not consist primarily of a prolonged battle between unified capital and organized labor. Instead, it expressed itself mainly through the influence of each class on the contested terrains of the federal government and American public opinion. The fact that the influence of labor in the industry manifested itself in this manner has been shown to be consistent with the claim that labor is generally involved in the development of industrial regulation in a RIS even though it may participate in a greatly weakened state with respect to the power of capital.

By recalling the notion of an institutional structure as a temporary stabilization of capitalist contradictions, it is possible to express the historical developments in the industry that were discussed throughout the case study at a very general level of analysis. Through its combination of repression and cooptation, the Steel Corporation managed to stabilize the structure of the steel industry during the progressive era. At the same time, the industrial structure changed as the class struggle manifested itself in the form of inconsistent government intervention in the steel industry and inconsistent public opinion about conditions in the steel industry. Although the Steel Corporation's regulatory program created a temporary stabilization of class forces during the progressive era, it was an uneasy equilibrium as the federal government and public opinion forced the Steel Corporation to strike a delicate balance between repression and cooptation.

If each institutional structure represents the temporary stabilization of the central contradictions of capitalism, then disruptions of this temporary equilibrium are responsible for the changes within each institutional structure and the transitions between institutional structures. In the background of the entire case study analysis has been the changing contradictory relationship of capital and labor and the relationship of each to the federal government and public opinion. The power of each class to shape public policy and public opinion was influential in shaping the development and performance of the iron and steel industry during the late nineteenth and early twentieth centuries. By tracing the historical movement of these relationships, the case study reveals how changes in these relationships disrupted the temporary equilibrium we know as the Progressive Era RIS without undermining its general stability.

Movements in the *relative* strength of capital and labor in the iron and steel industry with respect to the contested terrains of government and public opinion during the late nineteenth and early twentieth centuries represent the industry's changing structure. In particular, the relative power of capital in the iron and steel industry seems to have risen during the progressive era and declined in the years following that period in response to challenges from organized labor, the federal government, and American public opinion. Public opinion is a rather nebulous category, representing journalists, academicians, and professionals. Its reliability resembled that of the federal government insofar as it gave its allegiance to the steel companies at times and to the steelworkers at other times. Understanding the manifestation of the class struggle through government action and public opinion is necessary if one is to understand how the Steel Corporation was able to rapidly implement its regulatory program early in the progressive era and how its market share and profitability declined in the years following the progressive era. This declining performance of the Steel Corporation is thus consistent with the fact that regulationist institutional structures have a tendency to break up due to profit-squeeze complications arising from the growing power of labor and other social forces.

The period from 1876–1891 coincides closely with the late nineteenth century LIS. During this period, the Amalgamated Association enjoyed a significant amount of control over the production process and the conditions of work. It developed and enforced the sliding wage scale and contract system and enjoyed a measure of cooperation with employers. Over the same period, the intense competition between the iron and steel companies left capital in a relatively weak state. The next period from 1892 to 1901 is the period during which the mechanization drive was most rapid in the industry. It is also the period during which the two great battles took place for regulatory control of the steel industry. The Amalgamated Association was greatly weakened during the 1892 Homestead strike and finally defeated in the 1901 strike against U.S. Steel. At the same time, the federal government and American public did not represent strong forces for change in the industry.

During the progressive years from 1902 to 1914, the Amalgamated Association remained in a weakened state while muckraking journalists began to attack the long hours and poor conditions in the industry. Published during these years were John Fitch's contribution to the Pittsburgh Survey and William Hard's shocking article about the high number of fatalities at U.S. Steel's South Chicago steelworks. Upton Sinclair's novel, *The Jungle*, also addressed labor conditions in the steel industry and Charles Cabot's campaign for hours reform was initiated during the period as well. Hence, public opinion appears to have sided with the steelworkers early in the progressive era.

Also during the progressive era, the federal government became a significant player in the industry. Roosevelt's détente system lasted until 1908 when Taft took office and initiated an antitrust suit against U.S. Steel in part because of the TCI&RR acquisition. The establishment of the rule of reason in the case against Standard Oil in 1911, however, indicates in hindsight that the federal government would ultimately side with the Steel Corporation when the time came. The strong support of the federal government for the steel companies during most of the progressive era and the weakened state of the Amalgamated Association ensured an industrial structure that would permit the steel companies to implement the Steel Corporation's regulatory program without interference. Hence, no real inconsistency exists between the minimal government involvement in the steel industry during the progressive era and the expectation that the government will serve as a regulatory force in a RIS. That is, insofar as the Roosevelt administration created a political climate in which U.S. Steel could carry out its regulatory program, it participated in the capitalist program to restrain the free market during the progressive era. The issue, therefore, is not the presence or absence of government intervention but the role of government in the class struggle. This "class-domination theory" of the state, as Paul Sweezy has termed it (1970: 243), was foreshadowed in chapter 1 when it was pointed out that a laissez-faire government is entirely consistent with the existence of a RIS so long as it furthers capital's regulatory control of industry.

The stalled organizing drive in the steel industry after the 1909 strike against U.S. Steel was revived after the onset of World War I. The 1915–1918 period thus marked a turning point in the industry. The American labor movement took advantage of the wartime labor shortage to begin organizing the steelworkers at a rapid pace. Concerned about the consequences of management-labor disputes in the steel industry, the federal government encouraged the organizing drive by refusing to support the steel companies' open shop policies. The steel companies agreed to implement the basic eight-hour day and set up employee representation plans in an effort to appease the government. Public opinion was also critical of the industry during this time because it suspected the steel companies of pursuing excess profits due to wartime conditions. The passage of the bill providing for a government-owned armor plant and the failure of the steel companies to rouse public support in opposition to the measure demonstrate the strength of public opinion during the war. The federal government and public opinion thus favored the steelworkers during the war due to the enhanced bargaining power of scarce labor power.

By 1919, the balance of power had shifted again with the federal government refusing to demand concessions from capital in labor-management disputes. President Wilson's failure to convince Judge Gary to meet with union officials signaled the end of the government's commitment to the steelworkers. Although the National Committee for Organizing Iron and Steel Workers showed the extent to which the steelworkers had become unified in their fight against capital, the obstacles appeared too great in 1919. Public opinion, which shifted its allegiance during the strike away from the steelworkers and towards the steel companies, may have cast the deciding blow against labor, leading to its loss. The antiradical hysteria of the period definitely contributed to the shift in public opinion and gave the U.S. government the public support it required to justify the antiradical raids it ordered in Gary, Indiana in October 1919. Certainly, the strike movement suffered from its own internal problems as well insofar as the Amalgamated Association demonstrated its inability to abide by the principles of industrial unionism.

This overview of the historical developments in the iron and steel industry demonstrates the importance of the federal government and public opinion in the class struggle and in giving labor the ability to influence the regulatory structure of the progressive era, albeit in a limited sense. The contradictory movements of these social forces reflect the contradictory relationship between capital and labor. Although the Steel Corporation succeeded in stabilizing the industrial structure during the progressive era, the contradictions inherent in its regulatory program shifted the battleground of the class struggle to the public realms of government and public opinion. Although each entity served as an unreliable ally for the steelworkers, the public and governmental opposition to the twelve-hour workday ultimately led to its abolition in 1923.

A number of minor results have also been obtained in the course of this case study. One such result is that regulated characteristics begin to show up during the transition from a liberal institutional structure to a regulationist institutional structure. For example, regulated characteristics showed up in the late nineteenth century LIS in the form of the Amalgamated Association's regulatory program and Carnegie Steel's control of factor markets. Furthermore, because these elements arose within the context of an LIS, they took advantage of the free market environment rather than outright overcame it. The contract system and sliding wage scale were two regulatory innovations that took account of the free market structure by necessity. Similarly, Carnegie Steel's ability to pay for coke at cost was especially advantageous because all of its competitors were forced to continue their participation in a competitive market for coke.

Another result of interest is that efforts to control competition through capitalist combination may lead to new forms of competition that encourage even greater market instability. In the iron and steel industry, the drive to control price competition by means of consolidation led to an unstable situation of interdependence between primary and secondary steel producers. The motivation to expand into new product areas created an even more disastrous form of competition between corporate giants. The formation of U.S. Steel in the second phase of the industry's merger movement was the solution to this new problem. Cutthroat competition in an industry moving towards regulation may thus intensify with consolidation before it begins to slacken.

Another result has to do with the manner in which a regulatory leader in an industry manages to maintain that position throughout the duration of a particular RIS. The Steel Corporation, for example, refused to recognize organized labor as the legitimate representative of its workmen during the progressive era. On the other hand, it had little choice but to recognize the federal government and American public opinion as significant social forces affecting the industry. In response to these threats, the Steel Corporation may have voluntarily pursued a policy of relative decline to prevent government intervention. It thus allowed its market share to decline steadily after 1901. This policy of voluntary decline was the key to the Steel Corporation's survival after the 1907 TCI&RR acquisition and the breakdown of the détente system.

The policy of voluntary decline was also one the Steel Corporation needed to pursue relative to competitors so as to maintain regulatory control of the steel industry even if at the cost of lost market share and short-term profits. The rapid growth of Bethlehem Steel during the progressive era is the best evidence of this trend. Here we encounter an interesting contrast between liberal and regulationist institutional structures. An industrial leader in a LIS appears to be a technology innovator whereas in a RIS, the leader appears to be relatively slow to implement new technology. In the iron and steel industry, this tendency is best illustrated in the contrast between Carnegie Steel's rapid implementation of the open-hearth technology and U.S. Steel's failure to undertake production of the Grey beam. Of course, additional industrial case studies are necessary to establish the general validity of this observation, but the observation raises the troubling question of which institutional structure better promotes economic growth. By itself, this criterion suggests that a LIS promotes more rapid economic growth than a RIS, but it ignores the greater potential for liberal institutional structures to generate under-consumption crises. The fact that technological advance may raise the rate of output growth in a LIS may actually encourage an under-consumption crisis because it is generally not accompanied by a broad increase in purchasing power. It is also necessary to remember that the industrial leader in a RIS (e.g., U.S. Steel) may permit and even encourage the rapid growth of rival firms, which may offset the negative effect that its technological backwardness has on the rate of industrial growth.

A final result that is important to mention is the enhanced industrial performance for the steel companies within the context of the Progressive Era RIS. The regulated characteristics of that institutional structure succeeded in maintaining a high rate of growth of physical pig iron and steel output relative to the LIS of the 1920s in particular. The capitalist regulatory program of that period also led to the rapid growth of capital invested in the iron and steel industry as is expected in a regulationist institutional structure. Although not very stable, the rate of profit of the Steel Corporation was also highest during the progressive era and only began a downward trend late in that period and after the war. The independent steel companies, such as Bethlehem Steel and Midvale Steel, also enjoyed rapid growth and profits during the progressive era and World War I as well. Hence, the enhanced performance of the regulated iron and steel industry provides empirical support for the modified SSA framework, which suggests regulated periods exhibit better performance than free market periods.

Part of the institutional basis for the enhanced profitability of U.S. Steel was the price and wage stabilization program it enforced. Strictly economic factors cannot account for the considerable stabilization of steel prices that was achieved during the progressive era. Rather than price stability arising from free market activity, it was partly achieved as a result of the conscious regulatory control of U.S. Steel and the independent steel companies that followed its lead. The Pittsburgh Plus system was maintained throughout the progressive era because steel executives (e.g., Gary) believed that control of commodity prices would prevent the disruptions associated with the late nineteenth century economic crisis. It would then ensure a stable demand for steel and a high, predictable profit rate for many years. The flaw in this reasoning is that the central contradiction of capitalism (i.e., the capital-labor relation) was not eliminated. U.S. Steel's profit rate thus showed a downward trend during the first two decades of the twentieth century. The average annual rate of profit for the periods 1901–1910 and 1911–1920 were 12.14% and 9.24%, respectively. If the extremely high wartime profits of 1916 and 1917 are excluded, the average annual profit rate for 1911–1920 is only 7.44%. U.S. Steel's profit rate then reached its lowest point in 1921, in part because the steelworkers rose to challenge the dominance of its regulatory program during the 1919 steel strike.

Conclusion

The broad historical framework of social structure of accumulation theory has provided the theoretical tools necessary to understand the way in which the large steel companies acquired and maintained regulatory control of the American iron and steel industry in the early twentieth century. At the same time, it has shown concretely how the capitalist control of industrial regulation may lead to negative consequences for labor within the context of a regulationist institutional structure. The puzzling coexistence of the steel companies' domination of the steelworkers and regulatory measures in the iron and steel industry during the progressive era was resolved as soon as we acknowledged that capital succeeded in capturing the machinery of regulation primarily for its own benefit. When the steel companies did allow the steelworkers to share in the benefits of regulation, it was mainly in response to pressure from the federal government or the American public.

In chapter 1, a sharp contrast was made between the capital-labor relations of the Progressive Era RIS and the Post-World War II RIS. The power of labor in relation to capital was regarded as being considerably greater during the postwar RIS than the Progressive Era RIS. It is, therefore, possible to distinguish between two forms of RIS. One form of regulatory structure may be based on a complex balance of class forces such that organized labor, perhaps with the assistance of the state, can win modest gains for workers in terms of higher wages and better working conditions. In contrast, the regulatory structure may be established, controlled, and manipulated by the capitalist class for its own benefit while harshly repressing elements within the labor movement and other oppositional movements. It would be a theoretical mistake, however, to argue that regulationist institutional structures may always be distinguished sharply on the basis of this criterion. The reason is that it is necessary to remember the historical context when evaluating the character of each feature of an institutional structure. That is, the capital-labor relations of the progressive era were hostile when compared with the capital-labor relations of the postwar era yet they may also be viewed as a step towards the greater relative power of labor in the postwar era. That is, the modest

Conclusion 163

gains won by labor within the Progressive Era RIS were not entirely lost during the LIS of the 1920s.

The difference between the capital-labor relations of the postwar era and the capital-labor relations of the progressive era may then be of a more quantitative than qualitative nature. Consider the inclusion of the American Federation of Labor in the National Civic Federation. Although the AFL was rather conservative during the period, business leaders demonstrated a willingness to cooperate with organized labor on a scale that was unimaginable to them in earlier years. This tolerance for craft unionism was limited insofar as the NCF remained strongly opposed to industrial unionism and radical organizations like the Industrial Workers of the World and the Socialist Party of America. Nevertheless, the incorporation of the AFL into the progressive era power structure represented a considerable advance for the American labor movement.

In the years following the Great Depression, the working class enjoyed new gains as the CIO pushed the American labor movement beyond the conservative craft unionism of the progressive era. Industrial unionism thus became a feasible goal for the American working class and was finally achieved in the automobile, steel, rubber, and chemical industries. By pushing the limits set in the previous Progressive Era RIS, the CIO laid the foundation for an even greater increase in the relative power of labor in the Post-World War II RIS although radical labor and political organizations were still excluded from the power structure. In the case of the steel industry, the paternalistic welfare policies of the progressive era suggested a minimum level of recognition for the goals of labor that would help make possible U.S. Steel's recognition of the Steel Workers Organizing Committee (SWOC) in 1937. The general lesson to be learned then is that in social structure of accumulation theory, one must never study social structures of accumulation or institutional structures in complete isolation. The helpful analytical distinction between regulationist and liberal institutional structures cannot change the fact that institutional characteristics remain historically specific.

The contemporary relevance of these results should not be overlooked. As is discussed in the first chapter, the turn towards neo-conservatism in the United States and in other advanced capitalist nations is in many ways a reaction against the unrestricted markets of the neo-liberal era. Capitalist class interests, however, have sought to modify the global capitalist system to preserve and expand their own power while suppressing oppositional movements fighting to establish alternatives to free and unfettered markets. These capitalist-driven forms of intervention have potentially dangerous consequences for economic and political stability in much the same way that American capitalists' attempt to stabilize economic conditions a full hundred years ago sparked labor unrest. David Harvey has pointed out that the neo-conservative desire for greater domestic and international order has led to a preference for militarization as an antidote to the chaos of individual interests (2006: 58). Furthermore, neo-conservatives seek to restore a sense of moral purpose and higher order values in an effort to construct political consent around the neo-conservative agenda of maintaining and reinforcing capitalist class power. The long process of creating an electoral base to elevate the neo-conservatives to power began in the 1970s with the formation of Jerry Falwell's moral majority (2006: 59–60). Leo Panitch similarly argues that although neo-liberal ideology has made it more difficult to detect, the policies of globalization, rather than weakening the power of states has actually enhanced that power, for the United States in particular, by creating a new systemic relation between the state and capital (2000: 6). That is, globalization policies have "increased the scope for political leadership and discretionary intervention by central banks and finance ministries—a necessary step, given the (constantly) chaotic and (intermittently) crisis-prone nature of free markets" (2000: 6). The fact that the state is the leader in this effort to react against the chaotic character of the market in no way undermines the analogy to the paternalistically imposed order that capital established in the steel industry during the progressive era.

The paternalism inherent in the progressive era corporate welfare policies is similar in many ways to that which is represented by the non-governmental organizations (NGOs) and grassroots organizations (GROs) that have grown and flourished under neo-liberalism. Such organizations are not democratic institutions because they tend to be elitist, unaccountable, and define the interests of those for whom they speak (Harvey, 2006: 52). As non-elected advocacy groups of various kinds of rights (e.g., consumer protections, civil rights, the rights of handicapped persons), they have given rise to the belief that "opposition mobilized within some separate entity called 'civil society' is the powerhouse of oppositional politics" (Harvey, 2005a: 78).[1] The neo-liberal concern for individual opportunity and freedom has apparently influenced the missions of these organizations. Unfortunately, it has at the same time steered them away from tackling much broader issues related to the structure of social relations.

Part of the problem is that it may simply not be possible for capital to impose any sort stability in response to the difficulties inherent in a neo-liberal global order.[2] Enforcing a regulatory program in a particular industry is a simple matter in comparison with establishing a global regulatory program to establish a stable international order that also manages to strengthen capitalist class power. With global income and wealth income inequalities reaching levels not seen since the 1920s, one has to worry that the economic imbalances may become so severe as to generate a structural crisis of massive proportions (Harvey, 2005a: 188). Both Paul Volcker and Alan Greenspan are on record warning that economic imbalances in the U.S. are a growing threat to global stability (189). One can only hope that the growing opposition to the spread of neo-liberal policies will be able to accomplish what elite class power has been unwilling and unable to accomplish.

This study suggests a number of interesting directions for future research. One direction is an expansion of this research on the iron and steel industry to later periods in U.S. history. A case study of the iron and steel industry within the context of the Post-World War II RIS would be especially interesting in light of the findings presented here. The enhanced relative power of organized labor in the steel industry appears to have given rise to its own special problems during the postwar era. John Strohmeyer, who was editor of the Bethlehem, Pennsylvania, *Globe Times* for many years, explains how the United Steelworkers of America (USWA) obtained an important concession in 1956 that locked in past labor practices. The contract provision, which stipulated that past work practices could not be changed unless underlying conditions changed, gave the USWA the legal power to oppose the implementation of labor-saving machinery (Strohmeyer, 1987: 65). Known as clause 2B, this contract provision represents the postwar conflict between capital and labor for control of the production process, which ultimately left Big Steel incapable of meeting the threats of foreign and domestic competition that contributed to the postwar crisis of the 1960s and 1970s. An expansion of the case study to this time period might shed light on the specific reasons why the ability of labor to negotiate the terms of regulation in the postwar RIS failed to mitigate the negative consequences of contradictory capital-labor relations in the postwar era.

In addition to further research on the steel industry, this book has made an important methodological contribution that creates an opening for an unlimited number of concrete, industrial case studies in the SSA tradition. The modified SSA framework developed by Martin Wolfson and David Kotz has proven itself compatible with a historical and institutional case study analysis. Central to this approach is the notion of an institutional structure, which permits the generalization of SSA theory by accounting for stable periods of relatively slow economic growth. At the same time, it allows for the concretion of SSA theory by creating theoretical expectations about the nature of the institutions that form the basis of each period of capitalist stability. The application of this methodological approach to the American iron and steel industry during the progressive era is but one example of the way in which social structure of accumulation theory may identify the social forces responsible for the development of American industry in this century and the last.

Notes

NOTES TO THE INTRODUCTION

1. Corporations that refused to refrain from the abuse of their market power were disciplined. For example, the federal government ordered the dissolution of Standard Oil in 1911.
2. The hostility of capital-labor relations during the early twentieth century may be contrasted with the post-World War II SSA during which free market restrictions were also imposed and yet capital-labor relations were somewhat more cooperative. The extent of this difference is reviewed in chapter 1.

NOTES TO CHAPTER 1

1. As recently as 2008, McDonough (164) reported that "no consensus [exists] within the current SSA literature as to whether the current period is witnessing the consolidation of a new SSA." Furthermore, he regards it as the biggest unresolved issue for SSA theorists (2008: 170).
2. Hence, neo-liberalism is neither a crisis of the old SSA nor a new SSA but a new institutional structure altogether (Wolfson, 2003: 260).
3. Therefore, every social structure of accumulation is an institutional structure but not every institutional structure is a social structure of accumulation (e.g., the neo-liberal institutional structure).
4. This process of creating a large semi-skilled workforce, that David Gordon, Richard Edwards, and Michael Reich (1982) refer to as a process of homogenization, is discussed in greater detail in chapter 2.
5. The American Federation of Labor was a subordinate, conservative participant in the NCF during the progressive era. Its failure to implement meaningful labor reform forced it to enter politics in 1906.

NOTES TO CHAPTER 2

1. Rudolf Hilferding was the first Marxist to correctly identify the origin of promoter's profit within the context of Marxian value theory (1981: 107–116).
2. Aside from Roosevelt's evil trusts, "most of the other huge combines . . . discovered that, with a little diplomacy, they could hang on to most of their fiefdoms" (Micklethwait et al., 2003: 74).

3. "Wilson's victory [in 1912] signaled the beginning of a period of consolidation and stabilization of the new liberal state" (Weinstein, 1968: 139–140).
4. Unfortunately for workers, the Sherman Anti-trust Act was enforced against unions during most of the progressive era. For example, in the Danbury Hatters case (1908), the U.S. Supreme Court found the Hatters' Union's actions in violation of the Sherman Anti-trust Act, awarding triple damages to the anti-union D.E. Loewe & Company (Henretta et al., 2000: 653).
5. "The basic conception of the relation between the SSA and the investment decision draws upon the Keynesian concept of the uncertainty attendant upon investment decisions in a capitalist economy" (Kotz et al., 1994: 3).
6. Alan Dawley also argues that unlike European workers whose struggle for democracy made them class conscious, American workers had gained political democracy by the 1830s and so their "economic battles could be taken over by political parties that blurred class lines" (Zinn, 2003: 232).
7. This bias inherent in the structure of many organizations in the early twentieth century would haunt labor during the steel strike of 1919.
8. In 1902, English unions formed an independent labor party after a court decision found the Amalgamated Society of Railway Engineers responsible for business losses to the Taff Vale railway during a strike (Weinstein, 1968: 23).
9. By September 1917, 113 IWW leaders had been arrested for threatening to disrupt wartime production (Henretta et al., 2000: 726).
10. Attorney General Palmer ordered a series of raids, and with J. Edgar Hoover as the newly appointed director of the Justice Department's anti-radical division, 294 radicals were deported in December of 1919 (Henretta et al., 2000: 732).
11. Others argue that the real history shows that the working class defeated Taylorism on the shop floor and forced capitalists to seek out new and more acceptable means of labor control (Harvey, 1982: 112).
12. According to Gordon, Edwards, and Reich the mechanization of production proceeded more rapidly in consolidated industries because new consolidations created by the merger movement had access to larger pools of liquid capital for such investment (Gordon et al., 1982: 129).
13. From 1890 to 1920, the homogenization of the labor force and labor markets became more firmly entrenched as employers restored stability to the production process and renewed their control over workers (Gordon et al., 1982: 127).
14. The "consolidation of capital prompted a consolidation of labor" (Micklethwait et al., 2003: 72).
15. Worker resistance continued during the 1920s but was driven underground where workers artificially restricted output to rebel against employers (Gordon et al., 1982: 163).
16. The measure is an imperfect measure of the rate of profit because it excludes capital advanced for the purchase of raw materials and, more importantly, fixed inputs. It thus overstates the aggregate rate of profit. Nevertheless, it is the best measure available.

NOTES TO CHAPTER 3

1. McCraw and Reinhardt refer to Carnegie Steel's rapid adoption of any superior production method with apparent disregard of the short-term cost as the company's "scrap and build" policy (1989: 594).

2. "Capital grows to a huge mass in a single hand in one place, because it has been lost by many in another place. This is centralization proper, as distinct from accumulation and concentration" (Marx, 1990: 777).
3. This claim runs counter to Kolko's assertion that "[d]espite the ample amounts of watered stock available for new mergers . . . the steel industry in 1899 remained competitive" (1967: 31).
4. The desire for self-sufficiency was especially evident in the Moore group. National Steel provided crude steel for the American Tin Plate Company, the American Steel Hoop Company, and the American Sheet Steel Company (Hogan, 1971: 285). The Moore group thus became much more fully integrated than the Carnegie Company or Federal Steel (286).
5. "Gary deplored Carnegie's policy of aggressive price-cutting, and he considered Schwab a co-conspirator in this "offense" against business stability and harmony" (Hessen, 1975: 127).
6. As a loose federation of steel companies topped by a holding company, U.S. Steel also lacked a well-defined managerial hierarchy. Bethlehem Steel, on the other hand, possessed a highly efficient structure that allowed it to track costs and allocate resources rationally across product divisions (McCraw and Reinhardt, 1989: 613–614).
7. When the U.S. Senate ordered an investigation of the Tennessee acquisition in 1909, the Bureau of Corporations withheld key information in accordance with the détente system. As a result, the Senate investigating committee was unable to pass judgment on the affair due to lack of information (Kolko, 1967: 118).
8. In July 1917, Wilson announced that the government would begin the widespread fixing of prices (Urofsky, 1969: 208).
9. Goodwill is defined as the amount of the purchase price paid in excess of the market value of the identifiable net assets when a business is purchased (Porter and Norton, 1996: 841).
10. In 1909, for example, Gary finally did decide to cut prices to teach the independent steel companies not to undercut U.S. Steel's prices. Later that year, Gary allowed prices to gradually rise so that U.S. Steel's competitors would not fail (Cutcliffe, 1994: 154).

NOTES TO CHAPTER 4

1. "In former years the Amalgamated Association had some advantage over employers because the latter were not organized" (Fitch, 1969: 192). "Lack of cooperation between the different employers made possible a greater exercise of power on the part of the union than would otherwise have been the case" (192).
2. Although orthodox economists have typically denied the tendency for productivity-raising machinery to raise unemployment, it did not escape the careful inspection of David Ricardo. "I am convinced that the substitution of machinery for human labor is often very injurious to the interest of the class of laborers" (Ricardo, 1996: 270).
3. In addition, a sharp reduction in the wage differential between skilled and unskilled workmen occurred during the late nineteenth century. According to Novack and Perlman, the differential narrowed from 1869 to 1873 as the Bessemer process gained acceptance and again rather sharply during the period 1881–1885 (1962: 344).
4. U.S. Steel's business is highly cyclical in general with respect to employment, sales, and annual profits (McCraw and Reinhardt, 1989: 597).

5. "The production process . . . considered as the unity of the labour process and the process of valorization . . . is the capitalist process of production, or the capitalist form of the production of commodities" (Marx, 1990: 304).
6. Gerald Eggert is well aware of the contradictory nature and dual character of U.S. Steel's labor policy during the progressive era. According to Eggert (1981: xii), U.S. Steel only partially followed the new trends in the area of labor reform. It attacked unions yet supported certain benefit or welfare policies.
7. The welfare program is labeled "paternalistic" here because the steel companies considered it to be in the steelworkers' best interest, and it was designed and implemented without consulting them or their representatives.
8. Republic, Cambria, and Youngstown Sheet and Tube also followed with similar plans (Brody, 1960: 154).
9. According to Gulick (1924: 188–189), seven-day labor was eliminated on at least three occasions. Seven-day work was supposedly eliminated from Steel Corporation mills in 1907, 1912, and 1921, but Gulick (35) reports that it persisted at the Edgar Thompson Works in Braddock as late as 1924.
10. Martha Shiells offers another explanation for the persistence and then abrupt abolition of the twelve-hour day that finally occurred in 1923. She explains that immigrants preferred the long hours, but when immigration was greatly restricted by the war and then by law in 1923, the government was compelled to intervene (Shiells, 1990: 390). Eggert, on the other hand, identifies necessity rather than preference as the primary factor insofar as the steelworkers clung to the twelve-hour day. Their standard of living was already near the subsistence level and the shift to the eight-hour day would reduce their daily income by a third (Eggert, 1981: 94).
11. The twelve-hour day continued, however, but now with overtime pay for work beyond eight hours (Gulick, 1924: 106). When the war ended, the overtime pay ceased while the long hours persisted.
12. Brody goes further, arguing that the pressure the WLPB put on the steel companies ultimately cleared the way for the unionization of the steelworkers (1960: 213).

NOTES TO THE CONCLUSION

1. According to Nelson Lichtenstein, the emergence of a "rights" discourse in the 1960s and 1970s within the academy, social activist movements, and the judiciary had a "powerfully corrosive impact on the legitimacy and integrity of the union idea" as well (2002: 141).
2. David Kotz (2008) has recently suggested that rising household debt and the growth of asset bubbles may be becoming nonviable methods of promoting expansion and avoiding severe crises in the United States.

References

Aglietta, M. 2000. *A theory of capitalist regulation: The U.S. experience.* New York: Verso.

Albelda, R. and C. Tilly. 1994. Towards a broader vision: Race, gender, and labor market segmentation in the social structure of accumulation framework. *Social structures of accumulation: The political economy of growth and crisis.* Ed. D.M. Kotz, T. McDonough, and M. Reich. New York: Cambridge University Press.

Allen, R.C. 1981. Accounting for price changes: American steel rails, 1879–1910. *Journal of Political Economy,* 89(3): 512–528.

Barnett, D.F. 1994a. American Iron and Steel Institute. *Encyclopedia of American business history and biography: Iron and steel in the twentieth century.* Ed. B. Seely. USA: Bruccoli Clark Layman.

———. 1994b. Pittsburgh plus pricing. *Encyclopedia of American business history and biography: Iron and steel in the twentieth century.* Ed. B. Seely. USA: Bruccoli Clark Layman.

Barrett, J.R. 1994. Steel strike of 1919. *Encyclopedia of American business history and biography: Iron and steel in the twentieth century.* Ed. B. Seely. USA: Bruccoli Clark Layman.

Beard, C.A. 1986. The Constitution as an economic document. *Classic readings in American politics.* Ed. P. Nivola and D. Rosenbloom. New York: St. Martin's Press.

Berglund, A. 1923. The United States Steel Corporation and price stabilization. *The Quarterly Journal of Economics,* 38(1): 1–30.

———. 1924. The United States Steel Corporation and industrial stabilization. *The Quarterly Journal of Economics,* 38(4): 607–630.

Blair, J.M. 1972. *Economic concentration: Structure, behavior, and public policy.* New York: Harcourt Brace Jovanovich.

Block, F. 2001. Introduction. *The great transformation.* Karl Polanyi. Boston: Beacon Press.

Bork, R. H. 1978. *The antitrust paradox: A policy at war with itself.* New York: Basic Books.

Bowles, S., D. Gordon, and T. Weisskopf. 1988. Power, accumulation, and crisis: The rise and demise of the postwar social structure of accumulation. *The imperiled economy, book 1: Macroeconomics from a left perspective.* Ed. R. Cherry, et al. New York: Monthly Review Press.

———. 1990. *After the waste land: A democratic economics for the year 2000.* New York: M.E. Sharpe.

Boyer, R. and Y. Saillard. 2002. A summary of regulation theory. *Regulation theory: The state and art.* Eds. R. Boyer and Y. Saillard. New York: Routledge.

Brenner, R. 2002. *The boom and the bubble: The U.S. in the world economy.* New York: Verso.

Brody, D. 1960. *Steelworkers in America: The nonunion era.* Cambridge, MA: Harvard University Press.

———. 1965. *Labor in crisis: The steel strike of 1919.* New York: J.B. Lippincott Company.

Butler, J.G. 1912. Competition—Its Uses and Abuses. *Yearbook of the American Iron and Steel Institute.* New York: American Iron and Steel Institute.

Chandler, A.D., Jr. 1977. The visible hand: *The managerial revolution in American business.* Cambridge, MA: Harvard University Press.

———. 1990. *Scale and scope: The dynamics of industrial capitalism.* Cambridge, MA: Harvard University Press.

Chomsky, N. 2003. *Hegemony or survival: America's quest for global dominance.* New York: Henry Holt.

Cutcliffe, S.H. 1994. Elbert H. Gary. *Encyclopedia of American business history and biography: Iron and steel in the twentieth century.* Ed. B. Seely. USA: Bruccoli Clark Layman.

De Tocqueville, A. 1986. Equality. *Classic readings in American politics.* Ed. P. Nivola and D. Rosenbloom. New York: St. Martin's Press.

Dobson, J.M. 1988. *A history of American enterprise.* Englewood Cliffs, NJ: Prentice Hall.

Dwyer, K.M. 1994a. World War I: Government and the steel industry. *Encyclopedia of American business history and biography: Iron and steel in the twentieth century.* Ed. B. Seely. USA: Bruccoli Clark Layman.

———. 1994b. Steel strike of 1909. *Encyclopedia of American business history and biography: Iron and steel in the twentieth century.* Ed. B. Seely. USA: Bruccoli Clark Layman.

———. 1994c. Welfare Capitalism. *Encyclopedia of American business history and biography: Iron and steel in the twentieth century.* Ed. B. Seely. USA: Bruccoli Clark Layman.

Eagleton, T. 1976. *Marxism and literary criticism.* Los Angeles: University of California Press.

———. 2005. *The function of criticism.* New York: Verso.

Eggert, G.G. 1981. *Steelmasters and labor reform, 1886–1923.* Pittsburgh: University of Pittsburgh Press.

Fitch, J.A. 1969. *The steel workers.* New York: Arno Press.

Foster, W.Z. 1969. *The great steel strike.* New York: Arno Press & The New York Times.

Gordon, D.M., R. Edwards, and M. Reich. 1982. *Segmented work, divided workers: The historical transformation of labor in the United States.* New York: Cambridge University Press.

Gordon, D.M. 1994. The global economy: New edifice or crumbling foundations? *Social structures of accumulation: The political economy of growth and crisis.* Ed. D.M. Kotz, et al. New York: Cambridge University Press.

Gourevitch, P. 1986. *Politics in hard times: Comparative responses to international economic crises.* Ithaca, NY: Cornell University Press.

Gray, J. 1995. *Liberalism.* Second Edition. Minneapolis: University of Minnesota Press.

Gulick, C.A. 1924. *Labor policy of the United States Steel Corporation.* New York: Longmans, Green & Co.

Hartz, L. 1986. The concept of a liberal society. *Classic readings in American politics.* Ed. P. Nivola and D. Rosenbloom. New York: St. Martin's Press.

Hartzell, E. 1934. Profits in the steel industry. *The Accounting Review,* 9(4): 326–333.

Harvey, D. 1982. *The limits to capital.* Chicago: The University of Chicago Press.

———. 2005a. *A brief history of neoliberalism*. New York: Oxford University Press.

———. 2005b. *The new imperialism*. New York: Oxford University Press.

———. 2006. *Spaces of global capitalism: A theory of uneven geographical development*. New York: Verso.

Henretta, J.A., D. Brody, S. Ware, and M.S. Johnson. 2000. *America's history volume 2: Since 1865*. Boston, MA: Bedford/St. Martin's.

Hessen, R. 1975. *Steel titan: The life of Charles M. Schwab*. New York: Oxford University Press.

Hilferding, R. 1981. *Finance capital: A study of the latest phase of capitalist development*. Ed. T. Bottomore. London: Routledge & Kegan Paul.

Hoagland, H.E. 1917. Trade unionism in the iron industry: A decadent organization. *The Quarterly Journal of Economics*, 31(4): 674–689.

Hogan, W.T. 1971. *Economic history of the iron and steel industry in the United States*. Volumes 1 and 2. Lexington, MA: D.C. Heath and Company.

Hunt, E.K. 2002. *History of economic thought: A critical perspective*. New York: M.E. Sharpe.

Jessop, B. 1994. Regulation theory. *The Elgar companion to radical political economy*. Ed. P. Arestis and M. Sawyer. Northampton, MA: Edward Elgar.

Kolko, G. 1967. *The triumph of conservatism: A reinterpretation of American history, 1900–1916*. Chicago: Quadrangle Books.

Kornbluh, J.L., ed. 1998. *Rebel voices: An IWW anthology*. Chicago: Charles H. Kerr Publishing Company.

Kotz, D.M., T. McDonough, and M. Reich, eds. 1994. Introduction. *Social structures of accumulation: The political economy of growth and crisis*. New York: Cambridge University Press.

Kotz, D.M. 1994a. Interpreting the social structure of accumulation theory. *Social structures of accumulation: The political economy of growth and crisis*. Ed. D.M. Kotz, et al. New York: Cambridge University Press.

———. 1994b. The regulation theory and the social structure of accumulation approach. *Social structures of accumulation: The political economy of growth and crisis*. Ed. D.M. Kotz, et al. New York: Cambridge University Press.

———. 2003. Neoliberalism and the SSA theory of long-run capital accumulation. *Review of Radical Political Economics*, 35(3): 263–270.

———. 2008. Contradictions of economic growth in the neoliberal era: Accumulation and crisis in the contemporary U.S. economy. *Review of Radical Political Economics*, 40(2): 174–188.

Lichtenstein, N. 2002. *State of the union: A century of American labor*. Princeton, NJ: Princeton University Press.

Mandel, E. 1995. *Long waves of capitalist development: A Marxist interpretation*. New York: Verso.

Marx, K. 1990. *Capital: volume 1*. New York: Penguin Books.

McCloskey, D.N. 1973. *Economic maturity and entrepreneurial decline: British iron and steel, 1870–1913*. Cambridge, MA: Harvard University Press.

McCraw, T. and F. Reinhardt. 1989. Losing to win: U.S. Steel's pricing, investment decisions, and market share, 1901–1938. *The Journal of Economic History*, 49(3): 593–619.

McCraw, T.K. 1984. *Prophets of regulation*. Cambridge, MA: Harvard University Press.

McDonough, T. 1994. The construction of social structures of accumulation in U.S. history. *Social structures of accumulation: The political economy of growth and crisis*. Ed. D.M. Kotz, et al. New York: Cambridge University Press.

———. 2008. Social structures of accumulation theory: The state of the art. *Review of Radical Political Economics*, 40(2): 153–173.

Micklethwait, J. and A. Wooldridge. 2003. *The company: A short history of a revolutionary idea*. New York: Modern Library.

Murray, R.K. 1951. Communism and the great steel strike of 1919. *The Mississippi Valley Historical Review*, 38(3): 445–466.

Novack, D.E. and R. Perlman. 1962. The structure of wages in the American iron and steel industry, 1860–1890. *The Journal of Economic History*, 22(3): 334–347.

Panitch, L. 2000. The new imperial state. *New Left Review*, 11: 5–20.

Polanyi, K. 2001. *The great transformation*. Boston: Beacon Press.

Porter, G.A. and C.L. Norton. 1996. *Financial accounting: The impact on decision makers*. New York: The Dryden Press.

Renshaw, P. 1967. *The Wobblies: The story of syndicalism in the United States*. Garden City, New York: Doubleday & Company.

Ricardo, D. 1996. *Principles of political economy and taxation*. New York: Prometheus Books.

Seely, B., ed. 1994. Introduction. *Encyclopedia of American business history and biography: Iron and steel in the twentieth Century*. USA: Bruccoli Clark Layman.

Shiells, M. 1990. Collective choice of working conditions: Hours in British and U.S. iron and steel, 1890–1923. *The Journal of Economic History*, L(2): 379–392.

Sholes, E.C. and T.E. Leary. 1994. Tennessee Coal, Iron & Railroad. *Encyclopedia of American business history and biography: Iron and steel in the twentieth century*. Ed. B. Seely. USA: Bruccoli Clark Layman.

Sinclair, U. 1960. *The jungle*. New York: The New American Library.

Smith, J.R. 1908. The cost and the profits of steel-making in the United States. *The Quarterly Journal of Economics*, 22(2): 261–273.

Strohmeyer, J. 1987. *Crisis in Bethlehem: Big Steel's struggle to survive*. New York: Penguin Books.

Stiglitz, J.E. 2001. Forward. *The great transformation*. K. Polanyi. Boston: Beacon Press.

Stocking, G.W. 1954. *Basing point pricing and regional development: A case study of the iron and steel industry*. Chapel Hill: The University of North Carolina Press.

Stone, K. 1975. The origins of job structures in the steel industry. *Labor market segmentation*. Ed. R. Edwards, et al. Lexington, MA: D.C. Heath and Company.

Sweezy, P. 1970. *The theory of capitalist development*. New York: Monthly Review Press.

Temin, P. 1964. *Iron and steel in nineteenth-century America: An economic inquiry*. Cambridge, MA: MIT Press.

Thompson, F. and P. Murfin. 1976. *The I.W.W. Its first seventy years (1905–1975)*. Chicago: Industrial Workers of the World.

Thoreau, H.D. 1970. Civil disobedience. *American radical thought: The libertarian tradition*. Ed. H.J. Silverman. Lexington, MA: D.C. Heath and Company.

Tiffany, P. 1994. U.S. Steel antitrust suit, 1911. *Encyclopedia of American business history and biography: Iron and steel in the twentieth century*. Ed. B. Seely. USA: Bruccoli Clark Layman.

Tuttle, F.W. and J.M. Perry. 1970. *An economic history of the United States*. Cincinnati, OH: South-Western Publishing Company.

Urofsky, M. 1969. *Big Steel and the Wilson administration: A study in business government relations*. Columbus, OH: Ohio State University Press.

U.S. Bureau of the Census. 1960. *Historical statistics of the United States, colonial times to 1957*. Washington, D.C: U.S. Department of Commerce.

U.S. Bureau of Economic Analysis. 2003. National income and product accounts, table 5.1 (gross saving and investment). www.bea.gov.
U.S. Bureau of Labor Statistics. 2003. Consumer price index—all urban consumers. www.bls.gov.
Weinstein, J. 1968. *The corporate ideal in the liberal state: 1900–1918*. Boston: Beacon Press.
Wolff, L. 1965. *Lockout: The story of the homestead strike of 1892: A study of violence, unionism, and the Carnegie steel empire*. New York: Harper & Row.
Wolfson, M.H. 1994. The financial system and the social structure of accumulation. *Social structures of accumulation: The political economy of growth and crisis*. Ed. D.M. Kotz, et al. New York: Cambridge University Press.
———. 2003. Neoliberalism and the social structure of accumulation. *Review of Radical Political Economics*, 35(3): 255–262.
Wright, C.D. 1901. The National Amalgamated Association of Iron, Steel, and Tin Workers, 1892–1901. *The Quarterly Journal of Economics*, 16(1): 37–68.
Zinn, H. 2003. *A people's history of the United States*. New York: HarperCollins.

Index

180   *Index*

Printed and bound by CPI Group (UK) Ltd, Croydon, CR0 4YY
11/04/2025
01843992-0010